Strategies to Inspire Active Learning

Complete Handbook

Merrill Harmin

Inspiring Strategy Institute
105 Lautner Lane
Edwardsville, Illinois 62025

To Jesse Ken Harmin, 1957-1992

First 1995 printing
Inspiring Strategy Institute
105 Launter Lane, Edwardsville, IL 62025

Library of Congress Catalog Number: 95-77854

ISBN: 1-887313-03-6

The Inspiring Strategy Institute (ISI) offers teachers straightforward, practical strategies that are naturally motivating to today's students. The strategies develop active, self-responsible learning.

This book contains the complete selection of strategies currently available. It also contains a simple test teachers can use to assess how well they are doing at inspiring active, self-responsible learning. (See page five.)

Overall the book offers a modern set of teaching methods, methods effective with today's students and appropriate for today's realities.

For a list of other available publications, and for information about demonstrations and training programs, please contact:

Inspiring Strategy Institute
105 Lautner Lane
Edwardsville IL 62025

Tel 618-692-0177
Fax 618-656-5663

Complete Contents

Acknowledgements

Several people were responsible for producing these pages. I am particularly indebted to Dennis Bland, Doris Hanrahan, Lorraine Huntley and Marie Rehg.

Most of the strategies in the book come from the experiences, creativity and good will of practicing teachers. My role was rarely more than putting names on what teachers told me worked. Three sources call for special attention.

First, John Dewey, from whom I first learned that good learning and good living should and could be grown together. He is also the chief source for several of the strategies dealing with class climate and student project work, and for a good deal of the spirit pervading other strategies as well.

Then there is Louis E. Raths, my mentor in graduate school. He showed me practical ways to nurture the hidden potential in all students. He is also one of the main sources for strategies dealing with subject matter selection, thinking questions, and ways to encourage students that go well beyond praise and rewards.

And, finally, there is Grace Pilon, the creator of the Workshop Way®. Some of the strategies that teachers report most effective with today's students were adapted from her elegant classroom design. You may want to do what I did, observe some of the teachers around the county using the Workshop Way. It offers dramatic demonstration of what the profession now knows about teaching academic in ways that also develop students' personal strengths. To identity teachers or to obtain Pilon's publications, contact Workshop Way, P.O. Box 850170, New Orleans, LA 70185.

I apologize for being unable to identify all who contributed to this book's content. The source for so many teaching strategies seems lost in the history of the profession. Some of those I know are noted in the text or reference list. Here are others, including those who so graciously tested these strategies for us all:

Amy O'Donnell, Andy LePage, Ann Lowe, Anne Bailey, Anne Hyman, Anne Marie McMahon, Barbara Goldenhersh, Barbara Saul, Barbara Thielmann, Bertha Richardson, Besse Dale, Betty Hatch, Bev Reynolds, Beverly Douglas, Bill Gallagher, Bill Greive, Bill Shuey, Bob Reasoner, Bruce Maskow, Candi Cangelosi-Johnson, Carol Beatty, Carol Kreitner, Carol Little, Carol Norris, Carol Smalley, Catherine McGarrahan, Cathy Anise, Cathy Bay, Celeste Williams, Charles Pearson, Charlotte McDaniel, Cheryl Greaves, Chris Reinhart, Chris Skinner, Cindy Rueter, Claudia Herndon, Connie Dembrowsky, Crystal Lawler, Cynthia Hussain, Dale Paulus, Darlene McDaniel, Dave Thornburg, Dave Valley, David

Allsup, Debbie Mansin, Debi Stapleton, Debra Greenwood, Dennis Butts, Diana Taylor, Diane Frey, Diane Highlander, Diane Milner, Donald Baden, Donald Keefe, Donna Rakers, Dov Elkins, Elena Wallace, Ellen Edwards, Elizabeth Hall, Esther Wright, Florence Horne, Florine Epplin, Gail Dusa, Gail Mines, Gary Nunn, Gary Swalley, Gayanne Hoke, Gene Bedley, Guy Sachs, Hanoch McCarty, Hayman Kite, Heather Ketron, Helen Mings, Herschel Prater, Howard Kirshenbaum, Jack Canfield, Jack Schlueter, Jackie Bennett, Jacqueline Riggs, James Andris, James Comer, James Owens, Jan Ohlman, Jan Scanlan, Jan Witt, Jane Gregg, Jane Heitzig, Jane Holcomb, Jane Van Vertloo, Janet McCann, Janice E. Clark, Janice Hapgood, Jean Kauffmann, Jean Peek, Jeanette Tremoulet, Jeanne Swain, Jeffrey Boyles, Jill Schwear, Jo Thatcher, Joe Munshaw, John Hart, John Prieskorn, John Vasconcellos, Joseph Gentelin, Joseph Webber, Judith Albracht, Judy Kupsky, Julie Burch, Julie Corey, Julie Evans, Julie Wilcox, Karen Eastby, Karen Gitcho, Karen Herrington, Karen Rains, Karen Whisman, Kari Nairn, Karl Zilm, Kate Motley, Kathleen Gallagher, Kathy Burns, Kathy Matthews, Kathy Mayr, Kathy Smith, Ken Miller, Lana Rogier, Larry Hopp, Laurie Malone, Lawrence Kolhberg, Lellie Bryant, LeRoy Foster, Leslie Wehling, Linda Atchison, Linda Sauerwein, Linda Zoll, Linda Zorger, Lisa Kohlenberger, Liz Hand, Lynn Manning, Lynn Meyer, Lois Adomite, Lou Obernuefemann, Lovann Brown, Lynn Fox, Maralee Rivard, Margaret Grueter, Mariam Church, Marie Hackett, Marilyn Brown, Marilyn Richter, Marilyn Taylor, Martha Dieball, Marva Collins, Marvin Cohn, Mary Anne Dalton, Mary Kozlonski, Mary Martin, Mary Jane Ostanik, Mary Rader, Meg Dees, Melissa Sievers, Melissa Smay, Melita Bearinger, Michele Borba, Michele Morgan, Michelle Portwood, Miriam Harmon, Missy Sirtak, Nancy Bond, Nancy Johns, Nancy and Chick Moorman, Nathan Swift, Pat Jedlicka, Patrice Bain, Peggy Bielen, Penny Kennedy, Peter Pierro, Phillip Besonen, Ray Grinter, Rhonda Downey, Rich Revheim, Richard Tempko, Rick Galinas, Robert Rockwell, Robert Russo, Robert Shaw, Robert Williams, Robin Dermody, Ruth Ambruster, Sally Stumpe, Sandi Redenbach, Saville Sax, Scott Spencer, Shelley Fry, Sherry Wimmer, Sidney Simon, Stacey Lynn, Sue Burke, Sue Underwood, Susan Nall, Susan Kirchiner, Suzanne Rodgers, Tami Divitre, Terri Taake, Thomas O'Brien, Tom Fahey, Trudie Hotson, Valerie Meyer, Veronica Douglas, Vicki Valley, Vicky Summers, Vivian Rohleder, Wanda East, William Conway, Yolanda Williams, Yvonne Broger, Yvonne Halvachs, Yvonne Mitkos.

Overview: What Have We Here?

This book brings good news to teachers: We no longer need struggle with today's students. The profession now has available strategies that naturally draw them into active, productive learning. You will find a sampling in this book.

These strategies reduce the need to push and pull at students, or to rely so much on rewards and punishments. The strategies *inspire* active involvement, and they do so in a way that inspires the development of students' most constructive motives.

The strategies of this book are also quite doable, so teachers can readily test this proposition for themselves. Indeed, no strategy is included here unless many teachers at all levels of instruction, from kindergarten through college, tested it and found it both workable and effective, even in today's pressured classrooms, even with today's restless students.

For example, teachers reported that these strategies were effective in:

- Increasing time-on-task scores for both at-risk and gifted students.
- Modernizing a reading program so it satisfied more learning styles, including those of mainstreamed special education students.
- Reducing misbehavior in and out of classrooms.
- Restructuring a junior high into a thriving middle school.
- Helping new teachers get their classrooms running smoothly very quickly.
- Implementing an outcome-based curriculum in a comprehensive high school.
- Shift student attention from extrinsic rewards to intrinsic learning satisfactions.

The instructional strategies of this book are similar to strategies gaining ground in industry. They center on mutual respect, not bossiness. On collaboration, not isolation. On worker commitment to the job, not fear of failure. And most essentially, on the dignity of all, not praise and rewards for a few.

The most powerful factors in the world are clear ideas in the minds of energetic men of good will.
—*J. Arthur Thomson*

There are two basic ways to use this book:

1. **Ease teaching and improve learning** You might start by picking and choosing a few strategies to try in your classroom. I recommend beginning with the first chapters, for they contain the strategies most teachers find helpful at the outset. Experiment and see if these strategies help you draw more of your students into active learning more of the time — and with less struggle and effort.

2. Aim for a fully inspirational classroom Once you are clear about what distinguishes this inspiring approach to instruction from more traditional approaches, you might consider aiming to run a classroom that always inspires all students to develop their most productive, responsible selves.

I did not always believe that was a realistic goal for teachers. Yet the profession has advanced to the point where I am convinced that goal is now within reach of all teachers. Available now, for example, are straightforward methods for lecturing subject matter, organizing discussions, motivating disinterested students, handling classroom disruptions — and in fact doing whatever teachers must do — doing it all in ways that steadily inspire the best from all students.

The inspiring classroom

What does a fully inspiring classroom look like? The somewhat paradoxical answer: No singular way. There is no one way to be a topnotch teacher. Visit an inspirational classroom and you might see students in tidy rows with the teacher lecturing. Or you might see an informal classroom with lots of small groups. Yet an inspirational classroom will be clearly identifiable. It will give you the distinct impression that students are studying in ways good for them, in ways that bring forth their very best traits.

Let me be more specific. I would say visits to fully inspirational classrooms will reveal high levels of five qualities: Dignity, Energy, Self management, Community and Awareness.

DIGNITY Students will appear to sit tall and strong, feeling good about themselves, feeling confident about their work. We will not see students slouching about, as if down on themselves, without self-respect. Nor will students appear to be constantly on guard, worried about pleasing everyone or winning every game, as if their worth as humans depended entirely on pleasing others. We will see students appearing to have a quiet inner strength, sufficiently self-assured and secure to be able to relax and invest themselves unselfconsciously in their studies.

A comment: I personally believe all people, no matter what age, have a natural worth, a value beyond judgment, an essential dignity. And I suspect people nowadays are becoming more aware of their need to experience and express that dignity. Women show that. As do factory workers, the handicapped, and minorities. I see that awareness also growing in children. I would say a classroom that is to serve both good learning and good living, now and later, would do well to honor the dignity of all.

ENERGY We will notice that all students are busy, engaged, involved. The room will have a hum of activity. We will not see much waiting, restlessness, downtime. Students will not be hanging around, watching the clock, impatient, inactive, apathetic. Nor will students be working frantically, anxiously, stressfully, as if they were whipped into action. The room will flow with a comfortable aliveness.

Unless we find better ways to educate ourselves as citizens, America runs the risk of drifting unwittingly into a new kind of dark age.
—Ernest Boyer

All students are living centers of physical, emotional and mental energy. Those energies are meant to flow, move, get expressed. Instructional strategies that squeeze down those energies, that suppress students' aliveness, will not, I would say, do well at keeping students engaged in active learning. If a classroom is to be fully inspiring, it will somehow have to keep student energies flowing appropriately and comfortably.

SELF-MANAGEMENT The students will be self-managing, self-responsible, working along with self-motivation. We might, for example, see students making choices, starting and stopping on their own, or correcting their own work. The students will not always be following detailed orders, always proceeding passively. It will be as if students were saying, "I can manage my own work. I don't need to be told every little thing. If I need help, I know how to get it."

We humans are naturally self-regulating beings. We are not meant to be mere pawns of others, bossed around by others. If our instructional strategies are to flow with the best motives in students, they should not violate that self-managing impulse. Ideally, they should help students do better at managing themselves, assist them in becoming lifelong learners and mature, healthful, self-responsible citizens.

COMMUNITY We will also see students in comfortable relationships with other students and with persons of authority. Students will be getting along, listening to each other, giving acceptance and receiving acceptance, giving respect and receiving respect. They will not be teasing or slighting others. Or feeling isolated, rejected or disconnected from others. Nor will any student remain stuck in self-centeredness or resentments. Problems will come up, but students will get resolved in ways appropriate to respectful, community living.

Humans do not live alone. A classroom that is to bring out the best in students, and in teachers too, wants to get students learning in reasonable community with others, not in isolation, and not in opposition to others. We want to advance students' ability to accept and support others, even those very different from themselves.

AWARENESS Students will look thoughtful, alert, as if they know what is going on. Students will not look bored, groggy, as if they were plodding along with dulled awareness. They will not be handling the class subject matter mindlessly. Minds will be alive. We might see open-minded wonderment or narrowly focused concentration. Students will in one way or another be very conscious, perhaps aware of thoughts or feelings inside them, perhaps aware of the ideas or people around them.

Progress was all right. Only it went too long.
—James Thurber

All humans, of course, can be aware of memories, facts, emotions, colors, sounds, ideas, others, ourselves. We can be aware of future possibilities, as when we consider options for a story ending or our activities tonight. We can even be aware of possibilities not yet perceived by others, a knack characteristic of innovators. Furthermore we can choose which awareness to focus on:

"Should I continue to worry about tonight or get back to my book?" A useful definition of intelligence combines human awareness and self-management power: We are intelligent, we might say, to the extent we can self-manage our awareness. If we can open our minds to many awarenesses, and then manage to hold our attention on what we select as a focus, we are apt to produce results that would be called intelligent. In any case, a classroom that is to serve students now and into the future would do well to get students developing their innate awareness powers.

Targeting on DESCA with subject matter

For convenience, I call these five elements of inspirational teaching by their initials, DESCA. I have found that DESCA serves teachers very well as a specific, yet comprehensive, flexible teaching target. A bull's eye, in this scheme, would be a classroom that had every student handling the class subject matter with solid **dignity**, comfortable **energy**, appropriate **self-management**, feeling of **community** and open-minded, focused **awareness**.

When I am teaching, to give a personal example, I am very satisfied when I see students handling my subject matter with high DESCA. I conclude students are studying in ways likely to produce the best learning now and inspire the growth of the best lifelong learning and living habits.

I am less happy, and start hunting alternative instructional strategies, whenever I notice low DESCA. Perhaps low **dignity**, as when I see some students getting down on themselves, blaming themselves, losing trust in themselves. Or when I notice low **energy,** as when I sense apathy coloring the class mood. Or low **self-management**, as when I see students working only passively, doing only what they were told to do, or working without clear personal commitment. Or low **community**, as when I notice teasing, or some students feeling left out. Or low **awareness**, as when minds cloud over, boredom spreads, or responses become thoughtless and superficial.

And note: I am not satisfied with low DESCA even when students seem to be mastering the lesson of the day. My commitment nowadays is to keep my classroom running as a dignified, energetic, self-managing community of aware learners.

This collection as a guide to a DESCA classroom

This handbook could be defined in terms of DESCA. That is, you could use it as a guide to finding instructional strategies that inspire all students to unfold their dignity, release and channel their energy, improve their self-management, learn healthy community living, and develop the fullness of human awareness.

A teacher has the greatest profession. For through the hands of our instruction pass all members of every profession.
—*Jesse Stuart*

DESCA SCALES for Rating a Class

DIGNITY

1   2   3   4   5

No personal dignity Students slouch or mope, as if feeling unimportant, weak or hopeless. Or act as if they will be worthless without high success or others' approval. Little evidence of self-confidence, self-respect.

Clear dignity in all Talented or not, students sit and walk tall, speak up, seemingly self-assured, confident, secure. Much evidence students trust themselves and see themselves as valuable persons, worthy of respect.

ENERGY

1   2   3   4   5

Energy too low or high Mood too boring, slow, lifeless; much inactivity, waiting, apathy, time wasting. Or mood too frantic, stressful, exhausting, anxious.

Comfortable flow of energy The mood is comfortably alive. All students keep busy, engaged, active. No evidence of clockwatching. Time tends to fly.

SELF-MANAGEMENT

1   2   3   4   5

Students only follow orders No evidence of self-responsibility, initiative, self-direction, personal choice. Work is passive, without personal commitment.

All students self-directing Students make appropriate choices, guide and discipline themselves, work willfully, persistingly. Students not bossed.

COMMUNITY

1   2   3   4   5

Students self-centered Students act only for personal advantage, unconcerned with others' welfare. No evidence of teamwork, loyalty, belonging, kindness among peers or toward teacher.

Strong mood of togetherness Much sharing, cooperation, interdependence, mutuality. Students support one another and the teacher. No antagonism, rejection.

AWARENESS

1   2   3   4   5

Dull, mindless busywork Work is mechanical. Students seem unaware, or unresponsive, or narrow-minded, shallow. No thinking, concentrating or searching. Student talk is impulsive or uncreative, thoughtless. Much inattentiveness.

All students aware and alert Much concentration, observing, listening, thinking, noticing, evaluating. Students appear to be mindful, aware of what is going on. High level of attentiveness.

DESCA Questionnaire

Dear Student:

How was class for you today? Please check one item in each category.

Dignity

___ I had strong, good feelings about myself.
___ I felt OK about myself.
___ Unsure.
___ I didn't feel very good about myself.
___ I thought I was bad, hopeless or stupid.

Energy

___ I was always comfortably active.
___ I was sometimes active.
___ Unsure.
___ I was rarely comfortably active.
___ My energy was very low or too high and stressful.

Self-management

___ I made many choices, managed myself, felt self-responsible.
___ I was usually self-managing.
___ Unsure.
___ I rather drifted along.
___ I always felt controlled or bossed, not self-responsible.

Community

___ I felt I belonged in the group and was fully accepted.
___ I felt pretty good about being in the group.
___ Unsure.
___ I did not feel good about being in the group.
___ I felt only selfishness and rejection from others.

Awareness

___ I was aware and alert all the time. I did a lot of thinking.
___ I was aware and alert most of the time.
___ Unsure.
___ The class was dull.
___ I felt very dull, very bored.

You could also view the book as a collection of ideas for better meeting the needs of the students showing

- Low dignity: The ones with negative or low self-concepts.
- Little or impulsive energy: The lethargic or the explosive.
- Weak self-management: The insistent resistors or the passive followers.
- Unhealthy community relationships: The isolated, the lonely, and the antagonistic.
- Narrow or dull awareness: The narrow-minded and the non-perceptive.

Two forms can help you experiment with these possibilities. The first, the DESCA Scale, is useful for giving a self-rating to a class you have just taught or are now observing. Some teachers also give this form to students. They ask students to fill it out as best they can and thereby get an idea of student perceptions of a class. Teachers wanting the perspectives of young children often prefer something closer to the second form, A DESCA questionnaire.

DESCA is certainly not all of what defines a good classroom today. But I believe it covers the heart of it. Many teachers report its being a handy, flexible, encompassing target. Their reports suggest that as teachers keep tapping into these five human potentials, students increasingly sense that the teachers are on their side, on the side of the best they have within them.

The power of a personal plan

You do not really need this book. Once you get clear about a target appropriate for today's classrooms, such as producing high DESCA during subject matter study, you can find your own ways to hit that target more often, more easily, for more students.

But do pick a target. Don't try to do it all. When we are heading in one clear direction, we are in the position to make professional decisions and stick to them. We can say, "I will not do that. That will distract me from my main purpose." It's hard to make such statements when our priorities are unclear. It's hard not to respond to all the demands society would load on us. It's hard not to spin dizzily, getting nowhere.

A seed hidden in the heart of an apple is an orchard invisible.
—Welsh Proverb

If you do choose as your prime target the running of a high DESCA classroom, you can simply move ahead to create your own strategy package. When I conduct classes nowadays, DESCA is indeed my target. Let's say I teach a class in educational theory. Education theory then is my content target. DESCA gives me my process target. As our class proceeds, I want to see growth in group dignity, energy, self-management, community and awareness. I keep looking for strategies that will best do that and, to the extent that I succeed, our class does better at learning about educational theory.

You can create your own personal DESCA strategy package that way. Just keep aware of what is going on in the classroom as you teach. Perhaps keep a card on your desk: *How am I now doing at exercising and advancing dignity, energy, self-management, community and awareness of all students? Can I do better with this person? That one?* Keep asking the questions until they become knee-jerk reactions when you look out on your students. Then notice what strategies of instruction best serve you. As necessary, or as new teaching ideas occur to you, try new strategies. Keep creating your own way of teaching your subject with DESCA.

Most teachers find it easier to test these strategies and to avoid problems when they do not go it alone. Consider sharing experiences and problems with a support buddy or two.

If you take this path, take your time. Move at a pace that feels right. Yet stick to the campaign. Almost all teachers bump into old, limiting assumptions along the way. Old, limiting habits as well. It takes time to move past these obstacles. Remember what it takes to get to the top of the mountain. It's one step at a time.

Check your intentions

I recommend, too, being very clear about your intentions. It is easy to misuse any educational approach. Particularly consider holding two intentions.

- Intend to master the art of running a classroom that always and steadily serves both subject matter learning and long-term self-responsibility, as by always and steadily inspiring personal dignity, balanced energy, wise self-management, supportive community and expanded, refined awareness. A good start is to adopt the medical pledge: First, do no harm.

- I recommend you also choose to see every student — no matter how hopeless the student may currently appear to be — as potentially ready, and perhaps ready right now, to leap dramatically ahead. Do not ever give up on any student. Several teachers who have taken this DESCA path report this position as crucial to hold onto. It is, of course, true that none of us can ever be certain when another human is ready to make a major advance. There is more good in people than most of us know. Likely more than they themselves know. Intend to see more of that goodness burst forth at any moment.

Positive yet open expectations are central to this approach. In a way, all we need do is keep nurturing the positive motivations churning in every student while, at the same time, we stay open to the reality that some students will be unable to express those motives right now — and may in fact currently need strict external controls.

It is really not at all complicated, nor very new. Educational theorists have long recommended that we build our instruction on intrinsic, not extrinsic, student motivations (Dewey 1916, 1938; Guilford 1967; McLuhan and Fiore 1967). Yet the profession was not able to show us how exactly we could do that, especially with passive or pesky students. It was the rare teacher who could keep such students on task without relying on rewards and punishments, threats and scoldings.

What lies behind us and what lies before us are little matters compared with what lies within us.
—William Morrow

I hope this book demonstrates that strategies now exist that enable any of us to do so.

What can one teacher accomplish?

I recently read a study about a slum neighborhood in Montreal in which unemployment, violence and decadence generally were at extremely high levels. In the middle of that neighborhood was an elementary school. Researchers found that few children who went to that school ever improved their lifestyle (Pedersen, Faucher and Eaton 1978).

The researchers tracked down adults who had gone to that school twenty-five years earlier and found that, even after all that time, only 29 percent of the graduates had more than menial jobs or lived in reasonably decent housing. Thirty-eight percent of graduates suffered at the lowest levels of survival, typically homeless and unemployed.

Yet those statistics did not apply to all students who went to that school. They did not include the students who had a first-grade teacher called Miss A. The researchers noticed something curious about Miss A's former students. While only 29 percent of the graduates of most teachers broke free of their old lifestyle, a full 64 percent of the students who had Miss A did so.

Furthermore, while 38 percent of the students from other teachers were found to be living at the lowest levels of poverty, *none* of the students who had Miss A was found living at that level.

Graduates 25 years later	Students of Miss A	Students of other teachers
Living at lowest economic levels (Homeless, unemployed)	0 %	38 %
Living at reasonable levels (Steady work, decent housing)	64 %	29 %

Clearly, somehow, one first-grade teacher was having a dramatic, long-term impact on her students. She was doing much more than teaching reading, writing and arithmetic. My mind jumps to two other teachers able to inspire remarkable growth from unpromising students: Marva Collins and Jaime Escalante. You can think of your own inspiring teachers. The point: It is certainly possible to teach in ways that turn on students to their productive, healthful instincts.

When I'm inspired I dance to the music.
—Allison, 3rd grade

Now, I believe, any of us can do so. The profession now offers us a sufficient number of tools so we can teach whatever is our subject matter while we also help students reveal and express the best within them.

If you have doubts, I invite you to treat this as an interesting possibility and put that possibility to a test. I will be happy if the strategies on the following pages help you do that.

Chapter 1: High Involvement Lessons

Today's students can be a tough audience for a teacher. It's easy to feel we must be entertainers to hold their attention. The attention spans of students seem to be shrinking fast. Given this reality, how are we to conduct our lessons?

This chapter offers four strategies designed for this:

1-1 Action flow plans	1-3 Teaching in layers not lumps
1-2 Quick pace	1-4 Limited variety

The first strategy helps us plan lessons with plenty of involvement and movement. It also suggests a format for doing that. The next strategy helps us stay alert to times we need to quicken the pace, as when we notice some minds are beginning to wander. Quickening the pace is easier when we do not try to get all students to master a topic at one time, when we teach in layers, not lumps, which is the focus of the third strategy. Together, these three strategies help us add variety to our lessons. The last strategy helps us avoid too much variety. It helps us keep variety from becoming too confusing and unsettling to students or us.

Strategy 1-1   Action flow plans

> Use a variety of instructional strategies that flow smoothly, interestingly.
> **Purpose:** To keep all students actively involved.

As its name suggests, an action flow plan is high on energy and movement. The aim is to get enough action going so students get involved in learning without teacher threats or rewards. A typical action flow lesson flows with pace and variety. In one lesson there is some of this and some of that. If *this* does not capture the attention of a student, perhaps *that* will.

Each lesson often uses several instructional strategies, depending on what we want to accomplish at each step. Do we want students to think at this point? If so, how can we get them to do that? Do we want students to begin constructing personal meanings? If so, how do we get them to do that? We plan ahead for the instructional strategies to use at each point. Many such strategies are included in this book.

The pace of the lesson avoids lulls and hints of boredom. We keep momentum rolling. We want students to feel time flies, never drags. We want to avoid

Work consists of whatever a body is obliged to do. Play consists of whatever a body is not obliged to do.
—Mark Twain

interludes in which students have nothing to do. Therefore, we tend to move quickly, even when students have not yet mastered a topic. We plan to overlap content from day to day, so we know we always have future chances to improve mastery.

Here is an example of a lesson sequence in this action flow style.

Action flow plan one: Think-share-learn

1. **The question, all write strategy** Consider posing a thinking question to a class, such as, "What makes for a good paragraph?" or "What do we all know about planets and stars?" or "How can we tell the difference between a courageous act and a foolish act?" or "What are some ways we can dream up to make mental addition easier?" or "How might we improve the lunch room (or anything of interest to students)?"

   Then ask each student to respond to the question by making some private notes. Ask with confidence, expecting they will all do so. Don't worry if some do nothing at the outset. We want the flow of the action eventually to capture student attention.

   > [This is the **question, all write strategy**. The teacher asks a question, all students reflect and make their own notes. *Note: This strategy and all others in bold type are discussed in more detail elsewhere. Most of the strategies named in this chapter are detailed in Chapter Two, "Everyday Instruction Strategies."*]

2. **The attentive discussion strategy** When you see three or four students have already finished writing, announce, "Just one moment more," or say, "Just finish the thought you are now writing." Do not wait until most students finish. Keep the pace upbeat. Students will soon learn it's not important to write everything in their minds.

   Then say, "I'd like to have a few of your share your ideas. Who'll be willing to go first?"

   Invite responses and discussion. Yet don't let the discussion go too long. When you sense involvement may soon slump, move on. Better to have a discussion too short than too long.

   > [That is the **attentive discussion strategy**. It goes on only as long as it holds attention high.]

3. **The sharing pairs strategy** Say, "Please pair up with someone nearby and share your thoughts or notes. Just a brief time for this sharing. Go!" Say "Go!" as if starting a race. Zip up the energy level. Then let students pick their own partners, helping only those who can't manage. Allow students to learn this kind of self-management. Another time you can help students learn how to move into pairs efficiently.

   When you see two or three pairs have finished talking, announce, "Just one moment more please," or "Just finish the thought you are now on." And

Attitudes are catching. Children are extensions of us. When we make lessons come alive with what I call Hot Teaching, every child becomes a winner.
—*Marva N. Collins*

then firmly call the class together. Even if some students have not *started* talking on the topic, do not worry. When students eventually realize you do not give excess time for small group talk, they learn to move into their discussions quickly.

[That is the **sharing pairs strategy**. Pairs share their thoughts.]

4. **The attentive lecture strategy**   Without waiting for all pairs to be ready (we want *activity* to catch students up and *waiting* has no activity in it) say, "Who will share something you or your partner talked about?" That often leads to an attentive discussion.

You may then say, "Here are some thoughts I have about this." Let the words you send out call to order the students slow to disengage from sharing pairs. Do not repeat what you say. Do not frown. In time students will learn to come up to your quick pace. If you choose to share your ideas, talk only as long as the class attention remains high. Move to another strategy when you sense attention to your lecture may soon lag. Shorter is better than longer.

[This is the **attentive discussion strategy**. The teacher talks to a class only as long as students remain attentive.]

5. **Options for proceeding**   Again use the **question, all write strategy:** "You may have clarified or changed your ideas by now. Take a moment and make some additional notes to yourself or, if you like, draw something."

Or, return to the **attentive discussion strategy:** "Anyone willing to share reactions to what you just heard or share any other ideas you have?"

Or, do something else for a bit.

6. **The outcome sentence strategy**   The lesson could be concluded with, "Please think back over what we have done so far. We began with a question and did some thinking and sharing. See if you can get something for yourself from this lesson."

Point to the chart you had earlier posted or written on the chalkboard:

> **I learned...**
> **I was surprised...**
> **I'm beginning to wonder...**
> **I rediscovered...**
> **I feel...**
> **I promise I will...**

I get inspired when I am able to understand something without the help of anyone else. I feel smart.
—*Jo Ann, high school*

You might say, "Perhaps write some endings to phrases like these. You might write: *I learned...,* or *I was surprised...,* or *I'm beginning to wonder...,* or *I rediscovered...,* or *I feel...,* or *I promise I will...,* or anything like that. See how many outcomes you can get for yourself from this lesson. Go."

[This is the **outcome sentence strategy**. Students reflect on a lesson seeking to extract personal meaning from it.}

When three or four students have stopped writing say, "Just one more moment please." Alert students that the lesson will soon move on.

And then, if appropriate, "Anyone willing to read aloud one of their outcome sentences?"

Perhaps then, time permitting, "Sit with your partner again and take turns sharing one or two things you wrote."

Sequence One, the think-share-learn sequence, illustrates one high involvement lesson. The steps would, of course, need to be adjusted for various grade levels and subject specialties. The general format: Questions are raised to stimulate student interest, and only then does the teacher give information. This sequence contrasts with lessons that start with infor-mation, that in effect give students answers before they ask the questions.

Three additional sample sequences are below.

Action flow plan two: Practice-instruct-review

Format note   This sequence and the following sequences are presented in a more condensed format. It is a format I find works well when planning lessons. It helps teachers keep alert to the flow of the action. In this format, we indicate in a left margin: (1) the strategy we will use at each step of the lesson, (2) the approximate time we see the lesson consuming and perhaps (3) whether the class is to sit as a whole unit or in smaller groupings. On the right we list what the teacher will do.

1. Choral work:
   Whole class
   4-6 minutes

   Teacher shows cards containing math facts, chemical symbols, spelling words, proper language usage phrases, or any material students are to internalize. Students chant out each card in a rhythm led by teacher. Teacher turns cards briskly and encourages high energy with, "A little more power please."

   [This is the **choral work strategy.** Students chant together to review and memorize facts.]

2A. Guided practice:
   Whole class
   3-6 minutes

   Teacher poses a problem to be solved from yesterday's lesson. Each student works at desk. After students start working, teacher solves problem correctly on board. Students check own work. Focus is on student practicing. No expectation is held that all students must already have mastered the material. Teacher assesses the state of content mastery as the lesson proceeds. Extended discussion is avoided to keep the pace moving.

   [This is the **guided practice strategy.** Students write answers and check their own work.]

Boredom is the bitter fruit of too much routine or none at all.
—Brendan Francis

2B. If much confusion:
Think aloud
Whole class
5-10 minutes

If teacher notices much confusion, teacher works some problem aloud, after students have had a try. The aim is to model thinking that solves the problem. Math example: "Since I don't know what to put here, I think I'll try an estimate. I see I need something larger than six because… etc." Science example: "How should I approach this? How would it work if I…Oops, that doesn't work. Let me try…etc."

[This is the **think aloud strategy.** Teacher speaks aloud what goes on in his or her mind.]

3A. If understanding is low: Sharing pairs
5-10 minutes

Students are told to pick a partner and help each other or, if both understand, to create new challenges for each other. Teacher circulates and helps out.

3B. If understanding is high: Whole class
6-12 minutes

Teacher introduces easy example of new work, thinking aloud while working it out on the board. Teacher poses a similar problem for students to work at seats and then works the problem on the board, again thinking aloud. A slightly harder problem is then posed. Students work it and then the teacher works it on the board. The sequence continues at a pace that is comfortably forward. Extended discussions are avoided. Confusions are left to be handled another day. The lesson moves on *before* interest lags.

[This is the **think aloud strategy.** Teacher explains procedure step by step, saying aloud what might go on inside the mind as the problem is being worked through.]

4. Review test:
Whole class
4-8 minutes

To review and reinforce old work, teacher starts review test. Teacher writes problem one on board and pauses while students work the problem by themselves. After students get started, teacher puts correct work on board. Students correct own work. Teacher proceeds that way through a set of problems. No instruction is involved. Grading is not involved. The focus is on review, self-correction and personal challenge. The pace is sufficiently brisk to maximize student involvement.

[This is the **review test strategy**. Teacher poses a question, students write the answer, teacher gives correct answer and students check own work; teacher poses a second question and the process continues.]

Teachers inspire students by, "Good Luck!"
—Jeffrey, 3rd grade

5. Voting: Whole class *1 minute*	Teacher might ask: "How many did some good risking on today's review test? How many strength-ened old understandings? How many like the way they handled today's review test?" The idea here is to give a moment for students to assess their own learning processes or learning outcomes and to express themselves. No grades are to be taken. No rewards for excellence. No slights to those not yet excellent. [This is the **voting strategy**. Teacher asks questions beginning with "How many of you" and students raise hands.]

Action flow plan three: Cushioning-underexplain-learning pairs

1. Cushioning: Whole class *1-2 minutes*	"We will talk about something new today. Do not feel any need to understand this completely right now. We will review and help each other later on, so relax and let's just see what happens today." [This is the **cushioning strategy**. Teacher aims to reduce student anxiety and maximize a relaxed open-minded attentiveness.]
2. Underexplain and learning pairs: Whole class *5-15 minutes*	Teacher presents a concept or principle. Example: "There are lots of ways to get a balance beam like this to balance. You can move this center point or the position of the weights, as I am doing here. You can invent your own system, but one general rule that works is...." Explanation continues, but is brief, so perhaps only one-half the class understands. Then teacher says: "Now get together in pairs. Help each other figure out how to do this. When you both get it, work some practice problems. If both remain stuck, ask another pair for help." [This is the **underexplain and learning pairs strategy.** The teacher *underexplains* so many students have something to puzzle over. The teacher then gives time for pairs to help each other.]
3. Attentive lecture/discussion: Whole class *Time as appropriate*	"How did you do? What did you figure out? What questions still remain?" Discussion or explanation as appropriate, but no longer than whole-class involvement is maintained.

A good leader inspires people to have confidence in the leader: a great leader inspires people to have confidence in themselves.

—Anonymous

4. Ask a friend:
Individual work
*Time as
appropriate*

"Now please work on your individual sheets. Practice good thinking. If you get stuck, ask any friend for help."

[This is the **ask a friend strategy.** The teacher uses language that grows a feeling of community support in the classroom.]

Action flow plan four: Lecture-share-learn

1. Speak-write:
Whole class
2-5 minutes

Example of an extended lecture: "The Enlightenment, which took place more or less in the 18th century, was also called the Age of Reason. What happened was..." Teacher then continues until a natural break in the material is reached, but not more than 5 minutes. Teacher then says, "Take a moment and write the key ideas you heard so far or any questions you have."

2. Working alone
1-2 minutes

When three or four students have finished writing, teacher says, "One more moment please."

3. Speak-write:
Whole class
3-5 minutes

Lecture continues to next natural break point, but not so long that students cannot hold the material comfortably in mind. Then: "Again, please make some notes about what you heard or questions you have.

4. Alternate, as
above. *Time as
appropriate,
ending before high
attention slips.*

That sequence continues: Teacher talks very briefly. Then waits while students make notes.

[This is the **speak-write strategy.** Teacher lectures with pauses every few minutes for students to use for thinking and writing.]

5. Sharing pairs
*4-8 minutes,
depending on how
long sharing is
productive.*

"Pair up now and share a summary of what you heard, or what you consider important points, or what questions occur to you."

6. Lecture summary:
Whole class
2-5 minutes

"Let me summarize what I would most like you to get, what I see as the main points."

7. Attentive
discussion whole
class. *Time as
appropriate*

"Who would be willing to share ideas or reactions or questions?"

8. Outcome sentences
Individual writing.
2-4 minutes

"Reviewing the lesson, make note of some key things you were able to get from it. You can use the starter phrases: I learned..., I rediscovered, or any others on the outcome sentence chart posted."

*Be sincere; be brief;
be seated.*

—*Franklin D.
Roosevelt*

9. Whip around, pass option: Whole class whip around.
Time as appropriate

"Starting at this wall, let's whip around the class. When it comes your turn, read one of your outcome sentences or, if you prefer, say, 'I pass.'"

[This is the **whip around, pass option strategy.** Each student in sequence is invited to speak or to pass.]

In summary   These four sequence outlines are meant only to be suggestions. For some teachers and with some students, the above sequences might need major modifications. These plans merely illustrate a planning style that involves a fairly quick pace and lots of variety. The test for any action flow plan is straightforward: How well does it produce a lesson that catches all students up in learning activity and keeps the students active throughout the lesson?

Note, too, that the plans are not particularly new. Sequence one, for example, is similar to the "Think, Pair, Share" series developed by Frank Lyman at the University of Maryland (McTighe and Lyman 1988), and sequence two is similar to Barak Rosenshine's (1979, 1983) "guided practice" in his seven-step direct instruction model.

The three strategies that follow expand the suggestions included in the above planning strategy. They are valuable in whole-class lessons and, in fact, generally in teaching today's students.

Strategy 1-2   Quick pace

Notice when students are losing interest and promptly change the content or activity. **Purpose:** To avoid losing student involvement because the pace is too slow.

Life seems to be speeding up nowadays and students today seem to have absorbed that pace. Many students certainly have short attention spans and little patience for what is slow and deliberate. In any case, students usually stay more involved more of the time when we move fairly quickly through course work and lessons.

An example from my own teaching illustrates a classic error. In the past I would explain something, realize I could say it another way and then go ahead and use that new explanation. Then I would ask, "Any questions?" By that time all the students who got it the first time began to get restless. Was I about to explain it a third time?

The secret of being a bore is to tell everything.
—Voltaire

Sometimes a student would say, yes, he did have a question. Then I got stuck. Could I refuse his request for assistance? Usually not. Most often I would explain the topic a third time, making it difficult for students who already understood to stay alert.

It's like waiting in a slow line. It can be frustrating to wait for something you need. Nothing dampens the learning energy of a class more than waiting around for something that interests them, something they can dig their mental teeth into.

I have learned over the years to avoid saying, "Any questions?" When I slip and do ask, as I sometimes do, I might say, "How many others have questions and would like us to come back to this another time?" Or I might say, "Pair up with someone nearby and talk over your understanding with each other, helping those who still have questions." Either of these responses I find is less likely to slow the pace of a lesson.

More fundamentally, I search for strategies of instruction that give me alternative ways of helping students who have questions. In this book, as examples, see **learning pairs, ask a friend, sharing pairs, review test, support groups, class tutor, I say review.** I also recommend using small groups occasionally for reteaching material to students who need that.

The pace of choice, and especially with the restless students of today, is the quick pace, the pace of high involvement, the pace that keeps consciousness high, that does not let it slip low.

For a daily lesson, this often means lots of small steps, steps that involve a change in either topic or procedure. We make that change as soon as we sense a slackening of involvement, as when student attention dips or the energy in the room slips. The change is usually best made sooner, not later. Once students become disengaged it takes extra effort to get them fully involved.

We use the power of expectations on slower students. We expect dallying students to speed up to our pace. We do not slow down to theirs. We step ahead at a pace that energizes students' awareness and keeps as many as possible actively involved. We also run our classes in ways that allow us to return to topics again and again, so students expect that they can get it later if they do not get it now. Strategies for doing this are elsewhere in this book.

Do we ever want to slow down? Yes, in some cases. For some of us, those whose minds tend to snap along too fast, slowing down may be the wise adjustment. That is the adjustment to make, too, when topics require more than usual mulling. We might then pause longer, speak more deliberately. Or we might ask students to do some reflecting and note-making, or thought-exchanging with a partner. We might want to slow down, too, when students get too frazzled. Students occasionally need to be calmed and slowed.

The best preparation for being a happy or useful man or woman is to live fully as a child.
— Plowden Report

We must all learn to adjust speeds so they are appropriate to our students and topics. This is discussed by David Berliner, Jere Brophy and Barak Rosenshine, for example. But more of us are likely to belabor a point rather than to rush through it. We also are likely to re-explain a point rather than let it go for another day. So for most of us, most of the time, the speed of choice today is the quick pace.

A Teacher Comments

After you talked about quick pace I became very aware when the pace was too slow for some students. My biggest example was board work. I had some students putting work on the board while others in the room sat in dead time, just watching. Worse yet, I would ask the board writers to explain their work, which often produced more dead time in audience eyes. I discontinued doing that. When I have board work now I have all students doing desk work at the same time. And when I need something explained I do it myself and keep the pace moving.

—Vicki Summers, Math Teacher

Strategy 1-3 Teaching in layers not lumps

Plan to return to topics frequently rather than try to produce mastery at any one time. **Purpose:** To allow students to master a topic through a quick pace and lesson variety.

A quick pace need not result in superficial learning. We can avoid lack of mastery by returning frequently enough to a topic so students eventually learn it fully and deeply. We can overlap content and spiral ahead to mastery. We can teach in layers, not lumps.

For example, using sequence two above, students could handle material already presented by choral work, by engaging in some guided practice, by hearing the teacher think aloud and by completing a review test. It is not necessary to stick with one topic for long time periods to get students to master it. It may not even be desirable. We can teach much the same way we learned our native language, dealing with it again and again, allowing mastery to develop gradually.

If we adopt this strategy, then, we plan lessons that keep touching on prior material until sufficient mastery is reached. Several instructional strategies useful for teaching in layers are in the following chapters.

Strategy 1-4 Limited variety

Use enough variety to keep students involved, not so much variety that the students become insecure. **Purpose:** To give students the security they need to relax and learn.

If we succeed in giving the love of learning, the learning itself is sure to follow.

—John Lubbock

The **action flow plan** strategy calls on us to notice when class energy is slipping and to do something different. Perhaps ask students to work in pairs for a while. Or move from logical thinking to an artistic challenge: "Draw something as you think of this issue." Or perhaps toss out an oddball topic. We must use our own strengths, in responding to the fact that nowadays too much sameness will dampen student awareness.

Yet too much variety can raise student anxiety, raise fears. The modern world can be confusing and fearful indeed to students. Many of them need far more security and regularity than variety. Many of us too. We all work best within certain boundaries.

This strategy, then, would have us balance speed and variety with security and stability. I find the best results coming from lots of variety, but within comfortable, familiar forms. This recommends favoring a variety of strategies, but using and reusing the same ones so students become comfortable with them. It also favors keeping routines steady, as by always beginning class the same way, handling homework the same way, and so on. It recommends changing topics often, but within regular structures. Or changing sequences, but without abandoning familiar elements. We use variety, but within boundaries that maintain security.

The ideal of using the present simply to get ready for the future contradicts itself....We always live at the time we live and not at some other time, and only by extracting at each present time the full meaning of each present experience are we prepared for doing the same thing in the future.

—John Dewey

Chapter 2: Everyday Instruction Strategies

The focus of Chapter One was on how we can plan whole-class lessons that will catch up students in active involvement and keep them involved. Considering today's students, I suggest plenty of movement and variety. We usually get better results with a pace that is fairly quick and mastery that is approached in layers, not lumps.

This chapter discusses a set of instructional strategies particularly handy in conducting such lessons. Although many of these will be familiar, the descriptions below may suggest new ways to use them. As a group, they give us a flexible set of everyday strategies from which we can draw, a basic tool-kit for conducting high-involvement lessons.

Most strategies of this chapter were mentioned in Chapter One:

- Question, all write
- Outcome sentences
- Underexplain and learning pairs
- Ask a friend
- Sharing pairs
- Whip around, pass option
- Choral work
- Attentive lecture
- Speak-write
- Attentive discussion
- Think aloud
- Guided practice
- Review test
- Voting
- Simple discovery lesson

One other strategy mentioned in Chapter One, Cushioning, is not included here. Cushioning is not an instructional strategy as much as a confidence building strategy. It helps students stay comfortable with a layered-learning approach, with the fact that they may not achieve mastery at any one time. Cushioning is discussed in Chapter Three, **For Solid Student Confidence.**

Strategy 2-1   Question, all write

> Ask all students to write answers to questions before offering an answer or calling on one student. **Purpose:** To maximize the number of students who think about a question.

Our mistakes and failures are always the first to strike us, and outweigh in our imagination what we have accomplished and attained.

—Goethe

When dealing with groups of students it is useful to insert a pause between the asking of a question and calling on someone to respond. That pause or wait time, as Mary Budd Rowe (1974) calls it, is designed to give all students a chance to frame an answer in their minds. Without wait time more students are likely to sit passively, waiting for the students who are always ready to respond to speak up.

Two major problems are common with wait time. The first is that it's difficult for teachers to continue inserting those pauses. A teacher's instinct is to keep the class busy, and wait time can feel like an invitation to restlessness. The second problem is that many students cannot use that pause to get their answer precisely framed.

An option is to ask all students to note what they think an answer might be.

- "What was the name of the person who shot President Lincoln?" the teachers asks. "Please make a note of your answer."

- "Why might water boil at a lower than normal temperature? Write your best guess on scrap paper."

When all students are asked to *write* an answer for themselves, involvement tends to be high and thought tends to be precise.

The teacher might then say, "Who would be willing to read something they wrote?"

Since all students have had a chance not only to think but to write, and since they need not improvise an answer orally but can simply read what they wrote, more students are usually ready to speak up. Also, if there is a single correct answer to the question, all have a private response before them to compare with the correct answer. All, therefore, have more of an active learning opportunity.

Question, all write with personal slates Some teachers have students show their written work to the teacher. They may give each student a small personal chalkboard or what some students call a white board. "Three-fifths equals what percent? Write your answers on your slate. Hold it up when ready."

There are advantages to this procedure: Teachers can tell how well the class understands the problem. They can personally acknowledge those who are correct. They can also spot students who are working carelessly or not at all.

There are disadvantages as well: Slow students might be embarrassed at having to show imperfect work to the teacher. Furthermore, the emphasis of the strategy shifts from activating personal thinking for students to getting teacher-checked work. In terms of bringing out the best from all students, I prefer a personal thinking approach to a teacher-checked approach with this question, all write strategy.

People seldom improve when they have no model to copy but themselves.

—Anonymous

Strategy 2-2 Outcome sentences

Ask students to reflect back on an experience and write endings to such phrases as "I learned...," "I'm beginning to wonder...," "I was surprised...," **Purpose:** To get students to create meaningful learnings for themselves. Also to develop the habit of learning from experience.

We want students to learn. Yet we want those learnings to be *meaningful,* to make sense to them, not merely to be strings of words they remember. Moreover, we want students to be *life-long* learners, to learn how to learn on their own, to learn how to get meanings from experiences they have after they leave classrooms. This strategy is designed to serve those purposes.

This strategy can be built on most any classroom experience. A teacher might give a lecture, conduct a discussion or demonstrate a science process. A social studies teacher might use thirty minutes to tell anecdotes about an event in history, show a map of the region involved, and explain what he thinks about the event. The teacher might then say:

"Please reflect on the discussion and see what you can get out of it for yourself. Look at this chart I posted. You might write some endings to phrases like these. You might, for example, write: I learned... Or you might start off a sentence saying: I was surprised... Or: I'm beginning to wonder... Or any other such sentence. Think back over our discussion. See if you can find some learnings for yourself and write them down."

> **Outcome Sentences**
>
> I learned...
> I was surprised...
> I'm beginning to wonder...
> I'm getting clearer about...
> I rediscovered...
> I promise I will...
> I am feeling...

Many options then exist. Two that often work well:

- The teacher says, "Any one willing to read one of the outcome statements they wrote?" A few volunteers are heard. Teacher then asks students to pair up and share some of their outcome sentences with one another. The two sharing processes usually help students find learnings they themselves had not yet noticed.

- The teacher starts a whip-around, giving each student a turn either to read one outcome sentence to the whole class or to say, "I pass."

Either option could lead into a wholeclass summary discussion, with the teacher adding the points he would emphasize.

Our aim is to discipline for activity, for work, for good, not for immobility, not for passivity, not for obedience.

—Maria Montessori

Hints

- Use the strategy often, as by asking students to write outcome sentences on: each chapter they read in the text, the project each group just completed, a guest speaker's presentation, a current events discussion, a film, the unit just completed, their holiday vacation, the first week of school, the stories they read, each day's class.

- Keep an Outcome Sentence chart posted, so students have handy thinking starters whenever they are asked to think about what they learned.

- Consider adding other phrases to the chart, such as: I now realize... I would someday like to... I would conclude... I cannot agree with... I would like to find more about...

- Consider asking students to keep their Outcome Sentences in a Learning Log or use them as material for a student portfolio, which could later be used to summarize and illustrate the accomplishments of a student.

Note that this strategy does not expect all students to get the *same* learning from a lesson. The aim is to get meaningful, *personal* learnings. Said another way, the teacher does not want students merely to remember words or otherwise get superficial learnings. The teacher is aiming to stimulate students to think, digest information and create meaning for themselves. For more on this, see bibliographic references to metacognition.

A Teacher Comments

I used the Outcome Sentences strategy to wrap up our weather unit. After reviewing our unit, we charted as a group all our learnings. Then each child picked one that they liked and wrote it on a raindrop pattern. The raindrops were placed on our April bulletin board.
                                                                —Susan Willis

Strategy 2-3   Underexplain and learning pairs

Explain only enough to get some students fully understanding. Then ask pairs to work together to help each other understand or to further explore the topic. **Purpose:** To maximize thoughtful involvement in lessons and give students cooperative learning experiences.

Here is a strategy designed to get students to learn in a way that keeps them involved, exercises their thinking power and grows mutual support in a classroom. Imagine this part of a lesson outline:

I get inspired when beautiful music is played or when people say I look pretty.
—*Alissa, 3rd grade*

Whole class	To find 40% of a number, we can simply multiply the number by .40. For example, 40% of 200 could be done this way: $$\begin{array}{r} 200 \\ \underline{\times\ .40} \\ 80.00 \end{array}$$
Working alone	Try one by yourself. See what you think 40% of 120 would be.
Whole class and Learning pairs	How many got 48? While you were working the problem at your desk, I worked it here on the board. How many did it somewhat like I did it? How many found another way to get 48? (A long discussion is avoided here, to keep a quick pace.) Here are three more problems (writes on board). First work them by yourself. Then turn to a partner. Compare answers and help each other understand. If both understand, try creating a new problem for each other, maybe a harder one. Go! (When students start work, teacher begins working the problems correctly on board, so all can get help whenever it's needed.) Teacher scans class work often, answering questions with, "If both of you are stuck, ask another pair for help." When about half the pairs seem finished, the teacher calls, "Just a few more seconds." To keep an involving pace, there is no waiting for all to finish. Later lessons are used for necessary reteaching and review.
Whole class and Learning pairs	Looks like most of you got something like my examples. Here are three more problems, a bit harder. (Teacher writes a few problems that advance student work.) Again, work these problems alone and then compare with your partner. If both understand, you might challenge each other with something more difficult. Or write out a word problem I can use someday and put it on my desk. Go!

Genius means little more than the faculty of perceiving in an unhabitual way.
—William James

Note that the teacher in this example *underexplained* the calculation procedure. Many teachers do the opposite. They *overexplain*. They might explain something, ask, "Any questions," and then reexplain. Or they might notice some students obviously puzzled and then reexplain. Or explain the procedure in another way. After two or three such explanations, three results are likely.

- Boredom sets in for students who understood the first explanation or who understood before the lesson even began. And energy slumps. Awareness dulls.

- Boredom sets in for the students who cannot concentrate awareness on one topic too long, some of whom are known as the "slow" students.

- Boredom sets in for students who do not learn well from any teacher explanation, the ones who need to discover things for themselves, often from hands-on experiences.

To avoid such outcomes, this teacher used an *underexplain* approach and put students into pairs to work it out together, or teach each other, or check each other's ideas and correctness.

A useful guideline for this strategy: Explain until only about half the students understand. Then put students into pairs to check and teach each other, or to create new problems for one another. Leave them in these pairs for a fairly brief time period, not so long that confused students feel stuck in their confusion and understanding students get bored by their inaction. Bring them together for enough sharing and/or explanation to get the pairs going. Then repeat the cycle, if appropriate, perhaps slightly raising the level of challenge.

Students slow to get to work I generally recommend against prodding the students who are slow to get started. That is usually counterproductive in the long run. I prefer to move the lesson along quickly and give enough easy examples so students eventually and naturally want to be involved.

Forming groups Students are often best left alone to select their own partners. It is often a useful challenge to students' developing self-responsibility. Students who do not find partners by themselves might be helped to pair up, but might also be left alone or talked to later and encouraged to risk reaching out to others more often, to practice more initiative in such situations. For each student, the teacher considers what would be best in the long run. This issue and other common problems of group work are discussed further in Chapter Seven.

Applied to discovery lessons Discovery-type problems work well with this underexplain, learning pair strategy.

- A teacher might show students two or three correct examples of something and two or three incorrect examples. Students are asked to see if they can write the rule illustrated and/or if they can write additional pairs of correct and incorrect examples. This is similar to the "concept attainment strategy," see Joyce and Weil (1991).

- A teacher might demonstrate a scientific principle, such as how a candle flame reacts to insufficient air. Students are asked to write a guess for an explanation and/or to write a useful application of the principle illustrated.

- A teacher might give students a new paint brush, or any new tool. Or might challenge them to discover their own way to add fractions, do long division, or learn any useful skill. Or pose any provocative issue.

What is a classroom? A place for students and teachers. Students struggle, succeed, fail, give up, try again. Teachers struggle, succeed, fail, give up, try again.
—Esther Wright

In such cases, the teacher poses a problem and asks pairs to work together to solve it. After a brief time, if useful, the whole class could share progress, followed by pairs again resuming their work. Students who solve the issue could be invited to roam as "tutors" for students wanting extra help.

In many cases, as in the lesson on percent presented above, the students are best asked to work on the problem alone at the outset. That maximizes involvement. When some students seem to have solved it or when some seem to be getting stuck, the teacher might say, "Take your time, but whenever you feel ready, find a partner and help each other." Or if pairs are already set, "Whenever you see you and your partner are both finished, get together and share your thinking."

The power of expectations A hidden strength of this strategy flows from the expectations it communicates. The more it is used, the more students are likely to appreciate the fact that one responsible adult, this teacher, fully expects them to be able to think and learn and fully expects them be able to support and help one another. Even if students should never need the subject matter acquired or should one day forget its details, they may become more confirmed in believing that each of them is an able, positive person.

An additional example of the **underexplain and learning pairs strategy** can be found in sequence 3 in the **Action flow plan strategy**. Note that this strategy is similar to Arthur Whimbey's paired problem solving (Whimbey and Lochhead 1986) and Stan Pogrow's controlled floundering. See also work on inductive teaching as, for example, discussed by Jerome Bruner (Bruner and Kenny 1966).

A Teacher Comments

I tried using the Underexplain and Learning Pairs strategy to introduce a program in computers. It worked great! Those who knew a lot about computers just took right off. Those who didn't really caught on from their peers.

—Cheryl Miller

Strategy 2-4   Ask a friend

Encourage students needing help to "ask a friend." **Purpose:** To nurture a feeling of mutual support among students.

The shoe that fits one person pinches another; there is no recipe for living that suits all cases.
—Carl Jung

My first response to a student who asks what page we are on, or who asks me to repeat the homework directions, or who is unsure of how to complete a worksheet is usually, "Please ask a friend."

I find that comment serving me in several ways. It eases my load; many students have little difficulty getting the help they need from peers. It generates mutual respect and appreciation among students and builds a healthy, interdependent class community. It communicates that I assume others in the class can be "friends" if only we see them as such, which is usually the case.

Grace Pilon (1991), from whom I learned that phrase, notes that some elementary grade students invent confusion to get more chances to ask for teacher help. For such students asking one friend may not be enough. Moorman and Moorman (1989) offer the phrase, "Ask three then me." A teacher might announce to a class, "Whenever you are working at individual tasks and need assistance, please ask three others before asking me." Say a student approached afterwards, one might then remind the student, "Please ask three then me." Or one might simply inquire, "Did you ask three before me?"

A Teacher Comments

At first, some of the children found asking a friend difficult because they wanted an immediate answer from the teacher — they weren't sure they could trust all their peers for the correct answer. After the third time of Ask a Friend, the students became more trusting of each other.

—Miriam Harmon

Strategy 2-5   Sharing pairs

Ask students to pair up and share thoughts on a question or topic.
Purpose: To help students talk about their ideas and hear the ideas of others.

One way to get students actively involved with an issue is to ask them to talk about it. The most activity comes when they talk in pairs. In pairs, each is either a talker or listener. No one is left out. (See Chapter Seven for more on group size and selection.)

The sharing pair strategy not only invites active involvement, it also gets students putting words to ideas that may be a bit vague to them. The strategy also meets students' basic needs for social contact and freedom of expression.

Sharing can be used often and in many situations.

- **To share opinions** "Many people disagree about X. Before we discuss this as a group, please pair up and exchange your thoughts or questions with one person. Just a few moments for this."

- **To exchange understandings** as when students share their outcome statements on today's lesson or share what they did on homework.

- **During a lecture** to give students a chance to put ideas into their own words and thereby get more meanings from a lecture. "Take a few moments and share your reactions to what I've said so far with someone nearby."

- **After the question, all write strategy** on a question with multiple answers. "Please share your thoughts with a partner and then we'll get together and see what we all think."

No, you never get any fun out of the things you haven't done.

—*Ogden Nash*

- **In the midst of a discussion** to give many people who have something to say the chance to give voice to their ideas or confusion.

- **To add energy into the room** as when most students have been working alone for a while or have been mainly listening to others. "Take a few minutes and share your thoughts or your work with one other person."

A Teacher Comments

I tried Sharing Pairs when working with prepositional phrases in my slower English classes. We had been working with prepositions for a few days, and homework was going slowly. Instead of having students take work home, I asked them to choose a partner and do sentences together. Students were pleasantly surprised at the progress they made when they helped each other. This was a very productive class for everyone.
— Cathy McGarrahan

Strategy 2-6   Whip around, pass option

Ask a group of students each to take a turn responding to a question or, if they prefer, to say, "I pass." **Purpose:** To increase the number of students who speak up. Also to give students practice in managing themselves responsibly.

Sometimes we want to hear from lots of students, not just a few volunteers. In such situations, a teacher could say:

> "Let's whip down the row of students by the window. When it comes your turn, either give your thoughts or say, 'I pass'. There is no need to respond if you prefer not to."

The whip around, pass option strategy can be used with all or part of a class. It is especially useful when the issue addressed will likely be viewed differently by different people. It gives teachers an efficient way to get students sharing their different perspectives. Examples:

Some parents could do more for their children by not doing so much for them.

—Anonymous

- "We all have different ideas on X. Let's start with Bob and whip around the whole class, giving each person a chance to share one idea. You can always say, 'I pass', if you prefer. But first take a moment to think about what idea you might want to share. (Pause) Okay, Bob, please start us off."

- "Look over the *outcome sentences* you wrote about that chapter. I'd like to whip around at least part of the class now and ask you to read just one of your sentences or if, you like, say 'I pass'. Let's start today with Helen."

This strategy not only gives all students a chance to voice their ideas, it tends to raise the interest level of a class. Students often listen very closely to how others respond to an issue to which they too have a response. It also gives the students who are more shy a chance to get their ideas expressed and recognized.

In addition it poses a valuable self-managing choice to all students: Should I risk speaking up or risk saying "I pass"? For some students in some situations, risking saying "I pass" might call for the greater courage. In any case, teachers offering students the choice to pass invite them to practice managing their lives wisely and responsibly.

A Teacher Comments

I discovered that the Whip Around, Pass Option strategy makes students more responsible. I've used it quite a lot and have noticed lately that the students who passed because that was the "cool" thing to do are now participating. It has been really great to see the progression of these boys from everyone wanting to pass to 99 percent participation. It took a while, but the wait was worth it.

—Linda Prater

Strategy 2-7 Choral work

Flash a series of cards to which a class can respond in unison. **Purpose:** To get students to memorize material effortlessly. Also to heighten students' involvement and group energy.

Teachers of young children will often have students chanting material together, such as their a, b, c's. Many teachers report such a **choral work strategy,** as we have come to call it, valuable at all grade levels and for a variety of contents. Consider this:

1. Collect information you want students to internalize, such as chemical symbols (sodium fluoride = NaF) or proper language phrases (between you and me, he and I went). Print one item on a card and make a stack of such cards.

2. Hold up the stack and ask students to say each item aloud as you show it, speaking together. Read each card aloud yourself, moving through the pack briskly. Keep moving.

   Tell students you will use such choral work for a few minutes from time to time, so they can easily get material deep into their memories.

   The first day, include no more than ten or twelve cards. On subsequent days, as that material gets more familiar, you can begin to add new cards. If the stack gets too large, eliminate old cards. Yet from time to time, reintroduce old cards, to reactivate and deepen prior knowledge.

   The first time you do this, students will notice your confidence and, soon enough, most will be chanting out the cards in a choral style. After enough days, you can expect almost all to participate.

Always make speeches shorter than anybody dared hope.
—Lord Reading

You can make stacks of cards for any content you want students to internalize: States and their capitals, multiplication facts (7 X 5 = 35), tricky spelling words, formulas (Area of triangle = 1/2bh), or important health principles (a healthy breakfast).

Some teachers use cards like this each day. It usually peps up a class. It brings the voices in a room together, singing the people toward togetherness. That helps build a healthy community climate in class. It can also be a valuable change of pace. And little by little, as students internalize the material on the cards, they come to enjoy the confidence of calling out correct answers again and again.

Hints for choral work

- **Keep the cards turning** Do not worry that some students do not know the information on a card or say it incorrectly. Do not bother to make corrections. Repeating the same cards on many days gets students internalizing correct information.

  And do not worry that some students already know the information. If the pace is quick, they will enjoy being part of the group, using their voices, expressing their knowledge.

- **Back of card can be for you** By writing the same information on the back and front of the card, you can easily show students the information and see it yourself. After a bit, most teachers find they do not need to see that information. They do not have to chant along with students. Students carry it along well enough themselves.

- **Insert a pause for thought** Choral work is particularly effective for memorizing facts that come in pairs: A state and its capital, a chemical name and its symbol, or basic multiplication facts. For such information you can put one part on the front of the card, one part on the back. Sample instructions:

  > "Here are cards with our multiplication facts. I'll show each problem, like this." (Teacher shows, *4 X 5* =) "First we all chant that problem together. Then we have a beat of silence, so you can think of the answer, and then I'll flip over the card like this." (Teacher flips the card and shows, *20.*) "And then we all chant together the answer. Let's try it."

  > Teacher shows *7 X 6* = . Students chant together, *Seven times six.* The teacher pauses a beat, flips the card showing *42* while teacher and students together chant, *forty-two.* And the process continues for the set of cards.

Incidentally, some teachers are tempted to show only the "question" part, such as *7 X 6* = . They do not want to give students the answers. I do not recommend that procedure. I find it works better to show the question, give a beat for student mental activity, and then show the answer. Choral work aims for deep internalization of information and that is best done without worry about being right or wrong.

- **Uplevel group energy** An important benefit of choral work is in the group energy it generates. To get up that energy it's often useful for a teacher to intersperse choral work with calls such as, "Say it with power." "Speak up as if you mean it." "A little more energy please." "With more gusto."

- **Distinguish energy and loudness** When the noise level needs to be modulated, a teacher might demonstrate the difference between a soft, powerful voice and a weak, thin voice. We can even whisper with high energy. The teacher can then request voices with power but not noise. Students learn they can speak clearly and firmly, but not loudly.

- **Use sound variety** For variety, some teachers ask students to speak more or less loudly depending on how high the cards are being held at the moment. When the teacher holds the cards shoulder height, it means speak with a healthy volume. Waist high means speak strongly but with a whisper voice.

- **One say, all say option** I sometimes ask all students to respond in unison after one student has read the card aloud. Procedure: Hold up a card. Students willing to read it aloud raise hands; you nod at one. That student reads card aloud. You say, "Everyone" and then all repeat what that student says.

I occasionally use a similar procedure in other lesson formats.

> Teacher: "What is the definition of a noun?"
> Jacob: "A person, place or thing."
> Teacher: "Yes, a noun is a person, place or thing. All together class."
> All say together: "A noun is a person, place or thing."

- **Use it for emphasis** We can use the one say, all say option to reinforce any special content. Sample: "It is important to see the environment as one whole system. Together, please say that with me. (Teacher and students say, *The environment is one whole system.*) Let's say it again, with more power.
(All repeat, *The environment is one whole system.*) Yes, it is important to see that the environment is one whole, interdependent, active system that..."

A Teacher Comments

I tried Choral Work with my Essentials of Algebra/Geometry class. We were studying the names of the polygons. I would say, "A ten-sided polygon is called _____." The class would say, "Decagon." I went through all of them from three sides to ten sides, twelve and fifteen sides slowly. Then we went faster and faster through all the polygons. This was a great way for the students to memorize the polygons and to participate as a whole class.
—Cindy Huels

Personally I'm always ready to learn, although I do not always like being taught.
—Winston Churchill

Strategy 2-8   Attentive lecture

Watch students while lecturing and when attention begins to slip change either content or procedure. **Purpose:** To keep all students attentive in lectures.

This strategy is called an "attentive" lecture for it goes on only as long as it holds the groups attention.

Some educators would eliminate lectures. Lectures, they note, reduce learning to a passive process. I disagree. I have known teachers whose lectures can keep students actively involved for a long time. Most of us, unfortunately, cannot do that. But we can lecture well enough for short periods. And we will likely find situations in which that is the strategy of choice.

The key here is to watch for the beginnings of attention drift and shift before awareness falls too far. Pulling students from a pit of dullness is not easy. How does one make those shifts? There is no single formula, but here are examples of two transitions I often use.

- **The write-share shift**   If the lecture is rich with content worth thinking about, I often use a two-step shift. (1) I ask students to make notes on what they heard so far. "Perhaps write the main points, or your questions, or your personal reactions." When I see that one or two are finished making notes, I say, "One moment more." (2) I then ask all students to sit with a partner and share thoughts. While they do that, I consider what I might best do next. A discussion is often appropriate. Sometimes I can even resume my lecture. But sometimes I find it best to put the issue aside and come back fresh another time.

- **The quick review and out**   Sometimes the content is more routine or is essentially factual. It is usually inappropriate to ask students to reflect back on it and write thoughts, as in the shift above. I might then just quickly review what I covered and tell students we will pick up the material another time. Or I might ask a few students to restate one of the points they remember. Or I might simply say, "Before we turn to something new, please take a moment and review for yourself what we covered, perhaps noting questions that remain for you." The quick pace is important here. I do not want dullness to get deeper. I exit the lecture fairly quickly. Tomorrow is another day.

Strategy 2-9   Speak-write

Insert pauses in lectures and ask students to use pauses to note their reactions to what was said, a summary, personal questions or anything else. **Purpose:** To increase the learning power of lectures.

A teacher can also structure time for thinking during lectures. For that, I recommend the **speak-write** strategy. Here is a teacher introducing the strategy:

Let us open up our natures, throw wide the doors of our hearts and let in the sunshine of good will and kindness.

—O. S. Marden

"I will now talk to you for some time. I will use a speak-write procedure. That is, I will speak for a bit, until a convenient break in the material is reached, but not so long that you need to make notes while I am talking. I would like you to listen without being distracted by note-taking, and without being overwhelmed by too much material. So I will speak for perhaps three or four minutes.

Then I will pause for a minute or so. When I pause, your job is to write. What do you write? You have four choices. You may want to write a summary of what you heard me say. (Teacher writes on the chalkboard, 1 - SUMMARY.)

Or you may want to write questions about what I said. (Writes, 2 - QUESTIONS.)

Or you may want to write your reactions to what I spoke about. (Adds, 3 - REACTIONS.)

Or when I pause, you may write anything else you choose, or draw something if you prefer. Use the time to gather your thoughts in any way that works well for you." (Adds to the board list, 4 - ANYTHING ELSE.)

When I use this strategy, I then promptly begin the procedure, letting the practice of it demonstrate how I intend it to work. I do not invite questions about what I just said, which is likely to get me repeating my words and boring some students. Said another way, I use the **quick pace** and move right into my lecture, speaking for a few minutes, pausing for a minute or so for students to make notes, again speaking, then pausing for writing, and so on.

Often I follow several **speak-write** cycles with **sharing pairs:** "Now sit with a partner and compare thoughts and, perhaps, help each other clear up any confusion." That further helps students digest my lecture material. I often follow that with a whole class discussion.

In classes in which I lecture often, I post a small chart that reminds students of the four speak-write options. That reminds students how they might use the gaps between my presentation statements.

I once thought that if students were older and more mature, I would be able to speak longer than three to four minutes before stopping for writing time. I found that not to be the case. After three to four minutes I find both kindergarten and college students beginning to experience content overload and difficulty in maintaining attention.

There is nobody so irritating as somebody with less intelligence and more sense than we have.
—Don Herold

Incidentally, for very young children, those for whom writing is not possible or easy, I might say, "When I pause, you may write or draw something, if you like, or just sit quietly and see what goes on in your mind as you think back over what I said. Think it over for yourself."

A comment about visual aids: Some people recommend lots of visuals to augment lectures. Overhead projector notes. Chalkboard notes. Handouts, especially handouts with outlines, sometimes outlines with spaces in which students make notes as the lecture proceeds.

All these are valuable. They give students visual as well as oral input. They are especially valuable for the many students who learn more from seeing than hearing. Yet they do not remedy the problem of too much input, which is often the main problem of lectures. By themselves, visual aids do not give students the time they need to think and thereby to get personal meanings from lectures.

My recommendation, then, is to use plenty of visuals, including role playing and demonstrations if appropriate, but also to use plenty of think time, as by inserting silent pauses, using the speak-write strategy, or keeping a lecture brief and following it with the two-step shift outlined above.

Strategy 2-10   Attentive discussion

> Observe students during a discussion and when attention begins to slip change content or activity. **Purpose:** To keep all students involved in discussions.

Teachers often engage a whole class in discussion. But too often only part of a class will stay involved. The big talkers talk and the others wait for lunch. That leads to the first rule for effective class discussions.

Rule One

Continue discussions only as long as students remain attentive. Switch strategies as soon as group awareness begins slipping. With the attention span of today's students, that may come quickly, for it is the rare topic that holds them all for long. Sometimes, however, a discussion can be revitalized. For example:

- "How many of you basically agree with what Todd has been saying? "How many disagree? Are unsure?" That is the **voting** strategy. Which may be followed with, "How many people have something else to say? Let's hear from four people now. OK, you Tom, and then Jane, and then Sue and then Rick." I sometimes set up a group of speakers this way, which relaxes students who might otherwise worry about whether they should volunteer next and thereby increases attentiveness.

- "Please all take a moment to write or draw your ideas about what we have been talking about. What do you think about this now?" The **question, all write** strategy. Which might lead to, "Now turn to a neighbor and take two or three minutes to share your thoughts." The **sharing pair** strategy.

- "Let's use a class whip around. We'll start in this corner. When it is your turn, please say your ideas, even if it feels risky to you. This is a class in which we accept all thinking. Or, if you like, say with whom you agree. Or of course you may always pass." The **whip around, pass option** strategy.

We can't all be heroes because someone has to sit on the curb and clap as they go by.
—Will Rogers

- "Before we go on to something else, think back over the discussion and see if you can find some learnings or ideas for yourself from it. Let's sample a few and then decide if we want to talk more about this." The **outcome sentence** strategy.

Rule Two

The second rule is equally straightforward: Do not assume discussions stimulate meaningful thinking. They often do not. Often all that is stimulated is opinion exchange and thoughtless chatter. Discussions almost always work best as only a part of a more rounded lesson, as in this sequence.

1. First students think about the topic and make notes of their preliminary ideas.
2. Students pair up and briefly exchange thoughts.
3. A whole class discussion then follows, with volunteers speaking.
4. All students think back over the lesson and write outcome sentences, which may then be shared in a class whip around, discussed in sharing pairs, and/or placed in portfolios.

I find discussions rarely produce as much learning as their high reputation suggests. Most students seem to experience a discussion much like they do a lecture: as a set of statements that do not add up to personal meaning, at least not until the statements are mulled over and digested. And in the case of a discussion, since the statements are often disconnected, sometimes repetitious, the statements are often difficult to mull over and digest.

Other ideas for discussions:

1. **Provocative topic list** Consider making notes of discussion topics that work well. This can be a handy list for future reference.

2. **Student discussion leader** Perhaps ask a student to lead some discussions and to announce when he or she recommends the class shifts to something else.

3. **Visuals** Write key words, ideas, or numbers on the chalkboard during a discussion. It helps students maintain focus. In addition, some students see better than they hear, and most students benefit when more than one sense is involved.

4. **Chalkboard writers** Especially when a list of ideas is being generated from a class, use two chalkboard writers. Two students are asked to write notes on the board as the class mentions them. The two recorders take turns writing, so one is always ready. In the case of rambling student comments, it is useful for the teacher to suggest to the writers what phrase to write on the board.

5. **Maximize eye contact** Many students on the edges of a group or in the back of a room feel they are not noticed, not part of class discussions. Scan the group, walk about the room, or occasionally change seating to minimize this problem.

Every man must do his own growing, no matter how tall his grandfather was.
—Laurence Peters

6. **Circle seating** Or change seating, perhaps only for class discussions. Consider circle or semi-circle seating. The more students who face each other, without having others in front of them, and the closer they are to the center of group action, the more they are apt to stay involved.

7. **The nod of recognition** To get people other than the usual big talkers into discussions, perhaps announce, "Sometimes I'll ask for volunteers to answer a question. You will raise your hand, and I will not call on you or anyone else for a moment or two. I might just look at you and nod. That means I noticed you were willing to volunteer, so you can put down your hand. I simply want to wait a bit, to give more time for people to think before calling on someone."

Strategy 2-11   Think aloud

> Talk aloud while working out a problem, so students can hear how your mind is operating. **Purpose:** To give students a model of how they might think. Also to illustrate thinking is not always linear.

Students often misunderstand what's involved in thinking through a problem. Many assume answers should come quickly and easily, without making lots of errors, as answers seem to come to the fastest of learners. When that does not happen for them, many lose confidence altogether in their ability to think. They become learners who must be spoon-fed, able only to memorize.

We can, however, teach students that problem-solving is usually slow and messy, rarely quick and easy. No need to be discouraged when it is otherwise. Perhaps the best way to teach that is to model it. As an example, consider this teacher, thinking aloud as she works a problem on the chalkboard:

> Let's see here, I could divide six into the fifty. Wait a minute. Would that help me find my answer? What was the problem again? Find one-sixth of 50. Dividing feels right. Let me try and see if I get something that at least looks approximately correct. If not, I'll give something else a try.

> Now, let's see, six goes into fifty… hm. Six times five is thirty. Six times seven is, uh, forty-two. That will fit. Six times eight is, is… forty eight, which is more like it. Six times nine is bound to be too much, forty-eight is just two less than fifty. So I'll write eight here, two here and….

With the **think aloud** strategy, part of the metacognitive learning field, the teacher talks in ways that reflect real searching, errors, correction of errors, and whatever else goes on in the mind of someone engaged in thinking. It is an effective way to teach an intellectual skill, like math problem solving, and to teach that learning is not tidy and straightforward, a lesson reassuring to students reluctant to admit they are confused.

Thinking aloud is especially effective in promoting real-life problem-solving skills. Consider this teacher, who has just said that he will show one way to handle a communication problem.

Now how am I going to argue with him when I'm really scared? I'm not sure what will happen. I want to tell him how I feel but... I don't know... It feels terribly scary. Think I'll make some notes. That might help me keep my mind on this issue.

To start, what is my purpose? My main purpose is ... (he continues).

I wonder if I have thought of all my alternatives. I already wrote down three. (He points to the board where he had written out the three.) There are probably ideas I haven't thought about. Maybe I'll ask Jean if she has some ideas...

Now I have notes, but how can I decide? I'd rather forget the whole thing. Yet I remember my purpose is... (he continues).

A Teacher Comments

To show my special ed students how to read a new word, I use the Think Aloud strategy like this: "I know the story is about birds. And this word begins with an R. Maybe it's a kind of bird. Could it be a robin?" I find that with prodding my special ed students can think that way. After I show them how, they do just fine.

—Bruce Maskow

Strategy 2-12   Guided practice

Ask students to work out a problem, such as one requiring calculation, or to write an answer, as for a spelling word. As students begin, put the correct work on the board so students can check and correct their work or, if more effective, give the correct answer orally. Continue the process, usually with a minimum of discussion, so all students practice the content. **Purpose:** To involve all students in practicing and mastering subject matter.

We can explain a process to a student. Yet it is often more efficient and involving to students if we teach by posing questions that, little by little, lead students from easy or familiar examples to new understandings. We teach by means of guided practice. Such a process not only can teach subject matter but also can effectively exercise thinking and self-responsibility skills.

Language example:

Using the **question, all write** strategy, the teacher asks all students to write the plural of fox, a plural they already know. As soon as students begin writing, the teacher writes on the board, "foxes," so students can see the correct answer soon after they finish writing. Students correct their own work and, if necessary, make changes so their work is correct. Discussion is avoided here.

The man who makes no mistakes does not usually make anything.
—Bishop W. C. Magee

The teacher then calls out the next word, another easy word or perhaps one that may be less familiar or that may lead to a new plural-making rule. Students bend to write the plural of that word and, when they do so, the teacher writes the correct plural on the board. "If you didn't get this one, don't worry. The next one may follow the same rule," the teacher may say, aiming to reassure students and keep them alert to discovering new understandings.

The process continues at a fairly brisk pace, with extended discussions avoided. The emphasis is on students learning by practicing and observing and thinking.

While students are working, the teacher glances about, getting a sense of how well students understand. If understanding is low, the teacher inserts extra explanation comments as appropriate, and also strives to make subsequent words easy enough so students do come to understand.

Mathematics example:

Teacher poses a problem. All students work at their desks. While they do so, teacher works out problem correctly on the board. Students then check their work.

Extended discussions are avoided so as not to bore students who already understand and to keep the lesson one of learning from practicing.

The next problem is then posed and, similarly, correct work is offered so students can check themselves. The aim is to get students practicing familiar work and then gradually introduce new work.

The teacher might have on hand a previously-prepared list of easy to hard problems, so examples are readily available to lead the students toward understanding. The teacher might even have on hand previously prepared sheets of problems correctly worked out in large enough print to be seen by all.

In some cases, students who cannot grasp the correct procedure from the teacher's examples might be told they can ask a friend, or raise a hand for someone who understands to come over and assist them, or to ask the teacher. The teacher, however, avoids long explanations, preferring that students learn by reflecting on the examples.

The teacher might reassure students: "It will take some time and practice for everyone to get this perfectly. I'll try to give examples that show you how to handle key points. Take your time and you will get it."

Or the teacher might find it better to shift, temporarily or completely, from this self-checking practice to a strategy that involves more direct instruction, such as the **think-aloud** strategy or **underexplain and learning pairs.**

It is not the work ethic that's gone awry today. It's the work, the overwork, the lack of respect and the deteriorating relationship between worker and workplace.
—Ellen Goodman

The **guided practice** strategy is essentially a method of teaching by discovery, with students led ahead in appropriately small steps.

As long as students see the strategy as one of learning, not one that tests prior learnings, this self-checking practice is naturally motivating to students. Moreover, it is *intrinsically* motivating, not motivating because the teacher told them to strive for excellence nor because the teacher will check on their work. Indeed, no scores need be tallied. No grades given. Self-checking practice elicits students' natural desires to do well.

Sequence two in the **Action flow plan**/section of Chapter One contains an additional example of **guided practice.** A similar strategy, designed not so much for teaching as for reviewing and correcting prior learnings, called the **review test**, is below.

Strategy 2-13   The review test

Ask a question about prior material and ask all students to write an answer. As students begin, put correct answer on the board or, if more effective, give correct answer orally. Continue the process, usually with a minimum of discussion, so students can review their understandings and correct their misunderstandings. Work is not graded. **Purpose:** To involve all students in reviewing subject matter. Also to give students success experiences in school work.

The review test covers material previously introduced in class. The "test" is for the student alone: How many of the review questions can he correctly answer? The teacher assesses class understanding in a general way by scanning the room during the activity and getting a sense of how well students understand. However, the teacher's intent is not to assess learning but to have students review and clarify prior content in a way that is interesting and involving to all.

An example with spelling:

> The teacher asks students to write on scrap paper, first, the correct spelling of *generosity*. As the students begin to write, the teacher turns to the chalkboard and writes: **1. generosity**

> As students finish writing their versions of the word, they look up, check their work and, if necessary, erase and correct their writing, so each has the word spelled correctly.

> Without much delay, the teacher then says, "Two. Classic. The book was a classic. Classic." Students begin to write that word. As they do so, the teacher writes on the board: **2. classic**

> To avoid having any student inactive for long, the pace is brisk. The teacher expects students to speed up to her pace rather than her slowing down to theirs.

The more you do of what you've done, the more you'll have of what you've got.
—Anonymous

Students check their work. The teacher says the next word. And the process continues for ten spelling words. Without discussion to slow the process, the teacher has students writing each word and checking their own work.

The teacher might use some **voting** questions at the end:

- How many had all ten words correct?
- How many had eight or nine correct?
- How many have one or more words you need to add to your list of spelling practice words?
- When you get into your learning pairs tomorrow, drill each other with those words plus a few old ones.

An example with math:

"Problem one," says the teacher, writing on the board:
1. (a+4)(a+5) = Students begin to work the problem. As they put their heads down to write, the teacher works the problem on the board. When students finish their own work, they look up and see:

$$1. (a+4)(a+5) = a^2 + 4a + 5a + 20 = a^2 + 9a + 20$$

Students check their work and make corrections if necessary. Since the teacher notices two or three students are confused, he makes the next problem very similar to the first one, expecting that the model for the first problem, left on the board, will help them.

"Problem two," he says, as he writes: 2. (b+6)(b+3) = And again, as student begin to work, the teacher works it out correctly on the board. And the process continues for several problems, all without much discussion.

Such review tests can be held every day. They can include one or two questions from very old material, to refresh old memories. They can then move into recent material covered, to deepen understandings and, as students correct their work, clear up misunderstandings.

A **review test** can also be used to bring student attention to a topic, ready for new material to be taught. Before introducing longitude, for example, a teacher could have a five-question review test on latitude.

A **review test** is an efficient way to get students practicing and clarifying learnings. Students enjoy the strategy. With each review test, each student sees how much content has already been learned. Even for content not quite mastered, each student gets a chance to risk an answer and get the correct response without in any way feeling threatened.

I use a variety of **review test** questions in my graduate classes for teachers. My first two or three questions might be factual. For example, my first question might be, "What is the name of the psychologist we studied who wrote about a hierarchy of human needs?" When the teachers start writing their answers I would write on the chalkboard: *1. Abraham Maslow.* Following the strategy procedure, without discussion I would move on as soon as students checked the board, say "two" and give the next question.

However, after we got into the rhythm of the strategy, I might ask more complex questions, such as, "What are some purposes served by the outcome sentence strategy?" For such a question, I would not write an answer on the board. Rather, I would simply wait until teachers made some notes and then ask for volunteers to share one of their ideas. In that way, I could intersperse simple right-wrong questions with questions involving many correct answers. Again, the intent is to give participants a chance to review and refresh prior knowledge and, no small matter, feel good about having already learned something, all in a nonthreatening format.

Another example of the review test strategy is in sequence two of the **Action flow plan** strategy Chapter One.

A Teacher Comments

A slight variation of the Review Test strategy I tried is using the Review Test with Sharing Pairs. I have students work with a friend to try to get the solution to the problem before I put the answer on the board. This method is effective because it creates a lot of aliveness and community in the classroom.

—Cindy Huels

Strategy 2-14   Voting

Ask question to which students can respond by raising hands or giving another nonverbal signal. **Purpose:** To allow all students to respond quickly and easily.

Some questions call for verbal responses from students. Other questions call for students to raise hands to indicate positions. Such questions do not usually absorb as much time and therefore allow for a quicker class pace. I call the second questions, **voting** questions. Note these comparisons:

Verbal response questions	*Voting questions*
1. Does anyone have any questions?	1. How many have questions they would still like to have cleared up?
2. Are we ready to move on?	2. How many feel ready to move on?
3. Do you agree with what Ginger just said?	3. How many agree with Ginger? How many disagree?

Son: Dad, when I grow up, how will I know I've reached my full potential and if I'm truly successful? Father: Your wife will tell you.

—*Dick Browne*

In terms of keeping student involvement high, voting questions have two major advantages. They avoid inviting students' comments that can slow class progress. In addition, they make it easy for all students to participate in the questions raised, so all feel involved in class proceedings.

A more complex non-verbal response might sometimes be invited. Two possibilities:

- **Degrees of agreement** "If you agree, raise your hand all the way. If you half agree, raise it half way. If you disagree, point thumbs down."

- **Readiness to respond** "Hold up one finger if you have an idea but do not want me to call on you, just so I know who has some idea. Hold up two fingers if you are willing to respond aloud but are really not all that sure of your answer. Hold up three fingers if you are fairly sure and are willing to respond. Otherwise hold up a fist, so I'll know how many have no idea. I'll call on only those holding up two or three fingers."

A Teacher Comments

We used the Voting strategy several times last week. One example was in a science lesson. We were discussing properties of matter, specifically, sinking or floating. Each child tested one object by placing it in a tub of water. Before doing so, the class voted on whether the object would sink or float. This kept everyone involved and interested in the activity, which was rather lengthy. Second graders love to vote on anything!

—Ginny Beatty

Strategy 2-15 Simple discovery lesson

Get students to ponder a topic before giving information about it.
Purpose: To maximize student energy and awareness.

In a completely rational society, the best of us would aspire to be teachers and the rest of us would have to settle for something less, because passing civilization along from one generation to the next ought to be the highest responsibility anyone could have.

—Lee Iacocca

- Why would you guess I label the two lessons below discovery lessons?

  Science: The teacher has students watch what happens when she lights candles and controls the air by putting covers over them. She does not explain. Finally she asks students, "What explains what you just saw? Write some thoughts and then let's talk about them."

  History: This teacher sets up a mock convention in the classroom. Some students play parts of northern whites during the Civil War. Some play southern whites. A few act as black men, some free and some slave. No one acts as a woman. The convention is to debate what is to be done about slavery. The teacher's aim: Help students understand those times.

- Why label those discovery lessons? Clearly, the teacher does not start off by giving information. Rather, lessons begin by getting students to think things through for themselves.

It is tempting to start a lesson by giving information: "There are three basic kinds of moths...." Or: "Yesterday we did this with long division. Here is how to do the next step...."

Compare such lesson openings with: "Write down how many basic kinds of moths you would guess there are. How many wrote more than 10? Well there are only three, which are..." And: "Yesterday we went this far with division. Look at this problem. Try to figure out for yourself the next step, then pair up and share your ideas."

When we begin by stimulating thinking, and only afterwards help students discover and clarify understandings, student energy and awareness are almost always higher than when we give understandings without students having pondered the issues. The basic sequence: Pose a question. Invite thought and, perhaps, discussion. And *then* give information.

Sequence One in the first chapter illustrates this simple discovery strategy. In fact you may have noted that I attempted to use this strategy in this writing about it. The science teacher noted at the outset used it as well. As for the history teacher, I would not call that a *simple* discovery lesson. Too many concepts and too little student guidance existed. That is a more complex version of a discovery lesson.

Here are some examples of teachers who changed from traditional presentation openings to the simple discovery strategy:

- Before: There are several rules for effective poetry...
- After: Make a note of what you think makes for good poetry...

- Before: To add fractions...
- After: Get in pairs and see if you can invent a method for adding fractions...

- Before: Jefferson wrote this about democracy...
- After: Who is willing to try a definition of democracy?

Strategy 2-16   Experience before concepts

Give students a meaningful experience of a concept before talking about it abstractly. **Purpose:** To produce learnings that are real and lasting.

A teacher once announced that students with blue eyes in the class would thereafter get special privileges in that class. They could sit in the best seats, go first to lunch, run all the errands for the teacher. Brown-eyed students would get no such privileges, said the teacher. And for several hours the teacher did, in fact, insist on those rules.

After students experienced the dramatic, often distressing reality of living as half superior and half inferior citizens, the teacher announced it was all an experiment and led a discussion on it. What, she asked, can that experiment

Retired teacher to stranger: Do you know the way to the post office? Stranger: Sorry, no. Teacher: Well, it's two blocks down and one block to the right.

—Anonymous

teach us about discrimination, prejudice and the impact of group labels? The students leaped into the discussion with passion. They were deeply moved and learned some profound lessons.

That is a striking example of the strategy, **experience before concepts.** The strategy calls for a teacher to bring a concept into students' immediate experience *before* talking about it abstractly.

More common examples:

- A social studies teacher tells a story about Lincoln with which students can emotionally identify. The teacher then talks about the era in more general terms.

- A teacher shows students an advertisement for shoes at 30 percent off and challenges them to calculate how much a $45 pair would cost *before* students were taught how to do such calculations.

- Students are paired up. One is told to avoid eye contact while the other is told to explain something. That experience leads to a discussion of why eye contact is a valuable communication skill.

- A teacher asks students to pick an issue about which they have strong feelings and to write a letter about it to an official. That leads to a lesson on letter writing form and style.

Many of the examples in the **simple discovery lesson** can fit this strategy.

Why bother to help students experience a concept before talking about it abstractly?

- The strategy draws students naturally into a topic. It makes learning more interesting.
- It also leads to richer, more complete understandings and more lasting learnings.
- It meets the needs of students who do not learn from abstractions as well as they learn from emotional or concrete experiences.
- The strategy counteracts feelings that school is irrelevant. It makes schooling more real.

Note: **Experience before concepts** is a strategy for beginning a lesson. There is a related strategy appropriate for ending a lesson: The **application project** (15-3), the strategy of asking students to apply a concept *after* they learn about it.

Intelligence appears to be the thing that enables a man to get along without education. Education enables a man to get along without the use of his intelligence.

—Albert Edward Wiggam

Chapter 3: For Solid Student Confidence

If I wanted to learn something, say French or calculus, I would want a class in which I could relax and study with assurance. I would not want to feel nervous, anxious about looking foolish as I was learning, or worried that I might never succeed well enough. Such anxieties would slow my progress. They might even make me want to quit.

Yet many of our students suffer just such anxieties. Some are afraid of making mistakes, worried about what classmates will think of their blunders, worried about pleasing the teacher, or worried about ever being able to understand. Some are even unwilling to risk looking foolish or showing ignorance. That unwillingness squeezes down student energies, clogs up minds, restricts learning.

What can we do to get students unafraid of learning? How can we help them relax enough to wade into lessons with assurance, confident that one way or another things will work out? This chapter has three strategies for doing this, all of which I learned from the ingenious work of Grace Pilon (1988).

Strategy 3-1   Truth signs

Post signs that remind students of important truths about learning.
Purpose: To help students become wise, balanced, self-responsible learners.

The signs of this strategy are not the usual signs we see in classrooms. They do not tell students what to do (Think before you act. Respect the rights of others. Raise hands before speaking.). And they do not threaten (One infraction = ten minutes off free time). These signs remind students of important living and learning truths.

One teacher introducing truth signs

Look over the lesson sketched below. It illustrates words one teacher used to introduce these signs to a class.

1. The teacher points to a sign posted on the wall. The teacher reads it aloud:

> **Everyone needs time
> to think and learn.**

Just as the butterfly must leave the security of the chrysalis, so must the students leave the 'chrysalis' of the educational setting and rely on their own inner resources.
—*Micki McKisson*

Now let's read this together (says the teacher): *Everyone needs time to think and learn.* Let's say it again, with power. (Class repeats, with more intensity.)

Yes, it is true (continues the teacher). When we hear something or try something, we don't usually learn it right away. It takse a little time for us to make sense of it, get it inside us. Even if I say something simple, like my mother was born in England, it might take a second for you to make sense of what those words mean.

I want to post this sign on our wall so we remember it. It's an important truth. It can help us keep our learning climate healthy. You can use it to remind yourself to give yourself enough time when you want to learn something. You don't want to rush it. Why? Because, as the sign says, Everyone needs time to think and learn.

Let's read the words aloud again, together, to help us internalize it, get it more fully inside us. All together: *Everyone needs time to think and learn.* Again please, with more power.

  2. Let's look at another sign.

> **We each learn in
> our own ways, by
> our own timeclocks**

Let's say it all together. And again, this time with more power.

This sign, too, is true. We each learn in our own ways, no one quite like the other. Some learn best from words, some from pictures, some from experimenting, some from talking things out with other people. We each have our own favorite ways. It's true, isn't it?

And we each learn according to our own timeclocks, some fast, some slow. All of us only when the time is right for us.

I, for example, didn't learn to spell very well until I was much older than my classmates. My time to learn to spell just did not come when it came to most others. But later, when the time was right, I became a fairly good speller. You might have had a similar experience. How many of you tried to learn something, or were told you *should* learn something, but it just did not work until you were older, until somehow the time became right?

Yes, it is true that we each learn in our own ways and by our own timeclocks. We want to remember this sign. Let's say it again together, to get it deeper inside us. Again, this time with energy.

We will keep this sign in our classroom along with the first one, to remind us of this truth. Sometimes we forget it. We may think we *should* learn something the way others are learning it. But their way may not be the best for us. We have to search for our own best way to learn.

There is only one subject matter for education, and that is Life in all its manifestations.
—*John Dewey*

Or we may think we should have learned something *already,* because others have already learned it. That may just get us feeling down on ourselves. And that will make it harder for us to keep up our energy and keep on learning.

So please don't get down on yourself if you don't learn the way other people learn, and if you don't learn when other people learn. That would be foolish, for we each learn in our *own* ways, by our *own* timeclocks, right?

3. Here's another sign:

> **It's okay to make mistakes.**
> **That's the way we learn.**

Let's say that all together. And again.

And that, too, is true. Even the first time we walk, we stumble around, fall down, get up, try again. The first time we try anything new we are apt to make a mistake, until we get it.

It makes no sense to get down on ourselves when we make a mistake. We can eventually get so afraid of making mistakes that we are afraid even to try. And that is silly. For the truth is that it is okay to make mistakes. That's the way we learn. That's just what happens when we start learning.

All together again. Once more, saying it like you mean it! Yes, we want to remember that mistakes are not unfortunate when we're learning. They are necessary. It's the way we learn.

4. Now look at this one:

> **It's intelligent to ask for help.**
> **No one need do it all alone.**

I would say that, too, is true. Look, I don't have to be able to manufacture cars and grow food and construct roads and paint pictures and design shirts. I just need to know how to do what I do. No one has to know it all.

If I need to do something I can't do, it's intelligent to ask for help from someone who can do it. Then I get what I need and, often, the other person gets the pleasure of helping. Don't you sometimes feel good when you can be helpful to someone?

The apple tree never asks the beech how he shall grow, nor the lion, the horse, how he shall take his prey.
—William Blake

That's what a community of people does. They help one another. One person delivers the mail. Another mows the lawn. One cooks. Another builds. Old folks sit outside and smile on us. Young people play outside and act silly. It takes all of us to make a community. No one has to do it all alone. We can help one another.

In fact it is *intelligent* to help one another. It would be dumb for someone to try to do everything all alone. So, please, in this class, if you need help, if you don't know what to do, or you need someone to explain something, ask someone for help. It's *intelligent* to ask for help. Everything works better that way. We can become one happy team, one community that way.

So, all together now. Let's read that sign again, with lots of power!

5. Let's look at one last sign today:

> **We can do more and
> learn more when
> we're willing to risk.**

Let's say you want to do something. Try something new, or talk to someone, or speak up in class. What you want to do might *seem* like a good thing to do, but it can *feel* risky. That often happens to people. We want to do something. Our minds say it would be good to do it. But our feelings say hold it, it's risky! We want to back off.

What then? Are we not to act? Sometimes the risk is really too great. We might get hurt or hurt someone else. Then it would be smart to stop, not to do what we thought of doing. But sometimes the risk is really not that large. There is no real danger. It just *feels* risky.

What we can do, then, is call on our courage and go right through the anxiety. Speak out, if that is what we wanted to do. Or join a new group. Or jump into the swimming pool. Or whatever it is we wanted to do. The key is a willingness to act, even when it feels risky, even when acting will feel uncomfortable. Then all we need do is call up our courage and get started.

When we can call up our courage that way, we can do more and learn more. When we cannot, we often do nothing. We are stuck in inaction. We may not even be able to think straight about the situation. We may become limited to doing only what feels very comfortable.

But when we are willing to make use of our courage and risk, we can think about whether there is real danger or not and, if not, we can get going and do it, even though we know starting will be uncomfortable. That is why we can do more and learn more when we are willing to risk. That sign is just plain true.

Sometimes it helps to have support from others. It is often easier to take a risk when we are not alone. Can anyone here think of a time when having someone to support you made it easier to act?

Human nature is ever capable of improvement and never able of being made perfect.
—John Clare

By the way, did you know that all people have courage? Courage is a natural ability of people, like speaking and dreaming. Some people can call up courage easily. Some do not have much practice in doing that. Famous people, even movie stars, sometimes get anxious in public. But they are usually good at calling up their courage and getting out in public anyhow. Has anyone here once felt it would be risky to do something and, then, you called up your courage and did it anyhow?

It is easier to risk when we can call up the courage inside us, and it's easier too, as I said, when we do not have to go it alone. One other hint. It is also easier to risk if we are willing to accept *not* succeeding.

Sometimes it seems so important that we win, or come out on top, or get everything turn out just right — it is so important that we get nervous before we begin. A part of us does not even want to begin. We forget the simple fact that things do not always turn out the way we like. But if we can accept that fact, if we can remember that people sometimes win and sometimes lose, we won't worry so much about sometimes losing. If we lose, well, we can try again another time. It's usually not the worst thing in the world. And we can then more easily take the risk.

How many of you are sometimes very afraid of not winning? Anyone back off and stop trying in such situations? How many would agree that when people can accept winning or losing, however things turn out, they will be less nervous and, if they are not so nervous, might even be more likely to win?

In any case, I think you will find this sign true: We can do more and learn more when we're willing to risk. If there is something good for you to do in this class, I hope you will be willing to do it. Even if it feels a bit risky.

Let's repeat the sign together! And again, saying it like you mean it!

> **6.** We'll keep these signs posted as reminders for us and, from time to time, we will talk about them again. But now look back at all five.

Which ones do you feel good about? Which do you think might help you do good learning in this class? (Pointing to one sign.) How many feel good about this one? That's about ten people. How about this sign? (Voicing an approximate count for each sign, to acknowledge the students who raise hands.)

Finally, write me something that you got out of this lesson. You might write endings to one or more of our outcome sentences. (Points to list: I learned… I was surprised… I'm beginning to wonder… I rediscovered… I'm feeling… I promise…)

In general

We must of course each use our own style in introducing truth signs. And in choosing which signs to introduce. In my university classes, I usually present and post the five included in that lesson just outlined:

> Everyone needs time to think and learn.
> It's OK to make mistakes. That's the way we learn.
> We each learn in our own ways, by our own timeclocks.
> It's intelligent to ask for help. No one need do it all alone.
> We can do more and learn more when we're willing to risk.

We can learn something new anytime we believe we can.
—Virginia Satir

Regarding the risk sign, it is often useful to make a distinction between a smart risk and a foolish risk. I might tell students that I see a smart risk as one that would be good to take. A foolish risk might be dangerous, or hurtful, or in some way would not be good for oneself or for others. It would be foolish, I remind students, to call up courage and do something that should not be done in the first place. Some teachers have asked students to create a chart of smart and foolish risks and report that students enjoy doing so.

I have used a discussion on foolish and wise risks to lead into a discussion of smoking, drinking and sex. "Can you think of a time," I might ask, "when it takes more courage to say No rather than Yes?" I might then have students role play situations, aiming to solidify the relationship between risk taking and intelligent choosing in ways meaningful to them.

I do not recommend using more than six or seven signs in one classroom. I would not want to dilute the power of these signs. Other truth signs, however, may be appropriate. Some possibilities:

- Life is not always easy. It can call for a stretch.
- We each must live our own lives. No one can do it for us.
- It's not possible to know the full potentials of another or oneself.
- Life is one step at a time, one day at a time.
- If it happened, it happened. Let's go on.
- We can be a community, sometimes all for one and one for all, sometimes live and let live.
- We can accept and support one another. No one need be all alone.
- The hardest part of any job can be finishing it.
- There is no best in the world of humans.

Such signs, I would say, communicate important life truths. It is easy for most of us to forget these truths. It is often heartening, reassuring and strengthening to be reminded of them. (See research cited by Hart 1983; Caine and Caine 1991; and Marzano 1992.) Cushioning, the next strategy gives us a meaningful way to carry on such reminders throughout the year.

A Teacher Comments

I have a son, age 7, second grade, and a daughter, just turned five, preschool. Often at dinner we share information about our days, in particular, "What we learned in school." I have discussed the 'truth signs' you taught us with the children and tried to incorporate them into everyday living. One day last week my children were in the kitchen and I was in another room. I heard my son become exasperated with himself over something he had not done correctly. I then heard my daughter say, "Jed, it's OKAY to make mistakes. That is how we learn." Out of the mouths of babes...

—Patrice Bain

Learn from the past. Plan for the future. Live in the present. Rest in the afternoon.
—Anonymous

Strategy 3-2 Cushioning

> Before asking students to engage in activities, reinforce the learning truths with questions ("Is it okay if someone gives us a wrong answer today? Why?") or with reminders ("As you tackle your homework, remember you do not have to understand it all tonight"). **Purpose:** To cushion any student anxiety about learning and to expand willingness to participate fully.

Just because we post a sign that says it's okay to make mistakes, there is no guarantee students will not feel anxious about participating fully in class. As we know, it takes time to learn. Deep learnings often take long times.

Signs are best treated as only a first step in a process of reducing learning anxieties and growing a positive learning confidence. A steady offering of reminders and support is almost always necessary. Pilon called her strategy for doing this, cushioning.

Hear Mr. Jones:

> Class, before I ask my review questions today, I would like you to guess why I do not care if someone makes a mistake. Can you guess why that would not bother me at all?

> Adam: Because you want to know how much we know. Mistakes show what we don't know.

> Mr. Jones: Yes, you could say that. Anyone else?

> Ashley: As the sign up there says, it's okay to make mistakes, that's the way we learn.

> Mr. Jones: Yes, that's true. Anyone else?

> Frank: It shows we're trying, risking it, even if we don't know for sure we are right. And we learn more when we're willing to risk.

> Mr. Jones: Yes, all that is true. Our signs remind us of those truths. Now let's get to the review questions...

Even in the kindest and gentlest of schools, children are afraid, many of them a great deal of the time, some of them almost all of the time. This is a hard fact to deal with.
—John Holt

That is an example of cushioning. The intent is to *cushion* student anxieties that might pop up during the lesson, so students can relax, learn with confidence, learn fully.

There is a longer-range intent as well. It is to help students get deeply inside them the truth about mistakes — that mistakes are a natural part of the learning process, that they are certainly okay, and that we can reduce our fears of making mistakes by reminding ourselves of that truth. When we remind ourselves of that truth we also learn an important life-management skill. Thus we serve not only good classroom learning but healthful, productive long-term living.

Notice that the teacher above used cushioning *before* the lesson. That is significant. Imagine if he waited until *after* a student made a mistake and then asked the class if it was okay to make mistakes. The class might agree, "Yes, it is okay," but the student who just made the error might well be embarrassed, sorry he or she was the cause of such a discussion. Besides, not having begun with that discussion, the lesson might have been proceeding with students unnecessarily anxious about making mistakes. The most powerful use of cushioning is before lessons begin.

Day 2

Mr. Jones: Before we begin this lesson, I want to remind you that not everyone needs to learn this material perfectly today. Why do you think I say that?

Bill: Because it is new material.

Mr. Jones: Well, it *is* new. Yet I would say that even about old material. Why is it okay if some people have not learned something perfectly on *any* day?

Sue: Because we all learn in our own ways, by our own timeclocks. It might not be time for us to get something.

Mr. Jones: Is that true class? (The class agrees and the teacher continues.) Fine, so go as far as you can. It won't help you to feel bad if you fail to get it all today. Now to our lesson....

Day 3

Mr. Jones (He has just asked for the year of an event. Bob raised his hand.): Bob, before you give your answer, let me ask you, Is it okay with you if I say, no, the correct answer is a different year?

Bob: Yes, I guess so. Though I wouldn't *like* it!

Mr. Jones: I can understand that. Yet it is *okay* if you make a mistake, even if it's not entirely happy for you?

Bob: Yes, sure.

Mr. Jones: Can anyone tell us why it would be fine if Bob's answer turns out not to be the correct answer?

Bob himself answers: Because it's okay to make mistakes. As the sign says, that's the way we learn.

Mr. Jones: Thanks, Bob. Sorry for the delay. Now let me repeat the question and hear your answer.

Use what talents you possess: the woods would be very silent if no birds sang there except those that sang best.
—Henry Van Dyke

Day 4

Mr. Jones: Class, before we begin, let me ask, is it okay if some students fully understand this material and some are fully confused? (Several students say, 'Yes' and 'Sure.') Why is that okay? (Calls on Sue.)

Sue: We all need time to think and learn. Maybe some of us didn't have as much time as we need.

Mr. Jones: Thank you, Sue. Anyone else?

John: Some of us might not be interested in this so much.

Mr. Jones: Thank you, Cliff. Anyone else?

Jim: We all learn in our own ways, by our own timeclocks.

Mr. Jones: Yes, and how does that truth free us from feeling bad if we don't get this material right now? How does it make it okay for some of us to know it and some not to know it?

Tom: Maybe it wasn't our time to learn it yet.

Mr. Jones: (No one has another comment.) Thank you class. It is also possible that you didn't yet have your *way* of learning it. So no one need feel especially great if they learned this already and no one need feel especially bad if they haven't gotten it yet. A lot has to do with whether your time and way for learning has shown up. Anyhow, let's go at today's work with an accepting, open mind, helping each other the best we can.

Day 5

Mr. Jones: Today I'd like to start off by asking why you think it's smart to ask a friend for help if you are confused. Anyone?

Mary: We can't all ask you all the time.

Denise: Sometimes it makes me feel good when someone asks me for help.

Mr. Jones: Yes, thank you. Anyone else?

Michael: I'd say because we all learn more when we help one another.

Mr. Jones: Fine. Just remember that sign. Let's read it all together again. (He says aloud, and students join in.) IT'S INTELLIGENT TO ASK FOR HELP. NO ONE NEED DO IT ALL ALONE. Now for today's lesson...

Progress always involves risk. You can't steal second base and keep your foot on first.

—*Frederick B. Wilcox*

Cushioning steps

1. *Bringing a truth to awareness.* A cushioning could start by making a statement, "Remember it's okay to make mistakes as you get into today's lesson." But it's usually better to start with a question, "Why would it be okay to make a mistake in today's lesson?" Such a question calls on students to recall the truth involved: "Mistakes are okay because that's the way we learn." Our goal, after all, is more than reassurance for today's lesson. We care to promote lifelong reassurance. We want students to repeatedly call up that truth and internalize it deeply.

2. *Inviting participation.* The teacher invites students to respond, usually by calling out one or another of the posted truth signs. The teacher might probe for a sign he wants to emphasize: "Does the sign about risks touch on this issue?" All student comments are accepted.

3. *Moving ahead.* A concluding comment might be valuable, but more often the teacher simply moves promptly into the lesson. Cushioning is not intended to take more than a minute. Pilon, the creator of this strategy, recommends we keep cushioning very brief and use it very often.

Students who need reassurance and confidence in themselves will appreciate a moment of cushioning at least once a day. Others seem never to tire of it. Variety in openings helps keep the process alive.

Extra opening possibilities:

- Does everyone have to know everything today? Why not?
- Does everyone here have to get every answer right? Why not?
- I'd say it's okay if some people forgot what we learned last week. Why might I say that?
- Some of us expect too much of ourselves. How many are sometimes like that in a classroom? Do any of our signs help us with that?
- If you forgot your notebook, it is unfortunate, but does that make you a bad person? Why not?
- What if some people know a lot and others know a little? Does that mean that some people are better humans than others? Why not?
- I'd say the right answer is not as important as being willing to risk thinking and offering an answer. Can you guess why I'd say that?
- What is the best way to handle a failure? What would be the smart way to react?
- It takes courage to be willing to risk when you are not sure of the outcome. How many would agree? Disagree, anyone?
- No one can ever be me. And I cannot be anyone else. What does that say about how we can best learn here?
- My worth as a person does not depend on how much I know. Why do you think I say that?
- More than right answers, I need courage to hunt for answers. How about you?

Every individual has a place to fill in the world and is important in some respect, whether he chooses to be so or not.

—Nathaniel Hawthorne

- It sometimes takes courage to say, 'I don't know.' But sometimes that is the honest answer to a question. Can you say why it sometimes takes courage to be honest that way?

Extra concluding possibilities:

- No one knows everything. No one ever will. So relax and just get what you can from this.
- We are each intelligent; it is just that each of us is intelligent about different things. You will find your own intelligence as you go through your days.
- No one in life has to know everything. We each help each other. Our job is to live together as one helpful community.
- All people are unaware of some things. We are just unaware of different things.
- All human beings make mistakes. So, what will you make if you are a human? Mistakes!
- It's not mistakes that are important. It is what we do after we make a mistake. Right?
- Failing a task is not as bad as many seem to think. Can you imagine what would happen if people were always afraid of failing? So let's just forget about it and get into today's lesson.
- I'd like you to relax and use your full awareness here. Be a confident learner. No need to worry here. So risk jumping in wholeheartedly, thinking only of what you are doing. Trust that the outcome will somehow be okay.

The heart of cushioning

I like cushioning because it reminds students that it is all right to be human. It is okay to be oneself. Cushioning gives us a practical way to help people digest that truth and thereby accept themselves, blemishes, tempers and all else. That is often a very freeing learning. It is a good example of the truth setting people free, in this case free to get into academic lessons wholeheartedly.

A Teacher Comments

When I'm inspired I jump up and down.
—Jessica, 3rd grade

I'm using Cushioning throughout my calligraphy unit. It really seems to relax the atmosphere so students can concentrate more on improvement instead of worrying about mistakes.

—Sharon Matti

Strategy 3-3 Let them be

When you suspect students have not learned because they are not yet ready to learn, let them be, do not attempt to force something before its time. **Purpose:** To avoid discouraging students by expecting more than they can produce.

Most of us have had the experience of being asked to learn something when, for one reason or other, it was not the time for us to learn it. We might have been asked to tell time, or to understand graphs, or to sing on key, or to read, or to keep our lines straight.

Unable to learn what was requested, and especially if our peers were quite able to learn it or if we very much wanted to please our teacher, we might have felt bad, weak, stupid. Those are not feelings that lead us to become confident learners.

I recommend we be alert for such feelings. In our zeal to get our students to learn, we may overlook the possibility that, from inside the student, we are asking more than the student is then able to produce.

We already discussed the advantage of **teaching in layers**, **not lumps**. We can return to a topic another time, perhaps in another way, to avoid pushing students too hard too soon.

We can also remember that, when in doubt, there is wisdom in letting students be, even if we *cannot* come back to the topic. There is wisdom in not discouraging students.

More fundamentally, there is wisdom in communicating that we respect people even when we are disappointed with what they have produced. Modeling such acceptance is a fine way to teach students how to accept their less capable neighbors, which is a prime skill in healthy community relationships.

In summary

Truth signs, cushioning, and the **let them be** strategy drain unhealthy pressures from many students. They make life easier for those students feeling the need, to be the very best person in the group, or feeling they will not be a good person unless they do everything immediately and perfectly, or feeling obsessed by a desire never to disappoint Daddy. Letting students be themselves — especially when they know you would prefer they were more mature — communicates respect for their very selfhood and gives them the confidence to work without worrying about disappointing you.

As a result, these three strategies free up more of students' natural curiosities, their natural interest in knowing more of what goes on in the world, and their natural desire to do whatever they do easily and efficiently. Wisely used, these strategies build a sound base for learning with confidence.

The acorn is not a deficient fully grown oak, nor is the sapling an incomplete tree... You are in this moment exactly what you are. You do not lack anything, nor is there anything broken or missing. You have all the power and potential you need for further growth.

—Don Havis

Chapter 4: Beyond Praise and Rewards

Most young children seem to thrive on stickers, and approval, and praise and rewards are highly regarded as motivation tools at all levels of education. Yet when we look below the surface we may notice some unhappy side effects.

- **Addiction** Praise from teachers and rewards for work provide such easy pleasures that students can neglect tuning into their own motivations, delay the hard work of learning how to become self-responsible. Praise and rewards can be like watching TV: easy satisfaction from the outside smothering potentials for self-motivation and personal initiative. Or like eating candy: quick, strong taste satisfaction smothering the taste of more healthy nourishment. Like other addictions, praise and rewards can lead to endless desires for more of the same.

- **Unfairness** Many students notice that while some classmates get lots of praise and rewards, or get bright and hearty praise and rewards, they only get infrequent or distinctly pale doses. "We are not all worthwhile in this class," is the message received and, too often, "I am one of the unworthy ones." We can play a quite innocent part in this. Quite innocently we can react particularly positively to some students and not much at all to others.

- **Manipulation** "Look how good the first row is," says the teacher, with the intention of getting all the other rows to straighten up. The more subtle message: "The teacher is just saying that to get what she wants. To get along in life, it's okay to manipulate people like things." Not the best message for our future citizens, I would say.

- **Puffery** "Great answer!" gushes the teacher. Followed by Wonderful! Sensational! Super! Amazing!, and "Let's give a round of applause to Billy for remembering," omitting the words, "What I just said nine times." Exaggerated praise quickly devalues language and honest relationships. Puffery can also lead to students saying to themselves, "He must think I'm really dumb, expecting me to believe that nonsense," or "She must think I'm really weak, needing such hype."

Which can say more than this rich praise— that you are not alone.
—William Shakespeare

We can avoid these traps. We can support and encourage students without inviting these harmful side effects. Here are ten responses that seem to serve that purpose. For more discussion, see the work of Jere Brophy (1981) and others in the bibliography.

Strategy 4-1   Honest I appreciates

Telling a student you honestly appreciate something about him or her.
Purpose: To remind students that at least one adult appreciates them.

Consider a student who gives an excellent answer to a question. I might say, if I intended to shower praise, "Very good job, Shirley. The way you phrased your answer was excellent." Notice that is a "you" statement, really saying, "YOU did a good job." It carries the tone of one person judging the worth of another.

Or I could say, in the mode of giving rewards, "Extra credit for that, Shirley." Here the focus is not on the excellence of the work but on a payment for the work.

Alternatively, I could make an "I" statement. I might say, "I appreciate the way you phrased your answer, Shirley." In that case the intention is not to praise, that is, not to give a boost to Shirley's self-esteem. The intent is merely to communicate personal appreciation. It also is intended to be an honest statement, not a mechanical platitude, certainly not an empty exaggeration.

Some other words suitable for **honest I appreciates:**

- Thank you. (Which really means, "I give thanks to you.")
- I appreciate that.
- I like the way you said that.
- That makes me smile.
- I sure like your taking that risk.
- Thanks for giving that a try.
- I liked the look in your eye when you did it.
- Thank you very much for that.

"I offer you thanks" is essentially what this response intends to communicate, an offering of honest appreciation for what the person has said or done.

How do you respond if a student gives the *wrong* answer? Wouldn't it be hard to give an **honest I appreciate?** It is possible to say something like, "I appreciate your willingness to risk an answer." But more often I recommend simply giving the right answer and moving on, as the teacher does here with Keith:

> Teacher: What's the capital of New York? (Pause) Keith.
> Keith: New York City.
> Teacher: No, Albany is the capital of New York. What is the capital of Illinois? (Pause) David.
> David: Springfield.
> Teacher: Yes. What is the capital of New Mexico? (Pause) Etc.

I reckon there's as much human nature in some folks as there is in others, if not more.

—Edwards Noyes Westcott

Compared to praise and rewards, **honest I appreciates** are less likely to be seen as manipulative, judgmental or mechanical. Also, as long as all students get their fair share, they rarely have negative side effects. And since we can always find *something* to appreciate in everyone, although we must sometimes look hard to do so, we can meet this criterion. Sometimes I must think back over a few teaching days and seek to notice students who missed getting their fair share and make a note to myself to look for something, perhaps something they do or wear that I can express appreciation for. I can usually do that.

I find students reacting healthfully to **honest I appreciates** and to what I call **I'm with yous.**

Strategy 4-2 I'm with yous

Communicating an empathetic acceptance or understanding of a student's experience. **Purpose:** To help students understand that they are not alone.

Consider these teacher comments to a student:

- I might make that same mistake.
- Lots of us feel that way.
- I can tell you're worried about that report.
- I can see how you would do that.
- I think I understand how you feel.
- I'd be proud to be in your shoes.
- I can share your sorrow.
- I understand why you would do that.
- It sounds like that was a great day for you.

An **I'm with you** communicates: You are not alone. I am with you.

Often a student will say or do something that makes such a response appropriate, as in this example, which also happens to include an **honest I appreciate:**

Teacher: What's the formula for the area of a parallelogram?
Jane: Uh, is it, uh... LW?
Teacher: I appreciate that risk, Jane. I could tell you weren't sure and yet you did give it a try. No, the formula for the area of a parallelogram is BH.

An **I'm with you** is another alternative to praise and rewards. Many students feel alone and essentially inadequate, unknown and isolated. It can be deeply empowering for them to hear that at least one teacher is with them, understands, and expresses that empathetically.

Great tranquillity of heart is his who cares for neither praise nor blame.

—Thomas a Kempis

Strategy 4-3   Attention without praise

Simply giving time and attention to a student, as by listening carefully.
Purpose: To support and encourage students without growing a
dependence on others' approval.

Sometimes we accidentally fall into praising patterns. Imagine a young student
coming to a teacher with a drawing just completed. A caring teacher might
easily respond, "What a beautiful picture, Terry!" or "This is a lovely blue tree,
Terry," or "You printed your name just perfectly."

Yet sometimes the student would be quite satisfied with a response that showed
we care but did not include so much praise. **Honest I appreciates** or **I'm
with yous** can do that:

Honest I appreciates: "I really like this drawing, Terry. Thank you very
   much for showing it to me!" Or assuming it is honest, "Oh, I really
   appreciate how carefully you did this drawing."
I'm with yous: "I can see you are happy with this drawing! You have a
   big smile on your face, Terry. I would feel the same way if I did that
   drawing." Or "You look uncertain about your drawing, Terry. Am I
   right? When it comes to drawing I'm also not very certain. I like to
   hear what others think."

How else can we communicate that we really care for students, that we notice
each of them, that each is an important being to us, without relying on such
praise as, "good work" and "great job"? Depending on the age and personality of
the student and on our individual style, we might make use of:

Physical touch: A pat on the arm, hug around the shoulder, shake of
   the hand.
Warm eye contact: A look that communicates full personal attention.
Stimulating questions: Perhaps, "What a bright blue tree, Terry. Did
   you enjoy doing this?" or "Looks like you used lots of blue in this
   drawing. Do you like to draw with blue?" or "Thanks Terry. This is
   just fine. What would you most like to do next?"
Time for the student: Simply giving a bit of time to the student in
   whatever ways seem right at the moment, as in talking about a topic
   the student initiates, or in allowing the student to remain nearby for
   a moment while we talk with others.
Teaching: Providing instruction or guidance in ways that show we care
   what the student might next be ready to learn: "I'd like you now to
   try to draw a face, Terry. Are you ready for that?"
Greetings after an absence: Saying we missed students, that their
   absence made a difference.
Shows of concern: Any response that comes to us that shows we are
   caring and wonder if we can help, perhaps "You look tired, Terry.
   Everything all right with you?"

*Notice the difference
between what
happens when a man
says to himself, "I
have failed three
times," and what
happens when he
says, "I'm a failure."*
—S.I. Hayakawa

In short, we often want to show our care for students and to give them some attention. Many students, especially young ones, crave such care and attention. Yet we can provide it without inviting an addiction to our praise. We can often give students healthy attention without any praise at all.

Strategy 4-4 Plain corrects

> Simply informing a student that an answer is correct. **Purpose:** To confirm correctness without stimulating any distracting emotion.

- Yes, that's right.
- Okay.
- Yes, that's just what I wanted.
- Just right.
- Correct.
- Yes, thank you.

These are examples of what I call **plain corrects.** It replaces "Great job! You know your nose is in front of your ears" and other exuberant accolades. It treats students like intelligent, dignified people who prefer straight talk to overstatements. It gives a message cleanly: Your answer was correct. Let's move on.

A plain correct is a judgment; but, unlike praise, which often feels like a judgment of one's self, it is simply a judgment of a student response. It is an assessment by an expert, the teacher, of the accuracy of an answer and, as such, is quite helpful. The student now knows that answer is correct.

When we give students plain, unemotional corrects, we are simply serving as efficient answer keys: "Yes," we say, "you have that one right. Now to the next one…" We do not stir up emotions that might distract students from the intellectual work of learning.

Strategy 4-5 Plain incorrects

> Simply inform a student that an answer is not correct. **Purpose:** To inform students that an answer is incorrect without distracting emotion.

Everybody is ignorant, only on different subjects.
—Will Rogers

Similar to clean, unemotional feedback for correct answers is feedback for errors:

- No, the correct answer is Louisiana Purchase.
- No, that's not what I wanted. Please use adjectives like those on the board.
- You had the first name right. The correct answer is Thomas Jefferson.
- That's an answer for kidney. Bile is the answer for stomach.

With the **plain incorrect** response, the teacher simply gives expert feedback efficiently and then moves on. There is no hint in this response that students are so fragile they cannot handle a factual error.

On combining responses   Note that it is sometimes appropriate to combine judgments of correctness with **I appreciates** and **I'm with yous:**

> Right, Tara, and I appreciate your volunteering.
> Yes, Sheila. I know that was a tough problem for you to solve.
> No, Bob, the answer is 9. I can tell you're disappointed, but there is always next time.
> No, the answer is southwest. By the way, Tim, I like the power with which you spoke.

On drawing out answers from students   If I followed a common practice, I might follow a student error with a drawing-out process: "Keith, no, the capital of New York State is not New York City. The correct answer starts with an A. Want to guess? Try again. Want another hint?" However, I find that procedure often putting the student on the spot, often embarrassing, and therefore not particularly good for growing dignity. Furthermore, it clogs the quick pace I want for lessons. I would rather just give the right answer and move ahead.

On calling on a second student   Common practice might also have me calling on another student: "No, Keith, it's not New York City. Can anyone else tell us the answer?" I find that procedure often making the first student feeling inferior to the student who eventually gives the correct answer. I want to avoid pitting one student against another. Also, since I already have asked the question about New York, all students have already had a chance to think about it. I might as well give the correct answer and offer another question for students to consider.

Strategy 4-6   Silent response to errors

> Noticing an error or problem yet doing nothing about it at the moment.
> **Purpose:** To avoid responding in ways likely to be unproductive.

Sometimes the best response is no response, other than a mental note for oneself.

- John is giving a report of his work to the class. Several times he says "ain't" and "ain't not." The best response to those errors, I'd say, is often no response, other than to make a mental note that he and perhaps others need more practice in saying "isn't" and "is not."

- A student turns in a report that confuses <u>too</u> or <u>to</u>. Should a teacher mark that error? If so, two consequences are predictable. One, odd as it may seem, the student will continue making that error; all teachers have learned that marking such errors often fails to change future behavior. Two, the student will less willingly continue to write, sometimes to write anything for anybody, even for himself. Students rarely enjoy activities that lead to lots of corrections.

An endeavor to please elders is at the bottom of high marks and mediocre careers.
—John Chapman

The alternative? A **silent response.** Keep your observation of the error a secret. Remember the error and perhaps make a note to create an appropriate mini-lesson on another day for the whole class or a small group.

And at that time, do not say, "We need to review <u>too</u> and <u>to</u>. We have not mastered that yet." Or say anything else that may communicate to students, "You should have already learned this." Such a message is unnecessary and may stimulate discouragement. Simply teach the lesson as if it were never taught before. One way to reteach this lesson:

> "Here on the board is an example of <u>too</u> used correctly in a sentence. And a sample of <u>to</u> used correctly. It is, of course, easy to confuse the two. Each of you please write a pair of sentences like that on scrap paper. In one, use <u>too</u> correctly. In the other, use <u>to</u> correctly. Perhaps write about something that recently happened to you."

> Then perhaps: "Now please share your sentences with a partner. Check to see that the <u>to</u> and the <u>too</u> are correctly used in both sentences. If your partner wrote something interesting, you might also enjoy reading it. If both are unsure about what is correct, ask another pair of students for help."

> A second round of correct-usage practice could focus on a topic: "Now write sentences that deal with pets or animals." For fun and variety, the lesson content could even be shifted: "Here now are two math problems. Work them out alone and then see if you and your partner got the same answer. If not, help each other. If you both got it, try making up a harder one for each other."

In short, we need not point out an error to get students to learn. We can simply teach a lesson about the topic again. As long as such a lesson has a quick pace, it will be an easy review for students who already understand and, for those who do not, a chance to learn in a climate without a tone of failure.

It is not always necessary to keep silent about errors, of course. Once solid, accepting relationships are strong enough, we usually do not mind having someone point out one, or perhaps two, of our errors. However, when unsure, I recommend choosing the **silent response.** It is safer. Let's be like physicians who choose the medicine most likely to avoid harmful side effects.

Strategy 4-7   Praise and rewards for all

Offering praise or a reward to the group as a whole. **Purpose:** To encourage a group without slighting any student. Also to build group unity.

A major problem with praise and rewards is that some students get them often, others rarely. Worse yet, those who do not get them can experience despair: "Good answer," says the teacher to Jamie, one of the lovely winners of the class, while inside the heads of other students comes the reaction, "I only wish I were like Jamie, not like me."

The average number of words in the written vocabulary of a six to fourteen year old American child in 1945 was 25,000; the average number today: 10,000.

—Evelyn Toynton

Sensitivity to that potential hurt can invite teachers to lavish praise and to offer rewards to all. We want to make sure all get their share. Trouble is, students are aware beings. They can distinguish contrived, undeserved praise and inflated reward from the real thing.

I have heard it argued that given all the downsides of praise and rewards we should do away with them entirely. I would not go that far. I especially recommend praise and rewards when they can honestly be given to all:

- This group is making great progress. It's a pleasure for me to work with you.
- Let's give ourselves a hand for the way we handled today's lesson.
- You all are working so well together! I told the principal today how special you are.
- This class is going so well I'm giving you all a treat today.
- What a good group this is. Even though that material was hard, you folks stuck with it. I sure admire that perseverance.
- We did it right on time! This sure is a powerful bunch, isn't it!
- I'm proud that one of our own classmates, Nicky, won first prize. And I'm proud of the way you people supported Nicky. So I brought an apple today for everyone, in honor of Nicky. (Even when rewards cannot be distributed equally, I like to make sure everyone gets something.)

No one loses when praise and rewards are honest and directed to the group as a whole. No envy. No one left out. Besides, it nicely steps ahead feelings of community. It grows patriotism in classrooms.

Not all group praise and rewards are equally valuable, however. **Praise and rewards for all** can be used manipulatively, as when a teacher offers a reward only when students do what the teacher wants. A class party on Friday because of diligent work all week is often in that category. The motive of the teacher, then, is less to bring delight to the class, to show appreciation, or to share good feelings with the class. The motive is more to shape the behavior of students. Not only is that less generous, it adds to any tendencies students have to manipulate others. Not the best model to present students, I would say.

I prefer not to make group praise or rewards contingent on student behavior. I do not like to announce that *if* students do this or that they will get a reward. I prefer to give students a model of someone who likes to bring joy into others' lives, and not only when it is earned. Indeed, we might better model someone who brings joy into the lives of people who are *not* earning much, for they are often the ones most needful of it.

Give up sainthood, renounce wisdom, and it will be a hundred times better for everyone.
—Lao Tsu

Strategy 4-8 Honest delights

Expressing yourself when you are spontaneously delighted with something one or more students did. **Purpose:** To allow oneself to be spontaneously expressive. Also to demonstrate the reality that some individuals have unusual ability to generate delight in others.

The preceding strategies give us replacements for individual praise. Students get supportive feedback and encouragement, and we avoid problems of addiction, unfairness, manipulation or puffery. Does that mean that teachers are to suppress the spontaneous delights they experience? No, I would not say so. I can, for example, hear myself saying in a classroom:

* I like the colors on that shirt, Tom.
* Good risk taking, Mike.
* What bright eyes today, Zack.
* Real neat papers you wrote yesterday, Linda.
* What good initiative you took, Jim.
* I was delighted to see how you stuck with your friend, Terry.
* You were truthful, and that was not easy, Sam. I was very happy to see that.
* Great answer, Melanie. Very creative.

I call these **honest delights**. Unlike praise, they are not voiced with an intent to uplift a student. The intent is simply to give vent to a spontaneous joy that welled up in me. We could not be genuine without being willing to express such reactions. And I believe teachers should be genuine.

Honest delights are warmer, more infused with emotional energy, than are **I appreciates**. Yet no puffery should be included, no artificial ingredients. They are to be genuine, not exaggerated, and not used to manipulate others to behave in certain ways. Furthermore, an **honest delight** is not to be prolonged to the point that it causes embarrassment for the person involved and generates envy in those overhearing. An **honest delight** is not to be lingered on. It is to be expressed and let go.

> * Super design, Tony. I love it. Have you any ideas for your next project?

If you can read this, thank a teacher.
—Bumper sticker

Honest delights are especially appropriate for young students, for young students have a special need to know they can bring delight to the world around them. Perhaps that is why adults naturally smile at young children. It is nature's way of eliciting the response those youngsters need.

As with **I appreciates**, we must take care not to neglect some students when we distribute our **honest delights**. This is not too difficult, since delights need not be based solely on academic performance. We can find something in every student that will delight us if we wait long enough and look closely enough. If you would like help in doing this, I recommend making a list of students and checking the name soon after offering an **honest delight**, so you can notice which students are not getting a fair share. You can then be on the lookout for things about the needy people that honestly delight you.

Not that such responses must be distributed absolutely equally. Sooner or later students must learn that some individuals elicit a more positive response from people than do others. That's a fact of life. Having a bit of imbalance in the distribution of **honest delights** seems to me acceptable *as long as* every student experiences some of them and no student gets too many. It is the extremes we need to guard against. It seems to me far different to have some rich folk in a town of generally well-off people than to have some extremely wealthy people and others who have not enough for food and shelter. It is that extreme disparity with positive feedback that we see in so many classrooms today.

Each teacher will find somewhat different delights in students. Almost any delight is fine, as long as it is *honestly* delightful to the teacher and not embarrassing to the student or his peers: An article of clothing, the confidence with which a student strides, progress in holding a temper, promptness, shining hair, wise caution or adventurousness, and of course great answers and super projects.

Strategy 4-9   DESCA inspirations

Speaking up for the inherent dignity of students, appropriate use of personal energy, wise self-management, healthy community relationships and open awareness. **Purpose:** To inspire new growth in dignity, energy, self-management, community and awareness.

I have already suggested that we need not respond to everything students say or do. If a student flaunts his good looks and clothing, for example, we might well not say we appreciate today's new outfit. We might, indeed, generally avoid comments about clothing and looks. Such comments can encourage attention to superficial matters and, when overheard by others, can distress those unable to match the attractive appearance.

Similarly, we may choose not to respond to all superior work. I think of the outstanding high school students who went to top colleges and committed suicide after discovering they could no longer produce outstanding work. We may not want to overemphasize the importance of excellent work and underemphasize the importance of accepting people at whatever is their current reality.

Furthermore, some students define their worth in terms of what they produce, just as some adults define their goodness in terms of status or possessions. When students with such self-definitions do excellent work and we say we are delighted, we risk reinforcing that definition. And risk, too, hardening an assumption that if and when they cannot produce they will be less worthy humans.

The weakness of pure individualism is that there are no pure individuals.
—*Kenneth Boulding*

Generally, we may want to avoid comments about excellent products when we sense such comments putting at a disadvantage those who cannot produce excellently, students who are equally deserving of our respect and appreciation, of course. Democracy calls for a reasonable amount of equality among citizens.

Besides I believe there is something more valuable to note and publicly reinforce: Not the products of work but the process of living — the calling up of courage, the sticking to a tough task, the lending a hand to a stranger, the thinking through an issue. Not just the excellent students, but all students can stretch in those directions.

In general, I would not ignore many chances to comment about instances in which students strive to use their full potential or to accept themselves as they happen to be. I especially like to empower dignity, energy, self-management, community and awareness, which I remember from their initials, DESCA.

The chart below shows how we might use **I appreciates** and **I'm with yous** to inspire those five qualities. Note that I would want such comments distributed widely among students, not restricted to a few. If I sensed some students needed an extra dose of any such talk, I might talk privately to them, aiming to give them what they need without generating envy in others.

	I Appreciates	**I'm With Yous**
Inspiring Dignity	I appreciate the way you stand tall. • I really like the way you spoke up for yourself. • I enjoy the confidence you are showing. • I like the way you defended your friend. • I like how you said it as if you meant it. • I sure appreciate the way you look straight in people's eyes. • I like how you speak with authority.	I can imagine how you felt after speaking up that way. • I'm also proud of myself when I go that extra mile. • I think I know how you felt when you insisted on your rights. • It's sometimes hard, isn't it, to call on your will power? • There was a time when I, too, could not get all the courage I wanted.

You have to be either critically loving or a loving critic, but you should never be indifferent.

—John Gardner

Inspiring Energy	I like it when you: • Keep yourself active like that. • Get plenty of rest. • Stick to it. • Use your brain power. • Do it one hundred percent. • Pace yourself. • Speak with energy. • Go one more step when you are ready to give up. • Shine out like that. • Move right along. • Speak strongly but not loudly. • Walk briskly. • Relax to regain your strength. • Use your whole self.	I need rest too. • I enjoy moving about too. • I'm like you when it comes to taking initiative. • I like it when I look in the mirror and see my eyes shining as brightly as yours now do. • It's not easy to eat well all the time, is it? • I too sometimes have trouble getting myself up after I'm too down.
Inspiring Self-management	I appreciate it when you: • Start and stop yourself promptly. • Organize your own papers neatly. • Make a time plan. • Reach down for your ability to persist when you need it. • Control your impulses. • Rest when you need it. • Remember to take care of your leftover tasks. • Think it out for yourself. • Go past the first idea that comes to you. • Ask for help when you need it.	I too have trouble knowing when to speak up and when to say nothing. • We can each tell what is true for us, can't we? • I understand how you know when you have had enough. • Sometimes we must look twice to see what needs to be done, don't we? • I too must sometimes remind myself not to be negative. • I sometimes just take deep breaths, but sometimes I will also count to ten when I'm angry.
Inspiring Community	I really like it when you: • Remember you are not alone. • Respect the differences in others. • Find something to appreciate in people so different than you are. • Chip in like that. • Lend a hand. • Listen so well to others. • Do more than your share of the work without being asked to. • Call others by their names. • Accept compliments. • Care for those who need it.	I understand how you felt about cleaning up a mess you didn't make. • It's fun to cheer people on, isn't it? • I too like to show others my appreciation. • It's nice to reach out to newcomers, isn't it? • It's hard sometimes to keep searching for the good in others, isn't it? • It isn't always easy to tell people things they do not want to hear but that would be good for them, I know. • It feels good to me too when I can stand up for our class.

Without self-acceptance, we become convinced that we've got to depend on parents, doctors, drugs, and intimate partners for the answers. We ask, "Who am I to take charge of my own life, when I'm so inadequate?"
—Tom Rusk

Inspiring Awareness

Thank you very much for: • Being so alert. • Reading with an open mind. • Bringing your attention back when it drifted. • Ignoring the distractions outside. • Thinking back and remembering past ideas. • Noticing that someone needed help. • Noticing the nonverbal messages. • Keeping your attention focused. • Studying the details. • Opening to the big picture. • Wondering what else. • Noticing your feelings. • Enjoying those sounds. • Keeping a log of your thoughts. • Searching below the surface. • Noticing how things are going. • Seeing what is undone.

I too sometimes: • Like to look at colors. • Must stop and remember what I wanted to do. • Enjoy being in woods. • Wonder about my dreams. • Need to pull myself out of dullness. • Think about the past few days in my life. • Wonder about my feelings. • Notice lots of things on my mind. • Like to avoid feelings of guilt. • Find it useful to check the mood of the classroom. • Lose my sense of dignity. • Do not manage myself as well as I want to. • Go too fast without noticing it. • Need to stop and ask myself what's the next thing I want to do. • Think back over the day and wonder what I should do next time.

A Teacher Comments

I used to give rewards for everything. It got so the kids would do nothing unless they got a star or candy. No more. I use only I appreciates and honest delights. When a boy draws a picture now, I look him in the eye warmly and say, "I like it!" When a girl picks up the blocks, I smile and say, "Thank you!" It's all honest and polite and immediate. No big deal. The staff like it too and, somehow, the kids seem more self-composed

— Frances Fenton, Day Care Center Director

I was amazed at how empty my praise had become. So often I felt vaguely dishonest. Yet I too was addicted to praise. It wasn't easy to break the habit. I'm getting a non-praise habit, but slowly. I mainly ask opinion questions and respond with Thank yous. I'm surprised how easy the shift was on students. I put the following list on my desk and that is helping me.
1. Honest I appreciates — Thank you.
2. I'm with yous — I understand. You are not alone.
3. Plain corrects — Yes. Right.
4. Plain incorrects — No, the answer is...
5. Silent responses — (Just note for possible future instruction.)
6. Rewards for all — The group did well today.
7. Honest delights — Truly felt compliments. (Am I neglecting anyone?)
8. DESCA inspirations — Who's showing dignity, working with energy, exercising self-management, living in good community, striking out in awareness?

— Tom Clarence, High School History Teacher

Think about how hard it is to change yourself. Then you will understand how hard it is to change others.
—Anonymous

Strategy 4-10 Mental agility group

Form a small group for students needing better impulse control and give them fast-paced, easy-to-succeed mental tasks. **Purpose:** To sharpen awareness skills and show students they can get the impulse controls they need for good learning.

It is common, especially in elementary grades, to find a few students who have difficulty managing their impulses. They are often the ones acting disruptively. It is smart to help these students gain control over their impulses early on. Start a mental agility group early, and many future problems can be prevented.

The group is meant to be a special, temporary group. It might meet for ten minutes each day the first few weeks, continuing on if needed. Other students might be engaging in independent study tasks at the time.

Following the suggestions of Pilon, I recommend including no more than three or four impulsive students at one time and adding one or two more mature students, for a group size of no more than six. Include mature students partly to avoid getting the group typed as for "problem students." We do not want an air of negativity coloring the strategy.

To start off, I recommend **cushioning**:

- I will ask you to do some writing or to answer some questions and we will move fairly rapidly. Is it okay if I move fast? Is it okay if someone cannot answer a question? What **truth sign** tells us that's okay?

The next step is to get highly conscious involvement with a quick pace, as with:

- Make note of some things that are the same and different about a plane and a bird. Just a quick moment and I'll call on you. (See the thinking questions in Chapter 14 for suggestions.)

- Please think of something you once did of which you were proud. Let's do a quick whip around the group. Give an example, or say, "I pass."

- Point to people in this group with red in their shirts.

- Quickly, tell about something you like to do, or say "I pass."

- Who can tell us what Bob said he liked?

- What was the second to the last word Sue just used?

- Flip through your history book now. Pick one picture that interests you. Be ready to show it to us.

- Write two things you remember from a lesson this week or last week.

Often students see the teacher as someone who is "doing it to them"; hence, students get a sense of control only by actively resisting: by not listening, by not doing homework, and so on—behavior that translates as lack of effort.

—Janis Gabay

- Touch your nose with one finger, your left ear with another.

- Write something you are good at when it comes either to eating or some sport.

- Until I say stop, write as many pairs of words as you can that rhyme, starting with the letter A.

- Make notes or draw something about a time you had an urge to do something but stopped yourself, maybe because you thought it was not an intelligent thing to do. "Go."

As students write or speak, the teachers might see an extra chance to advance dignity, self-managed energy, awareness, or any important human quality:

- Jennifer, a memory challenge: I'd like to ask you if you can remember something you just wrote without looking at it. But first, tell me: Is it okay if you cannot do that? Why is it okay if someone cannot do something sometimes? Okay, Jennnifer: What is the second word you wrote?

- Billy, a listening challenge: Can you tell us what you heard Tom just say?

- Sue, a self-management challenge: Before you tell about one of your worries, let me ask if a worry crossed your mind that you decided *not* to risk mentioning. I ask that because I think it is smart to think about both what to say and what not to say. Anyone guess why I think that is smart?

- Tom, an awareness challenge: Keeping your eyes closed, can you tell what shirt Kurt is wearing?

- Tami, a dignity challenge: Can you repeat your answer with more power, saying it like you really mean it?

- Anyone, a self-managed energy challenge: Who can give an idea for keeping your attention on this activity when you notice it is starting to slip?

- Before we end this session, think of something you appreciate about someone in this group or yourself. Who would risk telling us something?

- A neatness challenge: Look at your notes and put your finger on any part you were able to do very neatly.

The greater a man is, the more distasteful is praise and flattery to him.

—John Burroughs

Perhaps set a timer for ten minutes and when the bell rings, instruct the students to return to usual classwork. No need to explain the purpose of the group. Students usually see the activity as simply another classroom activity. If students ask, I might say it is a group to practice quick thinking skills.

Chapter 5: Raising Standards of Excellence

I believe all humans have within themselves the capacity to appreciate excellence, beauty and perfection. Even the young man who does the sloppiest work for me recognizes excellent athletic play, beautiful young women, perfect battle plans. What gets students reaching for excellence in their schoolwork?

- Success plays a part. Students who fail at producing excellent work tend to give up. "I can't win anyhow. No sense really trying. I'll go through the motions so as not to get in trouble and let it go at that."

- Feelings of importance play a part. Students do better at tasks important to them — mastering a skill they care about, teaching a younger child, producing a class magazine — than they do at tasks in the category of "I couldn't care less."

- Absence of high anxiety plays a part. It is difficult to do excellent work when we are overly anxious, our minds more or less frozen, as when we are fearful of making a mistake, or we feel we must learn it right now.

- Choice in ways of working plays a part. If I can do something in my way, there are greater chances it will be done excellently than if I must do it the way someone else demands.

- Personal timeclocks make a difference. If I can do the job in my own time, when the time is right for me, there are greater chances it will be done excellently than if I must do it too fast or too slow for me, or before I am ready for it.

- Strong leadership often inspires excellent work. The high energy and constant support of a strong leader can get many students doing remarkably good work.

Teachers open the door; you enter by yourself.

—Chinese proverb

- Students can be brought to excellence by the high energy and constant support of a strong group. It's the inspirational power of teamwork.

- Less effective are rewards for top performance. Rewards and recognition seem to do better at keeping the good workers working than they do at motivating the mediocre and poor workers to raise their standards.

- Least effective of all are penalties for poor performance. Penalties rarely bring out people's best efforts, especially over the long run. Few students commit themselves to personal standards of excellence as a result of scolding and punishments.

Here are some practical strategies that are particularly effective in bringing students toward excellent workmanship.

Strategy 5-1   Assignments with choice

Include choice in assignments and assist students in making their choices intelligently. **Purpose:** To grow self-responsible work habits.

Many homework assignments are offered without choices. "Do the first ten problems on page 36." "Read Chapter 10 and be ready for a test on it."

Such assignments miss valuable opportunities, especially the opportunity to individualize instruction and to train students in responsible self-management. I recommend that homework assignments include appropriate student choices.

- Please do the first ten problems and as many of the next five as you choose.

- Read Chapter Six and write **outcome sentences** showing what you were able to get from the chapter.

- For tomorrow, read ahead in any story from our class library.

- Aim to create one or more real-life word problems based on this math work.

- From the list of words and phrases on the sheet I distributed, be ready to read aloud as many as you can.

- For homework, please think back over today's class activities and write a **like/might review.** First, list some things you *liked* about what you did. And then see if you can list some things you *might* handle differently next time.

- On the board is a set of information. Draw as many conclusions as you can from that information and be ready to share it tomorrow with a partner.

Choice invites the bright or interested student to do extra work, something students rarely do when assignments are without choice. More importantly, I'd say, assignments with choice give students real practice with a very real problem: Learning to make wise choices for oneself.

Consider a teacher talking about this issue with a class, a discussion that might well be divided into several portions:

Pity the poor teacher who is not surpassed by his students.
—Anonymous

- You will notice that in this class almost all homework assignments will include a choice. Sometimes the choice will be to do *more or less* of an assignment, such as how many words to learn. Sometimes the choice will be whether to do *this or that*, such as whether you should study new words or review your old words. In addition, you will always have the choice of how *well* to do what you do. You will always face that choice with a homework assignment.

- And you will always have the choice of whether or not to do the homework assignment at all. A teacher can, of course, insist that you do it. But you yourself and only you must choose to comply and do it. No one else can live your life for you. Is it ever smart to skip a homework assignment entirely? I'd say so. Occasionally more urgent issues come up. Anyone think of examples of this?

- I believe doing homework is important. It is important in terms of learning and also in terms of developing self-discipline. I want you to do your homework and do it well and do it every day. But I also want you to live intelligently, not to do everything everyone tells you to do just because they say so.

- When I talk about intelligent choices here, I am not referring to your moods or doing easy work. Sometimes you will not feel like doing your work. And sometimes it will be very hard to stick with it and complete the work. Is it intelligent to skip work in those situations? I would not say so. Can you guess why?

- Because homework is valuable for learning and for reviewing learning, you will have an assignment every day, from the first day of school to the last, including weekends. That will help everyone use non-school time for learning, and I hope you will do that. I encourage you to manage your out-of-school activities so you can do at least the minimum assignment every day. What helps students manage time this way? Let's brainstormsome ideas...

- Even if you put the time aside for homework, you may sometimes feel lazy, or get interested in a tempting distraction. That happens. But you can learn to say no to such distractions. I encourage you to learn how to do that. One of the main jobs you have at this point in your life is your schoolwork. Yet we all have impulses and temptations that can distract us from our jobs. What are some that might get students putting off homework? What are some ideas for making it easier to say no to such impulses and temptations and stick to our work?

- Then there is the issue of how *well* you do what you do, in this case your homework. Have you noticed that you do some things more carefully than other things? I am like that too. Can you think of advantages in learning how to do a careful job when it comes to homework, to do a job you yourself are proud of? Any hints we can think of to make it easier to do that?

The mind can only absorb what the seat can endure.

—Anonymous

After raising these points, few teachers would be wise to dismiss the issue. It is an issue that calls for a review and reconsideration. Here are some questions that might be used for revisitations, not all at one time:

- How many of you are finding you are doing more than the minimum homework some days? Do you ever *not* do that? How do you decide what is best for you to do?

- What ideas have you come up with for managing your time so you don't have to struggle hard every day to make time for homework? How many need more ideas or, perhaps, a support buddy, to help you learn the art of time management?

- How many have been aiming not only to do homework but to do it very well, seriously, carefully, doing work of which you are very proud? How many of you are perfectionists with your homework, are never fully satisfied and probably would be better off relaxing a bit with homework? What can we learn about the issue of striving too hard versus not striving hard enough?

- What are the temptations that are getting in the way of homework these days for you? Any tricks to share that help you say no to temptations that would not be good for you?

- How many have found you had a day when it was intelligent not to do any homework at all, when something else was really more important to do, when something made putting time into your homework not your best choice? Anyone willing to share an example?

- Homework sometimes calls for persistence, stick-to-it-iveness. How many are good at sticking to tasks, even when tasks are not easy or pleasant? How many are not so good at that? I wonder if we could list some things on the board that help people persist. Want to try some of these ideas? How about telling someone about your plan and, then, how things worked out for you?

When homework assignments contain choices for students, such discussions become especially appropriate. And, in terms of advancing lifelong learning and living skills, very fruitful, perhaps more fruitful in the long run than the homework itself.

Strategy 5-2 Learning challenges

All our knowledge has its origins in our perceptions.

—Leonardo da Vinci

Pose an assignment, not as a responsibility or chore, but as a challenge or opportunity. **Purpose:** To inspire high-energy work.

Young people nowadays can be said to have it too easy. Many could use more challenges. A challenge, as I use the term here, is meant to be perceived not as another chore or burden, but as an exciting, adventurous, stretching opportunity, a chance to be brave and reach and conquer. Appropriate challenges enliven students. Some excerpts from a lesson:

How many of you faced a really tough challenge and overcame it? Maybe trying something new, or working hard at something, or resisting doing something you really wanted to do but you knew was not smart to do. Perhaps you needed grit or spunk, or just plain determination, or lots of courage. Anyone willing to tell us about a time you succeeded at something that was a real challenge to you, even though it might not have been a challenge to other people?

Of those who overcame their challenges, how many found it invigorating, good for you? How many found it good for you even when you were not able to succeed, just because you *accepted* the challenge?

Yes, we usually experience a challenge, if it is appropriate for us, as positive. I would like to invite you to undertake more challenges in this class. Look at the next unit we will study, the one we introduced yesterday. I'd like to see if some of you feel up to a challenge with that unit.

- One challenge, for example, would be to target a number of items to master that are not easy for you and, then, to really go for it. To challenge yourself to master your items by a certain date. You might even set a quick deadline, if that will add zest to your challenge.

- Another challenge might be to create something related to that material, not items to master but, perhaps, something to build or dramatize. And then to do a masterful job with your creative project.

- Or you might challenge yourself to study the standard material but handle it in a new, challenging way, a way that is not normal for you, a way that will get you stretching out your skills and talents, or maybe your relationships.

- Anyone think of other challenges we could mention? Perhaps we can dream up more.

Some of you will not feel up to a challenge with this right now. I would say it is smart not to undertake a challenge that is not right for you, and smart not to undertake a challenge when the time is not right for you. Can anyone guess why I say this?

Yet we can all participate in this. In this next unit, the job of those of us without a challenge will be to be cheerleaders to the others. So take some time and think about whether you can find a challenge for yourself in the unit ahead, or whether you prefer to be a cheerleader, to support and encourage the challengers.

If you do accept a challenge, I challenge you fully to **strive and accept.** *Strive* fully, really go for it, give it your all. Then whatever the outcome, *accept* it fully, take what you get, without regrets. We all win some and lose some. That's life!

A new position of responsibility will usually show a man to be a far stronger creature than was supposed.

—*William James*

Elsewhere, I recommend that students be organized into **support groups**, into groups of perhaps four students who sit together for a month or more to support one another. If such groups are formed, students without challenges can be the cheerleaders for the support group members who have accepted challenges. They can encourage the challengers, ask about progress, even phone them between classes to inject spot doses of confidence. A teacher might lead a discussion on the importance of people having cheerleaders in their lives, how much easier it is to persist through difficulties when we do not go it alone, how much more we can accomplish when we are cheered on, and what kind of cheering works best for people.

What makes for an appropriate challenge?

- The timing is right. It must be the right time for that person. Sometimes the last thing we need is another challenge.
- The level of the challenge is right. The possibility of success must not be too high, not too low, with high and low defined for and, preferably, by the person involved.
- The challenge is freely accepted. A challenge unwillingly accepted will likely be a burden and chore. An appropriate challenge requires willing, personal commitment.
- The acceptance is invigorating, empowering. An appropriate challenge ignites new motivation, new energy, yet does not overwhelm. One is proud of it, glad to have it.

One challenge that is almost always appropriate, to all of us, is the challenge to be our best selves, the self that deep down we know we want to be.

Who reaps the rewards of challenges? Everyone. On completion, I do not recommend we applaud only the ones who succeed at their challenges. Public appreciation for only the winners slights, even depreciates, the students who did not make it. Similarly, recognizing only the students who undertook a challenge can diminish those who chose "not now," those who may wisely have opted out. If there is to be applause, I want it for all, for the class community: "Let's give ourselves a hand for the way we helped one another with those challenges!"

Notice how this second-grade teacher reviewed challenges with her class, using four rounds of applause:

> Let's see how our challenge went. First of all, how many are still working on their challenges, are not ready to call it off? Our job, of course, will be to continue cheering these folks on. Please stand, persistors! Let's give these folks a hand for their persistence!

> How many were brave enough to undertake a challenge that was not easy for you, whether or not you have been successful so far? Please stand and show us your courageous eyes. Let's give those folks a round of applause!

If we would have new knowledge, we must get a whole world of new questions.

—Susan Langer

How many were smart enough not to choose a challenge this time, because it seemed to be not the right time or not the right challenge for you? Please stand and show us your wise eyes. Let's give those folks a rousing round of applause!

How many of you either enjoyed getting cheered on by others, did some cheering or at least thought about it? Everyone please stand. Everyone, let's stand tall and cheerful and give ourselves a super hand! I'd say we all did a good job!

Strategy 5-3 Inspiring statements

A statement that inspires students to do their best work. **Purpose:** To ignite the power of students to meet learning challenges.

Imagine a teacher saying:

I care very much that you succeed in the future. I want you prepared to be a winner in your course work next year, even though I know it will not be easy to do that this year. So I want you to get this material down cold. Learn it backward and forward. Let's get to it!

As all coaches know, inspiring statements make a difference. Sometimes all the difference in the world. Inspiration, after all, has to do with bringing out the *spirit* in us. Once that is ignited, inner power, or what we might call self-motivation, flows naturally.

If you are unpracticed in cheering students on with inspirational comments, know that effective ones are rooted in honest care. They draw students with that care, touching them in ways only genuine care can touch. Sometimes, especially for older students, they are best made privately.

Inspirational statements stir up the best in others. They reach deep and say, in effect, "I'm with you." "I want this for you." "Working together, we can do the job." They do not say, "Do this for me." "I'm insisting on it." "It is required." They pull, rather than push at students.

When I'm inspired I feel invincible. Nobody can get me down or make me mad, because I know right then I am dictator of my own little world.

—Kurt, high school

- Pushing: "I want you all to master this material. It is extremely important. I will have no student of mine leaving here without knowing this backward and forward. You must do it."

- Pulling: "You will really need this material. I'm committed to doing whatever I can to make sure you get it, and get it well. Willing to come with me and go for it? It will be a challenge! Let's do it."

It is the care of one person for another that is the path which ignites deep inner power. That leads to the most inspired effort. And if the care is mutual, if the students in fact also care for the teacher, the inspiration flows along a highly charged path. It can be the path of inspired service, even love.

- Highlighting reciprocal care: "We are in this together. Yet I can't do the learning for you. You must do it. By now you know how much I care for you. If for no other reason, learn this for me. I want you to master this material perfectly. I want to be proud for you. Let's show the world we can do it. Here we go."

I just heard about an elementary school principal in Illinois, Frank Beczkala, who wanted to inspire students to do more reading. "If every student reads more," he announced, "I, who am deathly afraid of high places, will stand on the roof of this building and read aloud a story to those assembled below." The students met their challenge. And so did he.

Strategy 5-4 High expectations

Expect excellent work, even when there is no reason to do so. **Purpose:** To take advantage of the power of expectations.

As a teacher, I never want to lay negative expectations on my students. When, for example, I give an assignment, I fully expect all will do it, and do it with verve and diligence. When some do not, I fully expect that those students had good reason not to and, next time I give an assignment, all will *then* do it. I never assume any student lacks in personal willingness to learn.

There is, of course, good reason for that assumption. After all, when we expect the best we more likely get the best. If I were to expect my students not to study unless I gave them rewards and punishments, grades and tests, reminders and scolding, they might very well oblige me.

It is valuable, then, to keep expecting willing, self-motivated work. It is in fact one of our most influential, far-reaching strategies. If you have trouble doing this, consider these moves:

- Remind yourself that it is likely that your students engage after-school games and interests with spirit and dedication. Remind yourself that the capacity for cooperative, willful diligence exists in these young people, and it might well be possible to bring that self-motivation into class work. Perhaps remind yourself too of the advantages in expecting self-motivation to increase steadily.

  To activate more of that self-motive power, from time to time ask students about their non-school activities, their hobbies, teams, social activities, the events they really care about. Watch their energy.

  The **new or good** strategy serves this purpose well. With this strategy, teachers use a few minutes at the start of some classes to ask, perhaps, "Anything new or good in your lives? Anyone lose a hat, win a prize, make a new friend? Anything new or good show up for you recently?"

Consider the postage stamp: Its usefulness consists in the ability to stick to one thing till it gets there.

—Josh Billings

Teachers then invite a few students to comment. It's like verbal show and tell. The strategy encourages students to share their personal realities. It also builds community and gives all students a chance to shine with dignity. And, of course, it makes it easier to know and appreciate the unique humanness of each student.

- Notice that **action flow lesson** activities tend to get students working without any need for rewards or threats. Diligent, self-motivated work is possible. Assume that if you find enough strategies, you can steadily expand the amount of work students will do that way. Make the possibility of seeing all students working willfully, with persistent self-motivation, very real to yourself.

- Consider how few students would *prefer* to be poor readers, clumsy calculators, ignorant of what goes on in the world. My experience says that students *do* want to be skillful and informed in life. They see no advantage in being unskilled and ignorant. That is, their natural motives support learning. Many of them simply do not know how to get skills and knowledge in ways that fit their individual human styles.

- Experiment. Each day write a statement that affirms an expectation that you and your students will find a way to get learning taking place with full cooperative, self-sustaining energies. Choose words that feel right, perhaps something like, "I see my students working more and more willingly, more and more enthusiastically." As you write, visualize students studying that way. The more vivid and colorful your visualization, the sooner you are likely to see it showing up in the classroom.

Strategy 5-5   DESCA challenges

> Challenge students to stretch their capacity to live with dignity, energy, self-management, community and awareness. **Purpose:** To advance these human capacities.

Teachers can empower students profoundly by sprinkling the year with nondemanding but stimulating challenges along the five themes of DESCA.

Do you realize if it weren't for Edison we'd be watching TV by candlelight?
—Al Boliska

Dignity

Please stand tall when you make that announcement. When someone is being teased, I'd like to see more people aiming to defend the person. Look people in the eye. Speak up for yourself. Show your will power. Refuse to be put down. Say it as if you mean it. Walk away when people are gossiping negatively. Reach down for your courage. Stand up for what you believe in. Move ahead with confidence. Act with authority. Sit tall in your chair. Show your inner strength. Show you can take it. Remember mistakes do not touch your human dignity. Respect your ways, your timeclock. Even if it feels risky, please call up your courage and do what you think best.

Energy

Please keep yourself active. Watch that you do not get hectic; stay *comfortably* active. Stick to it. Apply your full self to it. Use all your brain power. Reach down for more ability to persist. Go for it. Make sure you get plenty of sleep. Eat well. Pace yourself. When you are ready to give up, take one more step. Put your all into it. Make sure you get enough exercise. Shine out. Walk briskly. Get yourself ready. Take initiative. Speak with energy. Move right along. Relax now to be strong later. Make your eyes bright. Speak with full energy. Use your whole self. Practice stepping with a joyful aliveness.

Self-management

Please control your impulses. Rest when you need it. Take care of leftover tasks. Think things through for yourself. Go past the first idea. Ask for help when you need it. You will know what's right. You can think for yourself. You will know what to do. You will notice when something needs to be done. Tell yourself you do not have to be negative. Proceed by your own timeclock. When you feel too low, get up and do something. When you are angry, slowly count to ten. Start yourself with will power. Practice starting immediately. Put things aside. Stop yourself with will power. Practice stopping immediately. Take control of your behavior. Organize your papers. Manage your own time. Look ahead and plan.

Community

Please respect the differences in others. Be all for one, one for all in this class. Listen to others. Help clean up. Do more than your share. Cheer people on. Show your appreciation. Accept compliments. Care for those who need it. Reach out to newcomers. Practice going out of your way for others. Look for the good in everyone. Accept all people for being who they are. Tell people when you do not understand. Be honest here. Stand up for our group. Let us know when we make mistakes. Think about how we can do better at being one supportive community. Do something extra at home. Help out your family. Do something good for the community. Pick up trash when you see it. Ask family members how you can help them. Connect to someone new.

Awareness

Please keep alert. Read with an open mind. Call up your intelligence. Reach creatively. When your attention drifts, bring it back, stay awake. Practice ignoring distractions. Recall past ideas. Notice when someone needs help. Notice nonverbal messages. Focus your attention. Look for the details. Open yourself for the big ideas. Look closely at details. Wonder what else. Notice your feelings. Enjoy hearing, seeing, feeling, smelling, tasting. Keep a log of your thoughts, dreams, feelings. Ask others for other ideas. Look below the surface. Notice how your days are going. Notice what is being left undone. Closely study colors and sounds. Notice when your mind goes dull. Notice where feelings show up in your body. Notice what's going on. When you are

Let each child be as a prince or princess in your presence.

—Gerald Jampolsky

going too fast, back off. Keep alert to the state of your body. End each day by asking what you liked and what you might do differently next time.

Strategy 5-6 Paper exchange

Students look at others' papers and, perhaps, make comments on them. **Purpose:** To allow students to see a variety of levels of work without raising student anxiety. Also, to allow students to help each other improve work.

A teacher might say:

> I would like you to pass the paper you wrote to someone else, but turn it over so you do not look at the paper you get until I say, "Go."
>
> You will notice that I piled a few extra papers here on the corner of my desk. These were done by other students. I will soon ask you to look over the paper you now have and, if you like, to make some notes on it. You might write some things you liked about the paper. You may note some suggestions for improvement that come to you, something you think might help. Or you might write a question or anything else you like. Just be constructive. Aim to be good to one of your friends in this class.
>
> Does that mean you cannot be critical or cannot mention errors? Would that be constructive? Would you like someone to note errors on your paper? How can we make this paper exchange strategy most constructive? (Brief discussion.)
>
> You may want to sign your comments, so people can come and ask for more if they like. But no need to.
>
> After you finish with your paper, please come up and put it on the bottom of this pile on my desk. Then take a new paper off the top of the pile and read it, making notes if you like, as before. Continue that way. Continue reading over others' papers until I tell you there's just a minute to go. You will have time to read over several papers, so no need to rush.

What is good about this paper exchange process? First, it gets all students looking over others' work. Most notice that some work is done better than theirs. If I include a few excellent papers in the initial pile on my desk, even the best students are likely to see other possibilities of excellence.

There is no possible method of compelling a child to feel sympathy or affection.
—Bertrand Russell

Furthermore, this comparing process is nonthreatening. No one need know what a student is thinking because there were extra papers piled on the desk, no student need wait for a paper to read. Students keep expanding their awareness while he reads another's paper. And each student can read an excellent paper as long as he or she chooses, seeking to understand what excellent work is. The focus is not on grading papers but rather on helping each other to do better.

The strategy is efficient. All students read and think all the time. Finally, this strategy can save the teacher an enormous amount of paper-reading time. One reason we want to read students' work is to give them feedback. Yet, as peer instruction keeps demonstrating, peer feedback is very often the most useful and understandable and the most easy, least threatening, for students to accept.

In some cases, it is helpful to instruct students in how they are to do a critique of papers. Examples:

- Underline all the words you think might be misspelled.
- Put a question mark in the margin whenever you read a part unclear to you.
- Draw a smiley face for the parts you really like.

The paper exchange strategy can be made into a homework assignment: "Read a paper at home." It can be used, not in the whole class, but in subgroups: "You people take papers from this pile, you from that pile." And it can be used as an optional activity: "When you finish the work you are now doing, take a paper from the paper exchange pile."

Strategy 5-7 Clarifying excellence discussion

> Discuss what excellent work is and is not, aiming to help students appreciate the advantages of having areas in their lives in which they strive fully and accept fully. **Purpose:** To develop personal standards of excellence and to reduce the frustrations of unrealistic expectations.

Some students assume excellence is an absolute. They assume that each person must produce excellent results or, unhappily, be a less than excellent person.

Life, of course, is not like that. What is excellent for one person may not be excellent for another. Yet teachers want to inspire students to hold to excellent standards so they at least know the *direction* in which to strive, so they do not slide into sloppy habits, low-level standards. How can we handle this?

One way, already suggested, is to make clear what excellent work is and then (1) to help students move toward it while also (2) helping them avoid getting down on themselves when they have not yet reached excellence. Many of the unenthusiastic students we face each day have become more or less down on their chances of doing excellent work and find it wiser to give up than to keep suffering the frustrations of trying.

The strategies of this chapter can be used to uphold standards of excellence *and* uphold the dignity and well-being of those still on the path toward excellence. Also very valuable are **truth signs** and **cushioning.** An open discussion of the issue can also be helpful. A teacher might pose questions like these to start such discussions.

I had a rough marriage. My wife was an immature woman. See if this is not immature to you: I would be at home in the bathroom taking a bath and my wife would walk in whenever she felt like it and sink my boats.

—Woody Allen

- What determines whether work is excellent? That usually leads students to see that it depends on the issue or subject. Excellent stories are viewed differently than is excellent piloting of airplanes.

- How are we to treat ourselves when we have not yet reached excellence? The truth here is that anything less than full self-acceptance makes further progress harder. Often makes it harder to get a good night's sleep, too.

- How are we to view people who do not care about reaching for excellence in some areas of their lives? This often leads to clarity about minimum performance standards being necessary in some areas (driving a car, working in an office, obeying laws against hurting others), even when excellence is not required. It also may lead students to see the unreasonableness of expecting a person to be excellent in all areas.

- What are the advantages of striving for excellence? It is usually more fun, of course, to play to win.

- How do you know when you are to be satisfied with your current work? Here I would aim to help students appreciate the advantages of not relying only on others' assessments but also of considering how they would judge their effort and persistence.

Other possibilities:

- Tell students your positive and negative experiences in attempting to do excellent work.

- Ask students to interview other adults about some of these questions.

- Ask students to evaluate, dramatize or illustrate the slogan: "Strive to do your best. Then accept whatever you get."

Strategy 5-8 Undone work response

> Avoid blaming students who fail to do required work and, instead, aim to respond in a growth-producing way. **Purpose:** To respond wisely to students failing to do their work.

Students will fail to do their work on occasion. Some students will not do their work on many, many occasions. We can count on that as much as we can count on cloudy days.

The first recommendation: Treat such events as noneventful. Do not get overly upset. Do not react as if your integrity is being violated, as if students are picking on you. Students are simply doing what students always do, and they would do it even if you were not you. It will not help if you get overly emotional. Chances are you will find the best way to react if you remain cool-headed. Treat students who fail to do what you asked them to do as representing just another teacher task to handle, just as you must handle lesson planning and grade giving. It's all part of the job.

Nothing in the world can take the place of persistence. Talent will not; nothing is more common than unsuccessful men with talent. Genius will not; the world is full of educated derelicts. The slogan "press on" has solved and always will solve the problems of the human race.

—Calvin Coolidge

The second recommendation: Avoid reacting in a way likely to do more harm than good. I, for example, do not want to scold, use sarcasm, belittle, punish or nag. That seldom works for long and, even when it does, is more likely to produce unhealthy resentment or guilt than it is to lead to the kind of cooperative, self-responsible study I want. I certainly do not want students concluding I see them as defective persons, or to withdraw from future learning activities.

In the long run, I find these reactions not serving me or students very well:

- **Warnings** "You know that if you don't do this you will suffer a more severe problem." Warnings more often produce a setback, not an advance in dignity, energy and self-management.

- **Punishments** "Since you didn't do your work you must suffer by...." Punishments produce results no better than do warnings.

- **Loss of learning chances** "You cannot participate until you finish that work."

- **Loss of basic privileges** "You lose out on fun or recess or participating with others."

- **Calling on parents** "I want this work signed by your parents."

Other responses are more likely to work in the long run. Some examples of such responses:

- **Respectful reminder** "Sean, please finish this paper later, before you start new work."

- **A next-time message** "Next time we have this work please turn it in by the requested time."

- **Inspiration** "Come on, Kelly, let's do it! I know you can! Please let me be proud for you."

- **Honest offer to help** "Was it too difficult for you?" "Any ways I can help you or get help for you?" "How about doing just the parts you can do?" I sometimes will use such questions, but not when such questions might sound sarcastic or belittling.

- **Honest I statement, with natural consequence discussion** "You agreed to stay after school to finish that work, right? Since you didn't do it, there are consequences we have to live with. For example, I now have more difficulty trusting your promises. More serious yet, you may have difficulty trusting your own word. It may have weakened your faith in yourself. Besides, you keep falling behind in your work. We need to deal with this situation."

The greatest evil that can befall man is that he should come to think evil of himself.
—*Goethe*

- **Respectful insistence.** "You sit there and finish that page," I might occasionally say.

  I sometimes *insist* that work be done and, occasionally, for students who might need that kick, insist it be done right *now*. Yet I want to insist only in cases in which I sense something deep inside the student himself or herself really wants to be able to sit and do what is required but, just now, cannot do it without my insistence. I want always to respect the dignity and self-management drives of students. Said another way, I want my insistence, when I do insist, to be *inspiring*, to bring out the best within students, not to be controlling, not to be denying, not to be disrespectful of the right all people have to their own lives.

  You might recall instances when someone insisted that you do something and, deep down, even if you resisted doing it, you knew it was good for you. The person was not diminishing you in any way. The person was rather challenging you to dig out more of your ability. The feeling of being respected was there. When I insist something be done, I want to be sure students know I am insisting for *their* welfare, not because of my stubbornness.

- **Acceptance of reality.** "I don't know what else to say. I have no constructive suggestion at this time. I know I cannot make you do something you choose not to do so let's put this problem aside for now."

  Sometimes I find it best to accept the reality that nothing I can legally do will get a student to complete an assignment right now. I see no advantage in getting bent out of shape when those instances occur. Nor do I want to bend an obstinate student further out of shape. When I have no construction option, I like to do nothing. I want to avoid loss and, accordingly, will back off from a confrontation to give myself time to find a constructive way to handle the situation.

The issue here is perspective. We want to keep in mind that our goal is not only to teach subject matter but to do it in ways beneficial to students. When we keep that in mind, we are less likely to handle undone work in ways that in the long run will do more harm than good.

Some cause happiness wherever they go, others whenever they go.
—Oscar Wilde

As teachers, we have much power, inherent authority. We can issue requirements. We do not want to abuse our power. We do not want to insist students fulfill requirements in ways that will slow down their growth toward mature self-responsibility. This strategy, then, calls on us to handle requirements in ways respectful of the rights and needs of our students. And when we cannot do that, temporarily let go of requirements. Avoid loss. Come at the work of promoting excellence freshly another time, perhaps another way.

Chapter 6: Everyday Group Strategies

Small group work has many advantages. It frees teacher time and energy. It makes for productive, active learning. Students who need explanations can get them more quickly and personally when other students do the explaining. Students who do the explaining strengthen their own understandings. It adds lots of variety into the classroom. And with group work students have many more chances to talk, take initiative, make choices and generally learn healthy living and learning habits.

Many forms of cooperative group work are available. Two basic strategies were included in Chapter Two:

> **Underexplain and learning pairs** Teacher explains material so only some students fully understand and then asks students to sit in pairs to help each other fill in the gaps and exchange and deepen understandings.

> **Sharing pairs** Teacher asks students to turn to a partner and, perhaps, to share opinions about a topic, to share what they did for homework, to share what they wrote in a **speak-write** lecture, to share their reactions to how a discussion was going up to that point, to share **outcome sentences**, or to share answers they wrote in **question, all write** procedures.

Note that both these strategies use groups of two students. That is the group size that maximizes cooperation. When three students sit together, one student often plays a subsidiary role and does not get equally involved. Furthermore, the pace of learning usually slows down. These difficulties mount as groups get even larger. Strategy 7-1 deals with issues of group size generally and the related issue of small group work. However, as you will see, the strategies of that chapter also favor groups of two. Teachers consistently report it as the size most involving for today's restless students.

Be confident, for the stars are of the same stuff as you.
—Nicholai Velimirovic

Much information on cooperative group learning is available. Experts on this topic include Robert Slavin and Roger and David Johnson. For more information on cooperative learning, you may want to consult their writings, some of which are listed in the Reference section.

Strategy 6-1   Paired reading

Students pair up and take turns reading to each other. **Purpose:** To maintain high involvement in oral reading.

"Pair up with someone," I might say, "and take turns reading the chapter to one another. One person volunteer to start. Read aloud for a bit. Then give the turn to the other person. In that way, take turns, back and forth, reading through the selection. If you come to something hard for you to read, just ask your partner for help."

Students usually enjoy paired reading. It is much more engaging than what is sometimes called round-robin reading, when one person in a whole class reads aloud and others are asked to follow along. Students do not usually tune out during paired reading, for they are either reading or staying ready for their reading turn. It can be used for most any reading material, fiction and nonfiction.

I prefer to give minimum directions, partly to allow for maximum self-direction and partly to allow for individual variation in talent. I find students usually know when, for example, to give the reading turn to their partners and how to assist a partner who needs help. When someone asks, "How long should we each read?" I might say, "You do not have to read exactly the same amount. Read as long as feels comfortable and fair for you both."

I'll usually give directions for what is to be done when the reading is completed. Possibilities:

- Afterfwards, talk over the reading and see what you think about it.
- Each person write in your journal some outcome sentences based on the reading.
- Identify some things you liked or found interesting. Be ready so each of you has at least one thing you can report.
- If you finish before I call time, you can begin the next reading or shift to some of your individual work.

Although **paired reading** is most often used in elementary schools, some high school teachers report it serving well as a change-of-pace activity, to give variety to a class period and to give special attention to portions of a text needing to be highlighted.

We should not only use the brains we have, but all that we can borrow.
—Woodrow Wilson

Strategy 6-2   Task group, share group

> Students work together to complete a task. Afterwards each student reports on work done in his/her task group to one or more classmates.
> **Purpose:** To maintain involvement in productive group work.

This is a highly involving, flexible small group activity. I learned it from Hanoch McCarty. It proceeds in two steps.

Step 1. Task group

Assign a group task. Samples:

- Make interesting sentences out of vocabulary (or spelling) words.
- Come up with three or four real-life applications of a multiplication fact, a science idea, or any general principle.
- Write in order of importance the government agencies we studied.
- Think of three or more alternative ways to handle a real-life problem.
- Write what you think is interesting about…(Lincoln, the UN, rivers, etc.)
- Create a set of problems and their answers dealing with…

Specify a time frame. Shorter is better than longer. A short time inspires students to start promptly and to move smartly. And assign a group size. Smaller is better than larger. The smaller the group, the larger the active role of each student. Pairs usually get the best results.

Inform students that when time is up, they will be put into pairs with someone not in their task group, to share a few of the ideas of their task group. "Make notes, if you like, so you are ready for that."

Step 2. Share group

When time for step one is over, instruct students to find one person not in their working groups, to sit with that person and then to take turns sharing some of the ideas of their task group. If I have task groups of two, I might say:

> Each pair, choose an A and a B. Ready? Now I'd like the A's to remain seated. B's please stand and find a new A person. B's then start and share with your new partner something about what you did or learned in your task group. Then A's, you take a turn and share what your task group did or learned. Not much time for this, so move quickly. Go.

They are able because they think they are able.
—Virgil

I recommend, as usual, a fairly quick pace. For high-level involvement and learning, it is almost always better to keep sharing brief.

A second or third set of **sharing pairs** is sometimes useful, as when a variety of important learnings is involved, or when quiet students could use more experience in speaking to peers. For extra sharing, when time is up you might simply say, "Now please find another partner and share either what you did in your task group or, if you like, some ideas that came up in your first sharing pair."

A whole class discussion might follow, or students could write personal **outcome sentences**, perhaps for a large group **whip around, pass option** activity or for inclusion in individual **portfolios.**

Some teachers prefer to give task groups a choice of problems. A teacher might say, for example:

> We talked about China. What ideas from China might be useful for us here in the United States? We might wonder, for instance, if our family life cannot learn something from Chinese family life. Let's see if we can't list two or three other possibilities on the board.

The teacher might then ask students to sit in pairs.

> Now each pair pick one of the topics we listed on the board, one of interest to you both. Think about the issue and the advantages and disadvantages of our country learning something from China. If your pair picked family life as your issue, for instance, consider what we might learn, including the pro and con effects that would have on our family life. Later we'll sit in new pairs so you can hear what other groups chose and thought.

A Teacher Comments

Students love to hear me read them stories. And I enjoy it too. But lately I often use Task Group, Share Groups. I ask students to pair up and take turns reading parts of a story to each other. "No one read too long, so both have turns. Yet please read at least one sentence. Ask your partner for help with a word, if you like, or just guess. When you are done, take turns giving answers to the questions I posted. The poster says: What happened so far? What do you predict might happen next? Have you any reasons for your prediction? For step two I say, "When I say Go, find a new partner. Take turns telling what you or your task partner guessed will happen next in the story. Just two minutes for this. Go." Somehow students really get up for this reading activity.

—Miriam Harmon, Second-Grade Teacher

Strategy 6-3   Option display

Small groups work on a problem aiming to construct a display that shows several options for solving the problem, the likely consequences of each option, and the group's recommendation as the best option. **Purpose:** To teach students how to attack problems open-mindedly and thoughtfully.

This strategy starts with an open-ended problem, perhaps:

> **In language arts:** How can we help the young students in our school who cannot read well? How can we best distribute the magazine the class produced? How can we reduce violence on TV?

If I despised myself, it would be no compensation if everyone saluted me, and if I respect myself, it does not trouble me if others hold me lightly.
—Max Nordau

In math: How can we remember all the geometry formulas? Keep track of the cost of a cart of groceries? Estimate the number of beans in a bottle?
In social studies: What might reduce prejudice nowadays? How might we help the poor in our area? Get more people voting in elections?
In science: How can we measure temperature without a thermometer? Provide better health care for infants? Dispose of all our garbage?

A teacher might collect a list of problems for this strategy from texts or other teachers. Problems could call for research or simply for creative thinking. One problem is then offered to the class. Or students could be allowed to select a personal problem of interest from a small list. This would lead to the option display procedure:

1. Small groups form Pairs usually work best. Larger groups have more ideas but also result in more passive participation. If the whole class were to work on one problem, groups could be formed in any way convenient. If students were offered more than one problem, individuals could select a problem that interested them; persons selecting the same problem could then be paired or placed in larger groups. Alternatively, groups could form first and then jointly choose a problem.

2. The option display is explained Here is one teacher explaining the elements:

> By next Monday your team is to produce a wall chart containing four elements.
> (1) On the top of the chart, a clear *statement of the problem,* in your own words.
> (2) On the left side of the chart, a list of three or more possible *options for handling the problem.* List as many reasonable ideas as you can identify by reading, thinking or interviewing friends and relatives.
> (3) On the right side, next to the option list, write the chief *advantages and disadvantages of each option.* Think ahead to the difficulties and benefits that would likely result if that option were implemented. Please think ahead to long-term consequences if you can.
> (4) On the bottom of your chart, write your team's *overall recommendation.* All in all, what would you think would be the best way to handle the problem? Sign your names to the chart. We will leave the charts on the wall for some time, so all have a chance to examine each other's ideas.

3. Review and conclusion Option display charts can be left posted long enough so students have chances to view them. This might lead to a group discussion on problems studied. Anyone get any new ideas from this activity? Anyone change his or her mind? All in all, what do you think is the best solution to the problem? Does the activity suggest steps you might take when you face a tough problem in your own life?

Strategy 6-4   Best choice debate

Pairs of students prepare either a pro or a con position on a controversial issue. Then a pro pair and a con pair join and explain their positions to each other and, finally, seek agreement on what would be the best overall choice. **Purpose:** To promote open-mindedness and a thoughtful sharing of perspectives.

Two meanings apply to debates. They can be seen as contests, win-lose battles, with an intent to put down others or to win over them. This approach leads to antagonism and distortion of information, not the best conditions for education's purposes. The meaning of debates I prefer is "to discuss by considering opposing arguments." Johnson and Johnson (1987) similarly talk of "constructive controversy." Consider a teacher introducing a debate on the issue, *"Should smoking be illegal?"*

> I would like you to get into pairs for this next activity. Please pair up with someone with whom you have not worked recently. I will arbitrarily assign half the pairs to take the Yes side of our question: You will perhaps need to pretend you strongly agree that smoking should be illegal. Half the pairs will be assigned the No position: You will strongly disagree. Let me outline the procedure we will follow.
>
> **Preparation time**   We will start with preparation time. During that time you are to work with your partner to understand your side of the issue very thoroughly, with reason and evidence, and to prepare to face an opposing pair later.
>
> **Debate time**   When you face that pair, you will be in four's and your job will be twofold: (1) To work together as a pair to get the other pair fully to appreciate your position. They may not clearly understand your position at the outset. In fact, since they were preparing the other side of the issue, they may be more committed to their side and have trouble listening to your reasons and evidence with an open mind. You will need, then, to practice a common life problem — getting people who think differently than you to understand your thinking. Note: Your job will not be to convince them they are wrong and you are right. Your job, as a pair, is to make sure they understand your side of the issue.
>
> The second part of your job: (2) To pretend you do not now understand their position. If you did not do this, they would have no practice in communicating effectively, which is the first task. That does not mean you have to be stubborn or argumentative. Don't go to extremes. This is not a conflict, beat-the-opposition debate. It's really a search for expanded, balanced understandings. So even if you fully understand the thinking of the other pair, pretend you do not. If you think it will not be too upsetting, you can even show some disagreement with their ideas so they get practice in communicating with people who have different positions. That's something we all must do in real life.

There's nothing wrong with teenagers that reasoning with them won't aggravate.

—Anonymous

Best choice time Finally, at the end, I'd like each quartet to see if they can agree on the best choice for resolving the issue. The question: Now that you four understand more about both sides of the issue, what do you think, overall, is best for all concerned? Make smoking illegal? Leave it as is? Or perhaps your group can come up with a third choice.

We do not want to get stuck in either-or thinking. We will just use this debate strategy to open up our discussions. Nor do we want to get stuck in selfish, what's-best-for-me thinking. We want to keep in mind what is good for us personally. But we also want to consider what would be best for others and put into words the best overall choice.

Hints for preparation time During the quartet discussions, you may face problems. What do you do, for example, if you and your partner do not cooperate and even contradict each other, making it hard for the other pair to understand your position? What do you do if an argument breaks out and people stop listening to each other? These and other problems might emerge. It would be smart to use some of your preparation time to talk about how you will handle such problems. Want to talk now about options for handling the two problems I mentioned? Want to identify other problems that might come up before we form pairs, assign positions and get into our planning time?

Sample issues for a best choice debate: Should possibly harmful fertilizers be outlawed? Should property and sales taxes be replaced by income taxes? Should children have an evening curfew? Should language in song lyrics that some people find offensive be censored? Should the minimum driving age be lowered? Should we require the metric system of everyone? Should children get an allowance? Should handguns be outlawed? Should the work week be limited to twenty hours so everyone can get a job?

Strategy 6-5 Support groups

> Students sit in stable groups, usually four's, and are encouraged to support one another. **Purpose:** To ensure that all students feel they belong and have access to peer support.

Support groups are ongoing groups that sit together and support one another. Group members might exchange phone numbers to help each other when questions come up about homework or to catch up when they are absent.

Few minds wear out; more rust out.

—Christian Bovee

Support group members might also read each other's portfolios and suggest improvements. They might share personal problems and help each other talk through solutions. Each group could also have a class task: Taking attendance, passing out books, etc. One person in each group could be responsible for, say, collecting support group papers for the teacher, handling group lunch money, marking absences for group members.

In general, group members are asked to sit together in class and to support each other in whatever ways they judge appropriate. The groups might remain stable for several weeks or even half a year. This often helps to create a strong climate of community in the class.

Fours are a good size for support groups. I generally recommend they be formed by some random method, so students learn to get along with all sorts of people. Before disbanding and forming new groups, I like to ask students to exchange **honest I appreciates:**

> Write your name on a card and pass it around in your group. When you get a card from one of your support group members, write one or more things you honestly appreciate about the person — what he or she once said, once did, once wore to class, the shine in the person's eyes, the way you were once helped, anything at all, anything you can say that you honestly appreciate about the person. In the future, you can take out your cards anytime you feel low. It may give you a reminder of your goodness.

Although support groups might also be used for instructional purposes, I prefer to focus groups on other purposes, such as keeping up with routines, building friendships and generally getting along. I treat support groups less as task groups and more as family groups, a stable home base within a class community. For instructional purposes, I use temporary sets of learning pairs, sharing pairs, task groups and the like.

Strategy 6-6   Project work

Alone or in small groups, students work for an extended time at a problem or task and, usually, produce a tangible product of their work.
Purpose: To motivate students to work on larger projects cooperatively and intelligently.

Some classrooms thrive on a steady diet of relatively complex, relatively long-term student projects. If you are unpracticed at it, you might want to experiment with ways to get it to work for you. The hardest part is often giving up control, trusting students to grow into the challenges. The best part is usually the spurt of energy and self-responsibility that projects produce. How to get started?

1. Identify the project

• Projects can start by forming groups around a **subject matter concept**: Plant growth, world government, weights and measures, sonnets, harmony. Or around an **interdisciplinary theme**: Designing an ideal city, graphing the answers to interview questions we ask of citizens, considering the health of senior citizens and how we might help with it, studying kite building, peanuts and their products, the measurement of time. Example:

It is well for people who think to change their minds occasionally in order to keep them clean.
—Luther Burbank

Our next unit is on rivers. I thought we could have one group studying the formation of rivers: How do they start? Where do they start? What is necessary for a river to last? Another group could study the local river: What can be discovered about that? A third group might identify the major rivers of the world and their characteristics. A fourth group could investigate rivers as means of transportation. There are other ways to approach rivers: Their contribution to the economy, the way they have been used by artists and writers, their connection to issues of ecology, the fish and vegetation commonly found. What other focus could a study team take?

• Projects can start with brainstorming of a list of what students **already know** about a topic. And then a list of what they might **want to know**. That can lead to a group discussion of what project groups might be organized.

• Teams can be organized around an **action project**, in which the focus is action, not studying. Groups could be formed, for example, by dividing up a project to produce a monthly class magazine:

Everyone can contribute writing and art work. You can use parts of your journals, even your doodles. But we need groups to put the magazine all together and get it out. We might, for instance, have a typing team. And a proofreading team. A team that takes care of the duplication. Another, say, for publicity and distribution. Or collecting material from parents and other classes, if we want that. I think we'll need people to manage the fund raising. They could also take care of the bookkeeping. Each of you could be on more than one team, of course. And maybe we'll need other teams. What do you all think?

Other **action project** examples:

Carrying out a tutoring program for younger students in the school.
Investigating alternative remedies for an existing problem in the
    cafeteria or community.
Managing a program for finding adults willing to consult in the class
    or accept students as temporary apprentices.
Comparing instances of loyalty and betrayal in history.
Conducting public opinion polls on issues of interest to each group.
Surveying expert opinion on drugs, health care, crime prevention,
    family values, etc.
Constructing a greenhouse for school use.
Creating exhibits showing space exploration past and future.
Designing and preparing a model of an ideal home or car or city.
Preparing an assembly for the school.

• Projects can be based on **student interests.** Example:

We will cover many topics in our class. Yet I would like you to practice learning on your own, perhaps to become more skillful or informed in an area that interests you. You could work at this personalized project alone

English spelling is weird...or is it wierd?
—Irwin Hill

or with one or two others. If you work with others, I want to keep groups small, pairs or trios at the most, so all of you have important parts to play in your groups. Most of the time you will need to work outside of class. But you might be able to substitute personalized project work for some class work. Speak to me if you think such a substitution would serve your best interests.

What can you design such a project on? Most anything you think would be fun or good for you. Overcoming procrastination perhaps. History of bicycles. Chess. Secret codes. Mark Twain. Labor unions. Heroines in history. Scuba diving requirements. Computer art. The concept of generosity, or imagination, or pantomime, or discrimination. Modern music. Improving your sleep habits. Perhaps improving your staying-awake habits.

Most anything you are serious about pursuing for a bit. Just check with me before you start. I'll ask you to draw up a provisional plan of action and to turn in, say, weekly progress cards. Then we'll go from there.

2. Set guidelines for project work

- **Clear timelines** Specific deadlines are a must, with limits better short than long. That keeps the pace quick and helps students learn to do the best they can in a short time.

- **Progress reports** For longer-term projects, progress reports are valuable. A teacher might request a weekly list of "What was accomplished" and "What specific plan have you for next week?" Each group could have a rotating reporter who would submit that report, with the names of all group members included. Or each student could submit a card each Friday saying, "What I did this week. What I promise to do next week."

- **Final product** Important, too, is that students have a final product to produce and are clear about what that is to be: A collaborative written report, personal **outcome sentences**, notes so each student can report task work to a classmate from a different task group (as in the **task group, share group** strategy), a chart of group ideas (as in the **option display** strategy), a personal assessment of the group report together with any "minority" viewpoints, or whatever. Not recommended are a series of oral reports to the class as a whole. Unless oral reports are particularly creative, as in the form of skits, they tend to be boring to many students. (See the **creative report** strategy for more suggestions.)

- **Avoiding copywork** Avoid projects that involve routine copy work from a text or encyclopedia. Rather than report on crime prevention, for example, try: "Summarize the opinions of three experts and interview at least five adults to see what they think of that expert advice." Or: "Design an ideal health center, including nutritional and illness prevention help." To reduce copywork, ask students, say, to: Interview. Compare opinions. Make a model. Design an ideal. Find contrasting views. Produce a mural. Prepare an educational debate. Create a dramatic presentation for another class.

"Come to the edge," he said. They said, "We are afraid." "Come to the edge," he said. They came. He pushed them...and they flew.
—Guillaume Apollinaire

On project power

As many teachers have long known, once smooth procedures are worked out, student projects offer unique advantages. No other strategy is as likely to grow self-management as well. Nor is any as likely to produce subject matter learnings as personally meaningful to students. Projects are also unsurpassed in producing learnings about life itself, including lifelong study skills and skills for getting along with others. In addition, student project work frees teachers from many routine chores and encourages students to exhibit high dignity, energy, self-management, community and awareness.

Note: The next chapter, on efficient group work procedures, contains other hints for supporting students during project work and for maximizing learning results.

Strategy 6-7   Task and team skill group

> Small groups work at a task while practicing an interpersonal skill.
> **Purpose:** To teach in ways that develop teamwork skills.

This is a most powerful form of cooperative learning. It advances not only academic learning but effective interpersonal skills. The strategy takes some time, however, usually a minimum of 45 minutes. This strategy was adapted from *A Guidebook for Cooperative Learning* by Dee Dishon and Pat Wilson O'Leary (1984). Four steps are involved.

Step 1. Assign individual tasks

This step could be done as homework. For example, each student could be asked to:

- Identify four or more new ideas from a text.
- Collect examples of a specified physics principle.
- Note personal recommendations for preventing waste in school.
- Create a poem.
- Draft a letter to an editor on an issue each feels strongly about.
- Seek real-life applications for a math procedure.

Step 2. Assign a group product that is to be built on the individual tasks while, at the same time, students practice improving a teamwork skill

It takes a whole village to raise a child.

—African proverb

Students are then told to work together in groups of two-to-four to produce one specific, tangible product, signed by all persons in the group. Possibilities (following the list above):

- A list from the text reading ranked by importance.
- A report of physics examples synthesized and augmented by any new ideas that came from group interaction.

- A list of individual ideas for preventing waste ranked by estimated long-term effectiveness.
- An illustrated booklet of poems.
- An improved version of the original draft letters.
- A poster showing a real-life math problem with a clear, illustrated solution on an attached sheet.

Students are also told that while they work in their groups, they are to practice a particular real-life skill, such as:

> Listening closely to each person. Taking turns. Reacting to others' comments positively. Returning to the task when they notice they are off tract. Disagreeing politely. Managing time. Asking for help. Being supportive. Sharing honest feelings. Keeping everyone involved. Paraphrasing. Helping without giving answers. Expressing honest appreciations. Listening with deep empathy to others. Disciplining unproductive impulses. Making everyone feel important. Making eye contact.

It's best for the assigned teamwork skill to be defined with many examples, so students get specific guidance in how they might practice it. A teacher might say, as an example:

> While doing this task I'd like you to focus on being supportive to one another. Let's brainstorm some things a person might do or say that would suggest the person is being supportive. And some things a person might say or do that might not be supportive at all.

> The class then brainstorms and produces a chart of items, such as:

Being supportive	**Not being supportive**
Nods	Does not listen
Smiles	Looks out window
Thanks others	Does not help out
Gives credit to others, etc.	Is slow to join in, etc.

If desired, students could be invited to select specific roles for their group work: Someone to be the group coordinator, time watcher, recorder, keeper of materials, etc. I usually do not recommend role assignments, however. I prefer to keep groups small enough so that all quite naturally have important roles to play.

Finally, students are told how much time they will have to produce the assigned product and practice the assigned skill. It's best if no penalty accrues to groups that fail to complete the task, for penalties can add excessive anxiety to the process. The activity alone can usually be made interesting enough to motivate active involvement.

If at first you don't succeed, you're probably just like the teacher in the next classroom.

—Mary Shanley

Step 3. Review the teamwork skill

After time is called, it's usually best to gather the class and first review the skill, while the experience is fresh, aiming to help students clarify what they learned about that skill.

One effective procedure starts with students making notes. The teacher asks students to think back to group time and note what they *liked* about what they did or what someone in their group did with the skill being practiced.

Students are next asked to note what they *might* do next time they have a chance to practice that skill. For example, they might try a new approach, or to do better at the skill.

Finally, students are asked to note some other places in their lives, perhaps with friends or families, where they would like to see people doing better with that skill.

The teacher might then invite a few students to share something they noted. This might lead to a very productive five-or-ten minute discussion.

Step 4. Review the task

The final step is to review the task, aiming at advancing subject matter understandings. Possibilities:

A teacher could lecture on the task and then draw out understandings from the group in an **attentive discussion**.

Students might post the results of their task groups so individuals could walk around and view each other's work, either then or in the future.

Students could be asked to pair up with someone not in their task group and to share their experiences.

Students might write **outcome sentences** about the subject matter and then share those in a discussion or a whip around.

Strategy 6-8 Rotating pairs

> Pairs of students share ideas or work briefly and then rotate, so each student can compare thoughts with two or three others. **Purpose:** To get students discussing with high dignity, energy, self-management, community and awareness.

A teacher asks Tommy what two plus two equals. "Four," he says. "Very good, Tommy." "Very good?" says Tommy indignantly. "It's perfect!"

—Quoted by Richard Kehl

Students might have thought about a question posed by the teacher. Or have written some **outcome sentences** based on a lesson or discussion. Or have their homework in hand. Or listed some things they each know or would like to know about a topic.

The teacher might then say: "Please pair up with someone nearby. Take just two or three minutes to share your thoughts. Go."

After time is called, the teacher might announce: "Please choose an A and a B in each pair. A's, in a moment I will ask you to walk around and sit with a different B. The B's will keep seated. B's, it might help if you would hold up your hand until you get a partner, so the A's know who is still available. When you get into your new pairs, again share your thoughts. You can even include thoughts you picked up from your first pair. Okay, A's, get ready to find a new partner. Go to it."

After time is called again: "Now it will be B's turn to find a new partner. A's, stay seated and perhaps raise your hand to help others find you, until you get a new partner. When your new pair is formed, again share your ideas. B's, please move now."

This rotating procedure can be continued with as many pairings as seem appropriate. The general aim is to give students the experience of sharing thoughts in a way inspiring to dignity, energy, self-management, community and awareness.

I lose all my inspiration when I encounter hate and ignorance. There are a lot of people in this world who are hurting, and who long for acceptance. These people need to be reached, but one of my own faults is that if someone is hateful toward me, sometimes I tend to lose patience and either hate them back or ignore their need.

—Michael, high school

Chapter 7: Efficient Group Procedures

Small group work does not always proceed smoothly. Some strategies reduce the problems substantially, however. Here are three to consider: Selecting group size, selecting members of groups, and hand raising signal.

Strategy 7-1 Selecting group size

For group work, generally select the smallest size feasible, usually pairs.
Purpose: To maximize learning, minimize confusion.

When forming groups, one consideration is group size, and generally smaller is better. I use pairs whenever possible.

Pairs maximize participation. Each person is either talking or being talked to. No one remains disengaged. Pairs easily start and maintain involvement, especially valuable with the short attention spans of today's students.

Pairs are less noisy than larger groupings. Two students can sit closely and hear easily. Pairs are also best for making eye contact, which facilitates honest communication and grows respectful relationships.

When an odd number of students are involved, I use one trio. I avoid forming trios, in part because two of the students often are more compatible with one another, leaving one student feeling left out. This is not good for either dignity or learning.

Sometimes students in a pair will have a task they are unable to handle by themselves. When that happens I instruct the pair to ask another pair for help. I prefer to give that instruction when I first organize groups. "When you are working in groups, always feel free to ask another group for help," I might say. "I want us all to be friendly and helpful to one another." Soon enough students know that whenever they get stuck they can always ask a friend. They need not come to me.

Fall seven times, stand up eight.

—Japanese proverb

I do not always use pairs, however. Sometimes more resources are needed than a pair is likely to have available. When a task calls for much creativity or many different perspectives, two students may not have enough to offer. For such instances, I usually use groups of three or four. Because I want to maximize student involvement, I prefer threes to fours.

Fours, however, are effective for **support groups.** Fours give students a fairly large set of ideas and chances to form comfortable friendships. Since there is not an odd number, it reduces the chances one student will feel uninvolved or left out.

Groups larger than four almost always lead to much passive participation. Even if discussion time is shared equally, which is rarely the case, most students must remain quiet most of the time. Involvement falls off dramatically.

Strategy 7-2   Selecting members for groups

Ask students to select their own group members and, only as necessary, assist them in doing so. **Purpose:** To form groups efficiently and grow self-responsibility.

In terms of time efficiency and student social learning, self-selection is my preferred mode. My most common instruction: "Pair up with someone near you. Go." Sometimes, to encourage students to sit with new partners, I will say, "Pair up this time with someone with whom you have not worked recently."

Self-selection has many advantages. It is efficient. Once students learn how to handle it, groups form quickly, and I need be involved only occasionally, as when one person remains without a group.

Self-selection also helps students learn how to take initiative in social situations. "We all need to learn how to start relationships," I might say. "Choosing our own group members will give us practice in doing this. Although reaching out to others may feel risky at first, practice will probably make it easier."

Self-selection also helps students learn how to accept or otherwise react when people reach out to them. I sometimes hear myself saying, "We all need to learn how to react when people ask us to sit with them. In this class, I'd like us to be kind and generous to one another. Does that mean you must always accept every invitation? No. We also need to learn to say, 'No thank you' when that is appropriate. When someone says that to you, just invite another person. I think that is far better than worrying over it. However, please do not say, 'No thank you' too often, or we may not all feel that we belong fully in our class. It is important to me that all of us here feel that we belong."

Few things help an individual more than to place responsibility upon him, and to let him know that you trust him.

—*Booker T. Washington*

Although self-selection is my preferred procedure, both in terms of time efficiency and its ability to give students chances to learn social skills, it has its difficulties. Here is how I might handle some common problems:

• Everyone keeps choosing the same friends. Cliques are beginning to form.

I most likely would tell the class that I want students to get to know and work with more than just a few others. At the same time, I would acknowledge the anxiety that some people feel when they are asked to reach out to new friends. I might say, "Today please practice calling up your courage. Risk asking a new person if you can work with them."

Occasionally I go to some groups and tell them not to sit with each other again for, say, the next two weeks. I explain that I want all students to get to know and appreciate each other. I am not too quick to say this, however. I am willing to give time for a secure, cooperative class climate to build. If I invest enough in climate-building strategies, I find before too long most anyone is willing to work with most anyone else. If I rush this process and push students to reach out too early, I find I slow the development of this group climate.

Nevertheless, I often do give students a structure for group formation, in part to mix students and in part for the fun of variety.

Pair up within categories "When I say, 'Go,' I want you to walk around and pair up. But pair up within colors. If you are wearing red, I want you to sit with someone also wearing red. If you are not wearing red, sit with someone not wearing red. Go." Other categories I have used for this procedure: Hair that touches your shoulder or doesn't. Wearing a belt or not. I have also said, "Hold up two fingers if you were born in an even-numbered month, one finger if you were born in an odd-numbered month, and pair up with someone in the same category."

Count-off procedure The count-off procedure is an old favorite. If groups of four are needed, for example, we divide the number of people present by four. That gives us the count-off number. (If thirty-two students were present, the count-off number would be eight and students would count off by eights. Then the four ones could be told to sit in this spot, the four twos in that spot, and so on.)

Playing card procedure Some teachers take an old deck of cards and, to form student pairs for example, make as many card pairs as the class needs, distribute the cards randomly among the class, and then ask students to find the person with the card that corresponds to their own.

Chalkboard procedure When students finish individual work at different times and need to form small groups, I sometimes use a chalkboard procedure. Here is an example, in this case, to form trios. It would be similar for pairs, fours, or any size groups.

> When you finish your individual work and are ready to work in a trio, write your name in this area of the chalkboard. If someone has already written a name, write your name under it. If two names are already there, erase both names, find the two people, sit together, and begin your trio work. The next person ready would, of course, see no names and write his or her name to begin a new trio group.

I was going to buy a copy of "The Power of Positive Thinking," and then I thought: What the hell good would that do?
—Ronnie Shakes

• No one wants to sit with John. Several times I have had to intervene and get him into a group.

I sometimes speak to a few of the more good-natured students privately, the ones likely to be gracious. I say that I notice not all students are readily being accepted by others when groups are formed. I ask them to go out of their way, please, to look for students being left out and to choose them, modeling for the class the supportive community spirit we want. I almost always find students willing to do such good turns. I may or may not mention John by name, depending on how much I trust the students with such sensitive information.

Alternatively, I might face the issue honestly with the whole class and then wait, allowing time to do its work:

> I've noticed over the last few days that some students are not chosen as quickly as others. Since we want to learn to get along with everyone and be kind to everyone, I would like you all to go out of your way to make sure everyone has a partner. We do not want anyone here to feel left out. I know you like to be with your good friends, but we want all students to feel that they are worthwhile parts of the class. Please keep on the lookout for classmates needing help or needing partners. Practice giving a hand to those in need. Let's build a caring, cooperative community here.

• Some students react to calls for good will by never refusing anyone. They feel they must always say yes when someone asks to join them.

I look for an appropriate time to talk to the class about the wisdom of not trying to please all the people all the time, about the wisdom of learning how sometimes to say "No" politely and respectfully, about the wisdom of respecting our own need sometimes to help others and sometimes not to.

> So say, "No, thank you," if you think that is best, all things considered. We all have to maintain our own limits, or we will not be very good for anyone very long.

> If people say, "No thank you" to you, respect their right to live their own lives in their own ways. Do not ask them why and do not fret about it. We all have our own ways. Simply walk over and ask someone else. You would probably not want to be quizzed about why *you* choose what you choose. Let's respect each other's rights here.

• The boys by the window keep gossiping and hardly do any work in their groups.

I would not want to complain, scold or threaten, for I find that to be counterproductive in the long run. I would probably do nothing the first time I noticed. But early the second time those girls sat together and delayed working, I might simply say, without rancor, just as someone responsible for their learning, "I need you to get right down to work."

I was successful because you believed in me.
—*Ulysses S. Grant (to Abraham Lincoln)*

If that simple authority statement did not work, next time I would inform the girls that, because I want everyone here to use learning time productively, I want them to choose other students to work with for the next two weeks. I skip the warning step I might be tempted to issue, such as, "I'll change your groups if you do not settle down to work," for that is usually heard by students as a threat, and threats, as I said, cause me more trouble than benefit in the long run.

• Slower students sit together and cannot do some of the academic work even if they wanted to.

I sometimes ask such students to pick different partners in the future. More often I instruct them to ask other groups for help whenever they feel stuck. The quicker students usually feel honored with such requests for help. I find, too, that the problem tends to vanish as the group climate grows more secure and cooperative. Eventually, slower students do not restrict themselves to choosing just their slower peers.

Some teachers prefer forming groups themselves, so they can mix student ability within each group or at least get some capable students in every group. And some teachers prefer to connect grades to group work, to motivate serious work. I find both unnecessary. Concerning grades, I find that a combination of quick pace, small-size groups and appropriate task assignments eventually motivates students to get and stay involved in group work quite as well as rewards and punishments and produces far fewer difficulties for me.

Strategy 7-3 Hand raise signal

To signal that it is time to discontinue small group discussions, tell students that you will raise one hand. All students who see your hand are then to raise one of their own hands, with the process continuing until all students see hands raised and know it's time to discontinue conversations. **Purpose:** To manage group work efficiently.

Disorder, of course, invites misbehavior, especially when students work in small groups. Here is a strategy that helps keep group work orderly. Imagine a teacher explaining to a class:

I get inspired when I see good looking girls.
—Clifton, high school

> When I raise my hand during small group time it signals it's time to stop the group discussions. Whenever you see my hand go up, please raise your hand. When you raise your hand, people who cannot see me will see hands go up and raise their hands. If you are talking when hands go up, please finish the sentence you have already started, but do not start a new sentence.

If something important is interrupted, which will sometimes happen, please remember what it was. I may simply need to give you new directions or ask you to speak more quietly. Even if there is no more time for you to continue your group discussions, if you remember what you wanted to say, you can say it to others later, perhaps during lunch or after school.

I suspect the hand raising signal works so well because it gives all students something to do — raise their hands — and does not focus on what a few students should stop doing — talking. The strategy is active and constructive. It can even be adapted to non-classroom settings, to signal it's time to put the gym equipment away, for example.

A Teacher Comments

I use the hand raising signal on the playground. When I need students to come inside I raise my hand, students who see me raise theirs, and soon all the hands are in the air. The students somehow enjoy going through the process, and I do not have to yell or complain. They just do it, and I wave them in. Works wonderfully well.

— Clara Bowles, Third-Grade Teacher

If you hear that someone is speaking ill of you, instead of trying to defend yourself you should say: "He obviously does not know me very well, since there are so many other faults he could have mentioned."

—*Epictetus*

Chapter 8: Basic Class Procedures

Organization is one key to effective classrooms. We must find ways to handle all the subject matter we must teach, the variety of students we must face, the time and materials we must manage, plus all the pressures and expectations others pile on us and, occasionally, we pile on ourselves. Various chapters of this book contain strategies for handling particular aspects of this. This chapter contains seven strategies more generally valuable: Intelligence call up, set of speakers, nod of recognition, once principle, class tutors, tutor training, student procedure mastery, physical movement, three structure weave, class workshop and consult time.

Strategy 8-1 Intelligence call up

> Remind students frequently that they are intelligent humans, each with a capacity to stop and think and make thoughtful, responsible choices.
> **Purpose:** To advance student ability to handle themselves intelligently.

Grace Pilon (*Workshop Way*, 1988) taught me the value of repeatedly telling students they were smart enough to solve problems on their own. Hear one first-grade teacher announcing that thoughtful problem-solving would be the style in her room:

> When things are not flowing smoothly in this class, I want you to pause and ask yourself, "What would be the intelligent thing to do?"

> So, for example, if papers are not being piled neatly, or a crowd is forming at the door, I might say, "What would be the smart, thoughtful way to handle this? Think about this and then go ahead and do what you think would be best."

> Let's use our brains. We want this to be a class in which we all learn how to think for ourselves. Let's grow our intelligence. I may remind you of this from time to time.

> If you were not a human with a human brain, you might not know what is best to do. But you have an amazing brain. You can think for yourself. You do it all the time at home.

> When things are not going right, pause and ask yourself, "What is the smart thing to do now?" Learn to reason things out for yourself. Humans can do that like no other animal.

Before I got married, I had six theories about bringing up children. Now I have six children and no theories.

—John Wilmot

Can anyone give an example of when something was not going smoothly, and you stopped and thought about what was best to do, or maybe what you had to stop doing, and you did that?

Incidents from an eighth-grade class illustrating how the **intelligence call up** strategy showed up:

Students fail to clean up on time:

Class, we're having difficulty getting everything cleaned up on time. How can we handle this problem? Let's brainstorm a list of ideas on the board. We are smart enough to find a way to solve this that will be good for us all. After the brainstorm, we'll see what we think is best.

Some students are avoided when the teacher asks the class to get into pairs:

Class, I'm having to use extra time to pair up everyone when I call for **sharing pairs.** I can understand that you want to sit with your good friends. But getting everyone involved is taking us too much time. Besides, I want us to learn to get along with everyone here. From now on, please reach out to all students, even those not near you. Be generous and kind. You will know when it would be a good idea to do that. Be aware please. Make sure everyone gets a partner quickly.

Preparing a class for the arrival of new students:

Here's a chance to exercise our brain power. We will get new students from time to time. What would be the best way to get them into the flow of our work? We could talk it over now and use our creativity all together. Or would it be better to ask a committee to think it through and give us a recommendation or two? What do you think is best?

A student asks a question about a non-vital issue:

You decide. (Said with a tone that conveys: "I trust you to exercise your awareness and self-management abilities wisely.")

Two students come to the teacher complaining about each other:

Talk it over, if necessary write down what options you have, and work it out yourselves. Use your creative intelligence. You both decide.

In short, the **intelligence call up** strategy has us often saying, "What would be the smart thing to do? Stop and think, and you will know what will be best." And we persist in talking that way, trusting that all students will eventually know we really mean it, all will come to believe it, and the intelligent way of handling situations will become second nature. Hold high expectations. Thereby enlist the power of those expectations.

The secret of education is respecting the pupil.
—*Ralph Waldo Emerson*

Assuring students they *are* intelligent

Some students, of course, do not believe they are intelligent. Perhaps parents confused grades with intelligence, or compared one child with another, or perhaps earlier class experiences did not fit the students' learning styles. Any of that may have led students to discount their ability to think and live intelligently. You may want to assure students that all humans have a remarkable intelligence.

How? The best way may be simply to keep using the **intelligence call up** strategy, until students actually experience themselves being intelligent. But you may want to find a way to help students distinguish human brain power from school grades.

I like to do this by telling about my father, who never got to high school, never did much reading, but who was one of the smartest people I ever knew. He knew what was going on, and he knew how to thimk. I tell about him and then I ask:

> What does it mean to be intelligent? It is certainly not a matter of being able to remember facts or solve school problems. Some of you can do that better than others. But *all* humans can do much more.
>
> All humans are aware. And all humans can manage that awareness. Look at that window. Now look at the ceiling. That is managing your awareness. You are directing your attention where you want it. All humans can do that. When you think about what to do next, you are simply managing your awareness, focusing your awareness on the options ahead. Being intelligent is nothing more than that, directing your awareness where you want it. The better you can manage awareness, and the more things you can bring into awareness, the more powerful will be your intelligence.
>
> In this class I would encourage you to practice that intelligence. Reach to become more aware of what is going on around you and inside you, including inside your head where, if you are patient enough, you will find lots of good ideas. And including the world around you where, if you listen and observe closely, you will notice many interesting events.
>
> And reach to become better at managing that awareness, focusing it for longer periods of time at one thing, looking more closely at details and looking more widely at the general scene. Practice that and you will learn how to use more of your native intelligence.
>
> In class, when unsure of what is best to do, pause and become more aware of what is going on. Then reach for all the ideas you can dream up. Perhaps ask others for ideas too. As our sign says, "It's intelligent to ask for help." After you get ideas about what can be done, imagine what will happen if this is done or that is done. That's what it means to think ahead. Think like that and your natural smartness will get exercised. It will help you to live an intelligent life. Like my father did.

What can be done at anytime is never done at all.

—*English proverb*

Strategy 8-2 Set of speakers

Request volunteers to speak and then, from all volunteers, choose the set who will next have turns. **Purpose:** To select speakers efficiently.

Rather than calling on one student at a time during discussions, I occasionally select a set of students to speak. "How many would be willing to share ideas?" I might ask. Hands go up and I point to some: "Let's hear from five people today. You be first. You be second." And so on. After the set is selected, I say, "Let's hear now from the first person." That gets a set of students ready to speak. All students can then relax and pay attention. The speakers know their turns are coming up and they know the order in which they will speak. The rest of the class knows the next bit of time is all organized, and they need not worry about whether or not to speak. More attentive discussions follow.

Choosing a set of students also makes it easier to avoid calling repeatedly on the same students and to notice the more tentative hands almost ready to be raised. I sometimes prompt more volunteers with something like, "How about some volunteers from those who have not spoken lately?" Or, "Simpson, I see you might be willing to be one of the speakers. Are you?"

I also like to use the **whip around, pass option**, sometimes down one row, sometimes around the whole class. That almost always produces widespread participation, assuming I have built a cooperative class atmosphere, an atmosphere that respects risk taking and appreciates the truth of the sign, "It's OK to make mistakes. That's the way we learn."

Strategy 8-3 Nod of recognition

Nod to indicate that you have noticed a student who has volunteered, and wait to give more time for other students to consider volunteering. **Purpose:** To maximize the number of students who will have time to volunteer.

Usually a few bright students quickly volunteer to answer my questions. To avoid calling on those few students all the time, I explain what I call the nod of recognition:

> Sometimes I'll ask for volunteers to answer a question, you will raise your hand, and I will not call on you or anyone else for a moment or two. I might just look at you and nod. That means I noticed you were willing to volunteer, so you can put down your hand. I simply want to wait a bit before calling on someone, to give more time for people to think about the question and to consider if they are willing to risk an answer.

Students seem to understand my motive and respect it.

We are so accustomed to wearing a disguise before others that eventually we are unable to recognize ourselves.
—La Rochefoucauld

Strategy 8-4   Once principle

Announce that from now on directions will be given only once and that students not hearing directions are to use their intelligence to find an appropriate way to catch up. **Purpose:** To teach students both to listen and live self-responsibly.

Imagine a teacher saying:

> Please, everyone look at me. From now on, I will say things only once. Page numbers. Directions. Anything like that. So please practice keeping yourself aware. If you miss what I say, find a way to catch up. Perhaps whisper to a friend, or watch and see what others are doing, or later catch what you missed. Call on your good intelligence. You will know the best thing to do. Now let's get started on today's lesson....

Note that the teacher said that only once. He did not say, "Any questions?" That might have led to a repetition of the message.

And note that the teacher began by asking all students to look at her. If a direction is to be given only once, it is fair to call for attention, so all students have a fair chance of hearing. Unnecessary confusion is prevented by giving directions only after a call for attention and an appropriate beat of silence.

Will procedures work if teachers say things only once? Yes, they will. When students realize that when they ask the teacher, "*When* was that due?" or, "*What* did you say the page was?" the teacher will only smile and say nothing, not even "I *told* you," or, "I say things only once," or, "Please check with a neighbor," students manage just fine. Students are far from stupid. If we expect students to manage the once principle, they will. In my experience, it is more difficult for the teacher to stick to the once principle than it is for students to learn how to live with it.

Strategy 8-5   Class tutors

Set up a procedure whereby individual students can get tutoring. **Purpose:** To give students who need extra assistance an efficient means of getting it.

I have been inspired by myself.
—Jeffrey, third grade

I find great advantage in peer teaching. It usually helps both the giver and the receiver. Furthermore, it helps not only with learning now, but in developing habits that will serve living and learning over the long term. One way to take advantage of peer instruction is to set up a tutoring program in a classroom, perhaps speaking somewhat like this:

> We all learn by our own timeclocks and in our own ways, of course. As a result, some of us will learn some things more slowly, some more quickly. That's not good or bad, any more than it is good or bad that some plants grow more slowly than others. It is just the way life works.

Another aspect of life is how we can help one another. And in our class, I want us to do that. I want us to live as a cooperative, kind community. So here is what I suggest.

Those of you who understand a topic and are willing to be class tutors on that topic, please sign the topic sheet I have posted in the tutor section over there. Then, when someone would like some help, they can look on that sheet and find someone to ask.

Notice that the sign-up sheet asks whether you are willing to help someone after school, as well as in school. You might do your tutoring on the phone, if you and the person you are tutoring agree.

I might also use those tutor lists. If I notice a few students whom I want to get extra help or practice, I might use a list to see what tutors I can put the students with. If I do that, I will tell the tutor exactly what it is that I want covered.

When students receive training in tutoring, many do better at both giving and receiving help and in developing the lifelong habits tutoring promotes. The following strategy suggests a way to provide such training.

Strategy 8-6 Tutor training

Teach students skills for effectively giving and receiving help. **Purpose:** To teach basic communication skills.

Students often need training if they are to be good tutors for one another. Such training also gives me a good excuse to teach important life skills, such as how to listen to others, how to discipline urges to upstage others, how to converse productively with others. Even without a tutoring program, since I often ask students to sit in pairs to help each other, I find it valuable to include tutor training in classes.

Below is how I might do this with a junior high class.

Whole class *1 minute*	I will often ask everyone to help each other with a learning, usually in pairs. And some of you may sign up to be special tutors for certain topics. But what does it take to help someone learn? I think you will find that, first, it takes good listening on the part of the tutors. If they are to do good jobs at helping others, they will want to listen to check what the others now know and to decide what might best help them.
Class and teacher brainstorm actions that distinguish good/poor listeners *8-12 minutes*	How many of you know someone who listens really well? Anyone know someone who is a terrible listener? Let's consider what good listeners do that terrible listeners do not do. Tony and Krista, will you write our ideas on the board as we think of them?

The first requirement for the growth of the individual is that the person remain in touch with his own perceptions.
—*Clark Moustakas*

Instructions and practice pairs *4 minutes*	Here are three key listening skills: (1) looking at you pleasantly (not looking out the window while you talk), (2) giving you plenty of time to think, and (3) not interrupting. When I give the signal, I want you to find a new partner, someone with whom you have not worked recently, and choose an A and B. The A will start. A's job is to talk about someone he or she knows who is either a fairly good listener or who is a very poor listener. B's job is to be a good listener. I'll signal when 90 seconds is up. Until then, B, do not take the focus from A. B will have a turn later. Get in pairs now. B, now start listening!
Review discussion *3-5 minutes*	How many A's had B's who did a great job listening, even though this was the first time we tried this? What problems came up? What did you all learn from this?
Second instructions and practice *4 minutes*	Let's reverse roles now. B's, you talk about listening, your experience just now, people you know, anything. A's, check the three key listening skills. Your job is not to steal the focus from B, but to be as good a listener as you now can be. 90 seconds. Go!
Review discussion *6-12 minutes*	How many B's had A's who already showed great listening ability? What can we say about this practice time? Was anything hard? New? Okay, that's enough for now. I just wanted to get us started on what I call tutor training. It's training so you can be better helpers for one another in our class. Next time I ask you to help one another, stretch yourself toward excellent listening skills.

After a day or so, I would want to review that listening lesson. I might do it simply by having a whole class discussion: Anyone become more aware of good and poor listening since we had our practice? Anyone practice becoming a more skillful listener? How many of the three good listening acts can you now list on scrap paper? How many listed 1? 2? 3? Please continue practicing, here or out of school.

Or I might use the **like/might review** strategy:

> Think back to times you listened to others in the last day or so, in this class, other classes, at home, any place. As you think about the listening you did, write one or two sentences beginning, "I liked the way I..."

> Thank you. Now as you think back to those listening experiences, see if you can write sentences that start "Next time I might..." You could write about doing things better, or differently, or anything else. Not a promise that next time you *will*. Just a sentence about what you *might* do next time a similar situation comes up for you. (I would then invite some sharing of notes written.)

The world could use more vision and less television.
—Anonymous

After that, at some appropriate time, I would have another set of practice pairs, this time focusing on disciplining urges to upstage others, that is, holding back one's own thoughts when others are speaking:

> A's, please pick a topic that you have pretty strong feelings about: What parents, teachers, police or the president should do, or should not do, what's wrong with this town or school, or your opinions on any controversial topic, anything. Tell B your topic.
>
> B's, you start this practice. Your job is to pretend your opinions are very different from A's. I'll give you two or three minutes to tell your "different" opinions to A. Speak as if you really mean it, with dignity and power, the best you can.
>
> A's, your job is to practice good listening. And to practice not upstaging the person who is speaking. Not interrupting. Not taking away that person's right to speak up. Not showing disrespect to the person. Put your own ideas on the shelf and just listen. While B speaks (1) aim to look pleasantly at him or her, (2) give your partner plenty of time to think about what to say, and (3) most important, do not interrupt. If you feel the need to say anything, say something like, *"Yes, I think I understand how you feel."* Or try a brief summary of an idea your partner expressed, *"As I hear it, you feel parents should never ground teenagers."* Go!

A few days after that, I would review as before, using an **attentive discussion** and/or the **like/might review** strategy:

> Anyone become more aware of holding back your thoughts when others were speaking? Anyone become more aware of when others failed to do that? Anyone risk practicing the self-discipline skill? Please keep aware of this skill and keep practicing, for it will help us be good tutors to one another in class.

My third and last step in **tutor training** would be slightly different.

Introduction and pair/trio brainstorming *3-5 minutes*	Some people are good at tutoring. What do they do? They might, for example, ask their tutee how they can best help. Or they might say, "Am I going too fast?" Or they might say, "Need a break now or some new practice problems?" Please sit with one or two others and write a list of what good tutors do. You may include my ideas or any others. Go.
Group reporting andclass summary *10-15 minutes*	Let's see if we can agree on which, from all your lists, are the top four or five. Too many items will give us too much to keep in mind as we stretch to be better tutors. Each group start by giving one idea for our board list. Then we'll vote and see which we agree are most important. Finally, I'll ask one or two of you to make us a wall chart, so we can occasionally review our Guidelines for Good Tutoring.

When I'm inspired I jump on my motorcycle and head for the trails.

—Adam, high school

Soon after training, if a real tutoring situation did not arise, I might invent a mini-practice exercise:

> Please pair up now with someone you do not usually sit with. Choose an A and a B. A's, I'd like you to pretend that you are not sure how to do long division. B, your job will be to be a good tutor and to help the person learn how to do long division. You might look at our Guidelines for Good Tutoring. I'll give you just three or four minutes for this tutoring practice. Then we'll look back and see what we can learn from it. Finally, we'll reverse roles and try again.

It's important here to pick subject matter both students are likely to understand fairly well. It is less important that the content be relevant to the class. For example, I have asked tutors to help their partners learn: How to add fractions. How to memorize three spelling words. How to remember what they read in a book. How to get from the school to the post office.

After the practice session, I might review by asking each person to write some **outcome sentences** and then have students share them, using the **whip around, pass option**. Finally, I might use the **learning challenge** strategy:

> I challenge you to keep stretching yourself toward tutoring excellence, and toward excellent communication outside of class, too. If you accept this challenge, keep track of how it goes. If you have a hard communication situation to deal with, perhaps ask a friend to be one of your cheerleaders. And from time to time you may want to let us know what progress you are making.

Strategy 8-7   Student procedure mastery

Spend enough time teaching classroom procedures early in the year so students can follow those procedures smoothly. **Purpose:** To train students to use procedures efficiently.

It is tempting to assume students will understand and follow simple procedures: "Pick a partner and talk over last night's homework." "When you replace your folder on the shelf, replace it in alphabetical order." But some students will neither comprehend well nor follow directions smoothly. The remedy: Over-teach procedures, especially for elementary school students. Aim for all students to feel absolute mastery of procedures and to feel good about that mastery. For young students, it's often wise to walk through a procedure, giving explicit instructions:

When in doubt, tell the truth.
—Mark Twain

> When I say, "Get a partner," first look around and make eye contact with someone. You can sit with someone nearby or not, as you choose. But if I ask you to pick someone with whom you have not recently worked, you might have to stand and walk elsewhere to make that eye contact. Then sit near that person, as close as you can conveniently, so talk is most quiet. Let's try that. Pick a partner with whom you have not recently worked and sit together. Please go do that now.

(After students begin to get settled) Let's talk about this now. Chances are some of you felt anxious about being left out, and felt it was risky to get partners. As I look around I see that some of you were in fact left out, and it was tempting to make a trio instead of a pair. Or to sit by yourself. Or to come and ask me what to do. Please go back to your original seats, and let's try this again.

This time, when I say "Go," take a risk and do not rush to sit with the first person you see. If most are paired up and you are still without a partner, look to see if anyone else is left alone. A person might have not been ready to risk today, so you may find someone sitting alone. That sometimes happens. Take your time and look closely, like a detective looking for someone. If you have done that and still find no one without a partner, please make one trio. Ask a pair if you might join them. Let's try it again. Please get yourself a partner with whom you have not recently worked. Go.

Similarly, the instruction, "talk over last night's homework" invites confusion, which invites noncompliance, which invites discipline problems. One teacher has a chart posted:

> **Homework Groups**
>
> Compare answers.
> Talk through disagreements.
> Help each other understand.
> Check with another group
>   if unsure.
> Support each other in
>   mastering the content.

Another teacher has a chart for writings when right-wrong answers are not central:

> **For Writing Homework**
>
> 1. Exchange papers.
> 2. Read thoughtfully.
> 3. Make helpful feedback
>   notes.
> 4. If time, talk over your
>   reactions.

I get inspired when I'm sitting outside and I feel the breeze blowing by my face. It feels great.
—Chris, junior high

The point: Spend enough time to make procedures perfectly clear and acceptable to all. Get students to enjoy their ability to follow guidelines masterfully and smoothly. The results in year-long procedure efficiency typically make that investment well worthwhile.

Strategy 8-8   Physical movement

Give younger students opportunities to move about. **Purpose:** To keep student energies from getting sluggish. Also, to give students more chances to learn to manage their physical selves.

Most young students sit too much. Their minds may get sluggish because their bodies get sluggish. What can be done about this? Some ideas:

- Do not pass out papers, but rather put three piles around the room and ask students to stand up and get their own. Perhaps twisting-stretching as they go.

- Allow students to stand and walk about whenever they feel like it, perhaps reminding them that it is not smart for people to bother each other when moving around the classroom.

- If you have quiet reading, encourage students to stand or even to walk while they read. Some teachers find students read better when they form a large circle and walk slowly while they read.

- If you use **sharing pairs,** invite pairs to stand while they work, even to stroll about if they can do that without disrupting the class.

- Pick a stand-twist-stretch exercise with which you feel comfortable. Lead students through it whenever you sense physical energies are getting dammed up.

- Have a team of students take turns leading the exercise, perhaps with their favorite music.

- How about an occasional round of Simon Says, Hokey Pokey, silly walking, or any movement game?

Strategy 8-9   Three structure weave

Blend whole class lessons, small group work and individual task work into the class time. **Purpose:** To keep student energies flowing, to enrich learning, and to assist students in learning responsible self-management.

I get inspired when I listen to Raps Bigest hits.

—BJ, second grade

The purpose of this strategy is to intertwine and balance three classroom structures: Whole class lessons, small group work and individual work time. Weaving these three structures helps us both to manage a classroom efficiently and to grow student self-management. The general recommendation: Avoid treating students together as a whole class too much of the time. Give them plenty of time to work alone or with a few others.

On whole class lesson time

Several whole class lesson strategies have been discussed elsewhere. Yet whole class strategies, no matter how artistic the presentation, limit student self-direction and usually eventually dampen DESCA scores. This may be exacerbated by the increasing need many young people seem to feel to live free of excessive domination. In any case, if your classes are typical, expect better work and more cooperation if you use only part of the time for whole class lessons. Also structure time for students to work either in small groups or at self-directed individual tasks.

I do not suggest a non-directive approach to such time. I do not find most students profiting from total freedom but, rather, from freedom from constant adult domination. I therefore suggest that the time away from teacher control be fairly well structured, as it is, for instance, with the **underexplain and learning pairs strategy, sharing pairs** and **paired reading.**

On small group time

As for small group work, some of it can readily be included in whole class lessons. The chapter on action flow lesson plans illustrated several instances in which students were asked, for example, to pair up and share ideas, or to pair up and help each other practice a skill. But such group work is somewhat controlled by the teacher, with the teacher at least starting and stopping the activity and prescribing its content.

Less controlled by teachers, and therefore more fruitful in terms of inspiring students to practice and advance responsible self-management, are such activities as **homework sharing groups, paired reading** and **project work.**

On individual task time

Many classes routinely include individual work time. This includes class time to begin homework. Time for work at learning centers. Time for work in a lab, in a library or at a computer. And time for work on individual learning sheets or projects. Students are relatively self-managing at such times. Including time for such activity in today's classrooms almost always makes a contribution to class dignity, energy, self-management, community and awareness. The strategy that follows makes use of such individual task time in an advanced form and is especially valuable.

The school where my father was principal, you couldn't drop out. You could leave, but he went and got you.
—*Asa Hilliard*

Strategy 8-10   Class workshop

Set a series of tasks so students always have their own work to do in the classroom and can keep busy whenever the teacher works with small groups or individuals. **Purpose:** To keep students engaged, to inspire self-responsible work habits and to free teacher time.

Pilon crafted a special format for individual task time. She calls it a class workshop. That workshop is made up of an extensive series of mini-tasks, each readily manageable by students, the whole comprehensively educational. Her tasks touch logic and imagination, review of old content and learning of new content, basic skills and extra enrichment, the abstract and the concrete, stiff challenge and enjoyable diversion. Pilon has prepared sets of such tasks for most grade levels, usually far more tasks than any one teacher will find necessary. (For Pilon materials, contact The Workshop Way, Inc., P.O. Box 850170, New Orleans, LA 70185-0170, phone (504) 486-4871.)

In her design, class workshop provides an ever-present core activity. Students can engage workshop tasks whenever they are not called by the teacher into a whole class lesson or are involved in small group activity.

Students can also proceed through the set of tasks at their own pace. However, there are more than enough tasks for any one day. Students are never expected to finish the whole set. Each does as many as time permits. As a consequence, students always have work to do and, except for those times they are in whole class lessons or teacher-led small groups, it is their own work. This provides a class design that steadily drives self-responsible work habits. It also frees teacher time for flexible small group work and much more individual consultation.

Strategy 8-11   Consult time

Set time aside for each student to visit briefly with teacher. **Purpose:** To help teachers monitor student progress and to give each student a brief time of full teacher attention and concern.

Intelligence appears to be the thing that enables a man to get along without education. Education enables a man to get along without the use of his intelligence.

—Albert Edward Wigga

Consult time is time in class for each student to sit with the teacher and to consult or report briefly on, say, homework just completed or progress with a personal project.

Teachers make time for this by arranging for the class as a whole to work at individual or small-group learning tasks. Each student, then, takes a few moments away from these tasks to visit and consult with the teacher.

Students could take turns coming to where the teacher sits. Or, if students are in small groups, the teacher could travel from group to group to visit with individual students. This group procedure has two advantages. When students meet with a teacher alone, many feel high anxiety; they usually feel less anxious when peers are sitting with them. Also, students often learn something when hearing others talking to the teacher.

What do students consult on? Some options:

1. Students could read one of the **outcome sentences** they wrote for homework. (See the **homework hearing** strategy.)

2. Students could read or talk about an item from their personal journals or consult on progress on a personal project.

3. If students were learning to read, each could read from a story or reading sheet.

4. If students needed to memorize a list of terms or formulas, each could recite ones recently mastered.

5. If the teacher simply wanted to get to know students better, students could be invited to talk about anything of interest to them, in or out of school. Teachers who choose this option might want to make consult time optional:

> I'd like to invite each of you to come chat with me during your individual work time. If you see I'm free, and if you would like, please leave your work for a moment or two and come sit with me. Perhaps tell me how things are going with you. Or tell me if you have any suggestions about our class or any questions I might help with. Just a moment or two. And not every person every day. But I'd like to spend a bit of time each week chatting with individuals, so I can better get to know you all. No need for you to do this. But you might want to risk it! It will help me get to know you better.

Consult time adds a fourth element to the mix of whole class lessons, small group time and individual work time. And it can be a worthy element to add. It adds a time for teachers to connect personally and meaningfully with each student, which of course can also be an occasion to clarify each student's progress or to offer brief instruction or support of some kind. And it adds a time for students to experience moments of personal, caring, full attention from a respected adult, something many students lack in this era of rapid change and fractured families.

A related report from the world of business: The Solectron Company was recently awarded the Malcolm Baldridge award for excellence in manufacturing. The quality and efficiency of work were both outstanding. Why? Perhaps, I would say, because Solectron makes use of the **consult time** strategy. According to Barron's Magazine (November 1991), every single employee chats informally and individually once every month with either the chairman of the board or the president.

Children are living messages we send into the future, a future that we will not see. In effect we are building the house of tomorrow day by day, not out of bricks or steel, but out of the stuff of children's bodies, hearts and minds.

—Melvin Konner

Chapter 9: For Opening a Class

There are many ways to begin a class. One, the **voting** strategy, was previously discussed. Using that, the teacher would ask a few voting-type questions to break the ice and gather the group's attention. Perhaps:

- How many of you have had a good day so far today?
- How many were surprised by the sudden rain?
- How many just love rainy days?
- Anyone wearing something new today?
- How many remember where we left off yesterday's lesson?
- Well, for today...

Here are five other strategies I often use at the outset of a class, sometimes in combinations, sometimes by themselves: Lesson agreement, immediate work assignment, motivational question, new or goods and risk reminders.

Strategy 9-1 Lesson agreement

> Outline plans for the lesson ahead and invite student agreement.
> **Purpose:** To maximize student cooperation.

I might ask for agreement with a day's lesson outline, as by saying:

> Today I planned to start with our homework. Then I thought we would begin our discussion on France. After that, there would be time for your group project work. And if time remains we could do some map work. How does that sound? Can we agree on that plan?

In our differences we grow; in our sameness we connect.
—Virginia Satir

Some students might have suggestions, of course. Some suggestions might even be worth a change of plans. The teacher, however, would make such a determination. The teacher has final responsibility. The intent here is not to expect all to agree. It is rather to use a moment or two to demonstrate respect for student intelligence, invite collaboration and hear suggestions, so we move ahead with maximum cooperation.

A teacher might present the class outline not orally, but by having it on the board. For older students, the outline might extend for a week or more, in which case the teacher would, of course, be asking for agreement with a longer plan, perhaps even with a plan for the whole course.

This **lesson agreement** strategy is similar to what Madelene Hunter called an "anticipatory set." Both point students forward to the lesson ahead. One difference is the invitation to accept the plan ahead which is part of this strategy. When we ask a class, "Is that okay with you?" we are, of course, asking students to be partners in taking responsibility for the lesson.

Strategy 9-2 Immediate work assignment

Organize work so students have something to do as soon as they enter the room. **Purpose:** To get students productively involved at the outset.

Some teachers instruct students to begin working on an assignment as soon as they enter the room, not to wait until the teacher calls the class to order. Students might be instructed to:

- Write in their journals, perhaps in response to a quote of the day that is posted.
- Work on the problems written on the chalkboard.
- Sit in pairs and begin checking each other's homework, perhaps against a posted answer key.
- Start work on individual tasks, worksheets at desks or tasks at learning centers.

The idea is to create immediate work so students waste no time and lose no energy waiting for activities to get underway. This procedure also gives teachers time for preparing lesson materials, taking attendance, or consulting with individual students.

Strategy 9-3 Motivational question

Ask a question, both to focus attention on a topic and to start students thinking. **Purpose:** To generate student interest in a lesson and to assist concentration.

Some teachers use questions to generate thinking and to focus attention on the lesson ahead: What would be an example of an antonym? What do you know about the reasons for the Civil War? Can anyone estimate how much faster a dime falls than a nickel? Once student interest is aroused, the lesson naturally proceeds more easily.

I get inspired when I ride my horse and go hunting.

—John, high school

Sometimes the motivation question can refer to an earlier lesson: What were the key points of yesterday's discussion? What did we say last time about a good diet?

Using the **question, all write** strategy with a provocative question helps get all students ready to jump into the lesson.

Strategy 9-4   New or goods

Ask students if anything is new or good in their lives. **Purpose:** To gather student attention and to build a healthy community climate.

From Jackins (1974) I learned the value of starting meetings by asking, "Who can tell us something new or good in your life?"

When I first use this strategy in classrooms, I usually give some prompts, to clarify the question. I might say, "Anything new or good in your lives? Anyone get a new compliment or a new car? Anything good happen lately at home or school?" Whatever is mentioned, then, is accepted. I usually simply say, "Thank you for sharing that," or, "I can sure appreciate that." After a few moments, I move into the day's lesson.

The intent here is not to raise issues for discussion, although it sometimes is wise to allow a discussion to follow, as when a student comment raises an issue important for many students to talk about.

The intent is to give students a few moments to share the happy or sad events in their lives. It allows students who may not shine in academic areas to announce good news in other areas of their lives — being on a winning team, for example. It allows students anguishing over an event — the death of a pet, for example — to vent distressing feelings. In many ways it brings a class together in deeper and more expansive appreciation of one another.

Besides all that, it opens a class with a positive, personal touch and usually brings student attention fully into the classroom. A good place to start a lesson.

Strategy 9-5   Risk reminders

Occasionally remind students how risking serves learning. **Purpose:** To encourage students to stretch beyond their familiar and comfortable learning zone.

The worst sin towards our fellow creatures is not to hate them, but to be indifferent to them; that's the essence of inhumanity.

—George Bernard Shaw

When the lesson ahead might be challenging to students, I sometimes will begin with, "How many are up for a risk today? How many are ready to do some new thinking? We have a tricky lesson today, an important lesson, so I want us to be ready for it. Can you stretch yourself for it?"

One of the **truth signs** I recommend, of course, talks of risking: "We can do more and learn more when we are willing to risk." It is useful, I find, to remind students of the need sometimes to reach beyond their comfort zone, to call up courage and move out into what may be difficult experiences. I use the **risk reminder** for that purpose.

I also use **risk reminders** in discussions. Quite often, to encourage students to reach for learnings, rather than saying, "Who would be willing to give an answer?" which tends to get the usual group of talkers volunteering, I will say, "How many would be willing to risk giving an answer?"

I say "How many" rather than "Who" because it tends to get more students volunteering. And I say "risk an answer" rather than "give an answer" because that better reminds students that open-minded thinking and full participation often involve risking, risking we might be wrong, for example.

I often add **cushioning.** I might ask, "Would it be okay if some choose not to risk sharing right now?" "Sure," students might say. "We each have our own ways and timeclocks. Besides, some of us may need more time to think."

And the stars come down so close, and sadness and pleasure so close together, really the same thing. Like to stay drunk all the time. Who says it's bad? Preachers — but they got their own kinda drunkenness. Thin, barren women, but they're often too miserable to know. Reformers — but they don't bite deep enough into living to know. No — the stars are close and dear and I have joined the brotherhood of the worlds. And everything's holy — everything, even me.

—John Steinbeck, in The Grapes of Wrath

Chapter 10: For Ending a Class

Some classes are best not ended but left incomplete, like a chapter in a serial film or interesting novel. Yet some classes end best with a wrap-up experience that helps students both review and advance learnings while the lesson is still fresh. Two strategies previously introduced are effective for this:

- **Outcome sentences** When understandings play a large part in a lesson, I often use the **outcome sentence** strategy. With this strategy, a teacher might point to a posted chart showing sample phrases, such as: I learned... I rediscovered... I was surprised... I'm beginning to wonder.... The teacher might then say, "Think back over the material we just covered. See what you can get for yourself from it that is meaningful to you. Write a few sentences, perhaps starting with words like those on the chart."

  Afterwards, a few volunteers might be invited to read aloud one of their **outcome sentences**. A whole row or section of the class might be asked to read one statement in a **whip around, pass option** strategy. Or students might simply be asked to file their notes, perhaps in a personal **portfolio.**

- **Review test** The teacher gives one question to the whole class, students write an answer at their desks, and the teacher gives the correct answer. Students check their work on each question before hearing the next question. The process continues through a series of such questions.

  If single correct answers to questions exist, as with math or spelling, the teacher usually writes correct answers on the chalkboard, so student thinking is minimally disturbed by classroom talk. If answers are more complex or subjective, the teacher either gives a correct answer or invites a few students to share their notes.

  The pace is rapid enough to keep class awareness and energy high. Discussion is minimized. When low understanding is noticed, the teacher might aim to make the next question overlap earlier questions, so students learn from the review practice.

  A **review test** could be used early in a lesson, to go over prior learnings, and also at the end of a session, to go over the day's new material. No grades are given. It is to be a non-threatening opportunity to review material actively and correct mistakes thoughtfully. The strategy also helps students appreciate the fact that they are in fact learning, are making progress. Students typically enjoy review tests.

It may be too late already, but it's not as much too late now as it will be later.
—*C.H. Weisert*

Here are two additional strategies teachers report effective: **Like/might review** and **thought/feel cards.**

Strategy 10-1   Like/might review

Students are asked to look back at their behavior and to write what they liked about it and what they might do differently another time. **Purpose:** To teach students to review their actions constructively, open-mindedly.

This two-part strategy gets students evaluating their participation.

In part one, students are asked to think back over the class, to what each of them did or did not do, and to write some sentences beginning with the phrase, "I liked the way I...." Examples: I liked the way I spoke up. I liked the way I took my time and changed my mind. I liked the way I did my outline.

As students begin to slow down their writing, the teacher might say, "Please finish the one you are on now." The second part is then announced. The teacher tells students to think back over the class again and this time to write some endings to the phrase: "Next time I might...." It's useful to give some examples:

> You might write, for example, "Next time I might volunteer sooner." Or, "Next time I might pick a topic that is easier." Or, "Next time I might not rush so much." Write anything you *might* do differently next time you have an opportunity like that.

The main intent of this strategy is to give students practice in reviewing their experiences constructively and thoughtfully. The "like" part of the strategy often gets students noticing their talents and appreciating themselves better. The "might" part gets them evaluating their behaviors and reminds them that one does not need to repeat past behaviors; one can live and learn, adjusting one's behavior appropriately.

No need for students to share their notes, but they might. Students might be asked to read one item aloud in a **whip around, pass option.** Or they might be asked to sit in **sharing pairs** and share some of what they wrote, although I always announce, "You can keep any part private if you wish." Often students like hearing samples of what others wrote in a like/might review. Such sharing tends to build an accepting community climate.

Bringing the student's world into the classroom is the most relevant act a teacher can perform.
—Marc Robert

Strategy 10-2 Thought-feel cards

Students are asked to note the thoughts and/or feelings currently in their awareness. **Purpose:** To promote healthful self-awareness. Also, when notes are shared, to build respectful group relationships.

This is a two-part strategy, usually making use of 3x5 cards or, perhaps, small slips of paper. A teacher might say at the conclusion of a lesson:

> On one side of the card just distributed note some of the *thoughts* now in your mind. These could be thoughts about anything. You will not need to share what you write. This is just a chance to look inside yourself and notice what thoughts you find there.

> Now, on the other side, write some of the *feelings* you currently find inside yourself. How are you now feeling? Again, you will not need to show this to anyone.

Once the class climate is secure enough for students to handle this strategy honestly, it serves several valuable purposes. For one thing, it helps students learn the distinction between a thought and a feeling. Some students are not sure of that distinction. As a result they have difficulty keeping their emotional reactions separate from their reasoning power. Those are the students who will have special difficulty using their minds to manage their impulses.

This strategy also gives students a chance to vent their feelings and thereby get ready to move ahead to whatever is next with a clear mind. It also suggests that writing is always a safe way to vent one's feelings, in that way teaching a useful life skill.

Thought-feel cards also cultivate self-awareness and self-acceptance. If the strategy is repeated from time to time, say, every few weeks, many students will learn something interesting about how their lives are going.

After the writing of cards is completed, I sometimes ask volunteers to share some of their thought-feel notes, perhaps in a discussion format, or a **whip around, pass option**, or in **sharing pairs**.

At other times I will collect the cards, instructing students not to sign their names. I might then shuffle cards and read one side aloud to the class, as a kind of feedback to what is going on inside others in the room. I take care not to reveal who wrote anything and not to read something that I think might be troublesome to anyone.

A man who finds no satisfaction in himself, seeks for it in vain elsewhere.

—La Rochefoucauld

I may read the cards aloud immediately on receiving them. Sometimes I will just pick a few to read aloud the next time the class meets. This feedback procedure to the class helps some students to feel they are not alone, not defective, not peculiar. They come to see that others in the class have the same unspoken thoughts or feelings. Even if I do not read them aloud, this feedback also helps me know how my teaching is being received. It helps me plan for future classes.

A Teacher Comments

I was doing a tutorial when a thunderstorm occurred. The students lost all interest in what we were doing. I took advantage of the situation and had everyone complete a Thought/Feel Card. Then we did a Whip Around. Everyone felt so much better. Several students had been frightened, and the activity helped them see that others felt that way too.

— Holly Goldsmith

A teacher affects eternity; he can never tell where his influence stops.

—Henry Adams

Chapter 11: Homework Strategies

Homework. The word brings as much joy to the average student as a toothache. Even for the teacher, homework is often a tedious, tiresome procedure. Yet homework can be one of our most efficient, flexible and potent teaching tools.

One homework strategy was presented earlier, **assignments with choice.** To return to that strategy here, consider these homework options:

- **Common assignment** "Do 1 to 10 on page 46." There are advantages to this. All students do common work and we know what it is, which makes it easy to review the work later in the group as a whole. Yet there are disadvantages: Some students are asked to do more than they need, some less than would be good for them, and all miss chances to practice responsible self-management. Some other options to consider:

- **Flexible assignment by amount** "Do at least the first three problems, more if that would be good for you." Or, "Do as many as would best serve your learning." The big advantage here is that students are regularly asked to consider what would be good for them. This gets them ready to ask that question of themselves in later life, which is especially useful when impulses or friends are tempting them to do things *not* good for them.

- **Flexible assignment by learning** "Read the chapter and write some **outcome sentences**, as many as you care to." Or, "Pick some of your difficult spelling words and practice writing them correctly." Such assignments give room for students to do more or less, as the material and their personal situations vary.

- **Flexible assignment by time** "Study the material for at least twenty minutes, more if that would be good for you." Or, "Decide how long you want to work on the assignment. Set a timer and then stick to your commitment and do it."

- **Creative assignment** "Design an assignment on that work that would be good for you." Or, "Pick partners and prepare assignments for each other. Later exchange work and help each other check what you did."

It is clear that giving students choice in the matter of homework has certain advantages. The advantage many teachers report is the improvement in the quality of work students do. Less obvious, and

Do what you can, with what you have, where you are. What better can you do?
—*Theodore Roosevelt*

perhaps more important, is the opportunity it gives us to help students learn habits of self-responsible workmanship.

Three other strategies follow: **Homework sharing groups, homework hearing** and **homework unlike class work.**

Strategy 11-1 Homework sharing groups

> Homework groups, usually pairs, meet in class to review and correct completed work. **Purpose:** To maximize academic learning. Also, to advance self-responsibility.

This is a strategy for handling completed homework. It shifts the process away from "checking to make sure it was done" to "using completed work to deepen and expand learning." The strategy calls on students to share their work in some way.

- If right-wrong answers exist for the homework, **learning pairs** might be used to go over the previous night's homework. Pairs of students compare answers, teach each other when confusion or errors arise and, if both are stuck, ask other pairs for assistance. When both students understand the material, and if there is sufficient time, students could be told to create new problems for each other.

   In cases where correct answers are unlikely to be revealed by the process of comparing work, correct answers could be provided by the teacher. They could be posted or put on the chalkboard. Or a student or the teacher could read aloud answers before the homework sharing groups begin.

- **A junior high history teacher** asks students to come to class each day with one or more **outcome sentences** they got from the evening's reading homework. Often then, but not every class period, he says, "I ask students to sit in fours and take turns whipping around the group, sharing at least one of their **outcome sentences** and, after each has had a turn, discussing what they learned informally."

   He reports: "I find students read more seriously and learn more when they have a few minutes to tell others what they learned. They hear others' perceptions, which are often different from their own. They hear about ideas they never thought about. They also seem to learn more and learn, too, that others' points of view are different and worth listening to."

- **A second-grade teacher** asks students to be ready each day to read at least one new paragraph to another student, and to read it with feeling and meaning. In class, then, students are told to find a partner they have not read with recently and to take turns reading their paragraphs to each other. Partners are to listen and, afterwards, to comment on how well they heard and understood the reading.

Prove that you can control yourself, and you are an educated man: and without this all other education is good for nothing.

—R. D. Hitchcock

Reports this teacher: "I recommend students read from a story book but allow them to read from anything they want. In this slow class some even pick a comic book. One always reads from the daily newspaper. I want them to get in the habit of reading whatever is meaningful to them. Some need to practice aloud reading many times at home in order to do well in class, and I send letters home that tell parents how I want them to help. Mainly, I say, do not push the child. Do not remind the child of that homework. Allow the child to ask for help. Do not *offer* help. Help the child learn responsible initiative. Then help the child read the paragraph until he or she feels comfortable and ready for the next day's oral reading. Do not tell a child when he or she is ready. Let children learn to judge that."

- **A high school English teacher** uses homework sharing groups to give her students more feedback on their writing than she has time for. Sometimes she has students pair and read aloud to each other what they wrote. Sometimes she has all students pile homework up front. Students then have ten minutes to get a paper and write a critique in the margins, doing as many papers as time allows. Some homework papers get more than one critique. The teacher includes lessons on how to be an informed critic and distributes a form, "How to be a useful critic." "Many students," she reports, "learn more from the critiquing process than they ever do from the writing process."

- **A college teacher** asks students to prepare mini-lessons based on something they got from their homework reading. In class, then, students form random trios, a timer is set, and each person has, say, five minutes to give his mini-lesson to two peers. The task is to teach the two others something about the material. The two listeners are to respect the time of the speaker and not to interrupt with their own ideas. When the timer rings, the next person is the presenter. After all three have spoken, an extra five minutes is set so each trio can discuss ideas informally.

Homework sharing groups often benefit from occasional discussions of process: "How did the groups go today? How can we do better next time?" Students might write **like/might review** notes: *Today I liked the way I...* and *Next time I might....*

I lose all my good inspiration when I try hard to do something but I fail at my attempt.

—Dale, high school

Note that no teacher evaluation of homework is included in this strategy. Learning takes place quite naturally, without any need for teacher evaluation. The natural desires of students to understand and share work leads to the advance in knowledge.

The emphasis here is on the *process* of learning, not on *what* was learned. The content is controlled by selecting what students are asked to read. The students are then left to manage the process. This process focus seems to work particularly well with today's restless students. Also, not at all incidentally, it seems to promote healthy lifelong learning skills.

In terms of the **DESCA** target, with **homework sharing groups**: Dignity is respected, actually enhanced as students have chances to be of service to peers. Energy is high, each student playing active roles the entire time. Self-management is exercised; students choose how seriously to prepare, what ideas to present, how to manage their presentation. Community spirit is fed and awareness grows as students listen, assist each other and hear each other's point of view.

Strategy 11-2 Homework hearing

A procedure whereby you meet briefly with each student to hear about homework completed. **Purpose:** To advance self-responsible work habits and give each student a bit of personal attention.

This strategy gives each student a moment or two to report work done directly to the teacher. Here's how a high school biology teacher set this up:

> As you know, part of the time each Friday you will be in one or another work group. During that group time, I will take turns visiting each of your groups. When I join yours, please discontinue your work temporarily. Then, each of you please take a moment to read me something from your homework journal. You can read any one or two of your recent learnings or tell me about a question you have. Others will just listen in as you and I do this. This will give me a chance, each week, to visit with each of you personally. It will help me keep up with how you are doing.

An elementary school teacher used a different system for meeting with each student:

> As you have seen, each day you will have time to work individually in the classroom, as when I give you individual study tasks. One thing I will do during that time is ask you to come to this sharing table, in alphabetical order. When you get here, you will have a chance to read me the words you mastered for homework. Here's the way it will work.
>
> I will be sitting at one side of the table. Opposite will be five chairs for five students. When you see a chair is empty, please temporarily move from your individual work to that empty chair and wait a turn to read your homework words. I will hear the words from the student in the end chair. When that student is finished, he or she simply goes back to individual task work. When that happens, the other four students slide over. That's how a chair gets to be empty. Keep aware of when your name is coming up, and if you are next in the alphabet, come over and sit in the empty chair.

An unusual amount of common sense is sometimes called wisdom.
—Anonymous

Have your homework with you, for when you eventually slide into the end chair, your job will be to read aloud, with as much confidence as you can muster, the words you worked on for homework. Let's walk through this procedure to get the idea more clearly.

Note that with this strategy the teacher speaks to one student at a time while other students sit nearby. This allows other students to listen in and, perhaps, learn something from the student-teacher dialogue. It also helps some students feel less intimidated, as they might if they had to meet with a teacher alone, without peers nearby. From the point of view of efficiency, it reduces time between student reports. Teachers find they can go through a class of thirty students in thirty minutes this way.

How is the teacher to respond to each student? I recommend:

- **Easy eye contact** We want each student to be clear that he or she has inviolable self-worth, an essential value, one that need not be earned. Eye contact that is warm and accepting can affirm that self-worth. When a student is ready to report to you, then, the first move I recommend is a look that is easy and accepting, inviting of whatever eye contact the student is willing to engage. You need say nothing. Just look warmly, openly at the student's eyes, open to the person inside the face you see.

- **Supporting responses** When a student gives a report, I recommend encouragement that does not rely on praise or rewards. I personally like: **Honest I appreciates. I'm with yous. Plain corrects. Plain incorrects.**

- **Cushioning** It is occasionally useful to call on the **cushioning** strategy, especially in cases in which a student reporting (or sitting nearby listening) might need a confidence boost, and also generally to inoculate against learning anxieties and to keep deepening learning confidence. Examples:

    Before you begin, Jill, would it be all right if you made mistakes in your homework? Why would that be all right?

    Matthew, before you start, tell me if you think it would be okay if someone did not understand a thing about today's homework assignment, not one single thing. Why might that sometime happen?

    You have no homework for today, Terry. Well, we each have our own ways and timeclocks, so that sometimes happens. Do you remember what the sign about that says? Can you find a way to have your homework ready for tomorrow?

    First, I want to ask Josh, what if someone did not have time to learn this material yet? Can you think of a sign that would explain why that sometimes happens? Thank you, now please tell me about your work for today.

Anytime you see a turtle up on top of a fence post, you know he had some help.
—Alex Haley

• **Self-management stimulators** I like to use occasional comments designed to stimulate attention to personal work habits. I've highlighted key phrases in the samples below:

> You did more than the minimum required. *Do you feel good about yourself for having done that much?* (Which might be followed by...) Thanks, Ellen, I was just wondering.

> It seems to me you did your work very carefully. *Did you deliberately choose to work very carefully this time?* (Which might be followed by...) I see, Ian, I was just curious.

> You have nothing to report for homework. That sometimes happens. *I wonder how you feel about not having work today and if you feel okay about it?* (Which might be followed by...) Thanks, Bill. I just wanted to know.

> You have nothing to report for homework. *Please take a moment and ask yourself if you are willing to do what it takes to have tomorrow's homework completed.* (If yes, perhaps...) Thanks for thinking, Patti, I'll see you tomorrow. (If no...) Thanks for thinking, Patti, I'll see you tomorrow.

> You do your homework very well every day. *Is it hard for you to say no to temptations that want to distract you from your work?* Thank you.

> You have not done very much. *I wonder if you could use some hints or more support for managing your time or for saying no to unproductive impulses. Can I or one of our classmates help in some way?* (Perhaps followed by...) Would you be willing to ask for that help? Will you do so? Will you sometime tell me how it worked out?

Such self-management stimulators call for an artistic touch. If possible, I suggest joining with other teachers for practice and feedback until you feel comfortable with them. Note, however, that one need not use self-management stimulators to extract large benefit from the **homework hearing** strategy. It simply adds an extra nourishing element.

Finally, a reminder that the focus of **homework hearing** is not on grading students' work. I recommend simply making mental notes of which students need extra help or what learnings need extra review. The focus is rather on demonstrating that we respect the value of the homework they do.

This strategy gives each student a minute or two of personal, fully respectful attention. For some students, a regular dose of such attention from an authority figure can make the difference between a life of essential self-esteem and a life of assumed worthlessness.

I hope I die during an inservice, because the transition from life to death would be so subtle.
—*Mary Shanley*

Reports a high school Spanish teacher:

> I changed my approach to homework. I decided I wanted all students to know they were not less worthy if and when they did not do homework. Since, in Spanish, homework is *very* important, this was a *very* risky experiment for me. But I did it, and guess what? Eventually students started doing more — not less — homework. They also did it more willingly. I no longer struggle with students about homework, although I still find myself slipping. I must learn patience with students even as I am beginning to appreciate how I can teach them to be more patient with themselves. Something about once a week giving each student a chance to show me what they learned without worrying that I will judge the work or correct or in any way be critical has changed something important for us all. Now they *like* to show me their stuff.

Strategy 11-3   Homework unlike classwork

Design homework assignments that are distinctly different from class work. **Purpose:** To make homework more interesting to students.

Many students find homework uninteresting simply because it resembles class work. One remedy is to design homework assignments that are related to class work but somehow distinct. Possibilities:

- Make up new problems we might use for class drills.

- Draw something that illustrates something related to our class work.

- Pick one or more words we mentioned and look them up in a dictionary or encyclopedia or ask someone in the neighborhood about them. Note what you discover.

- Cut out parts of speech from magazines or newspapers.

- Each day write at least one new sentence in your journal.

Strategy 11-4   How read discussion

Those who can, teach. Those who can't, go into some less significant line of work.
—Anonymous

Help students see that different ways of reading exist and that it is wise to choose one's own way. **Purpose:** To make it easier for students to read profitably.

Ask a group of excellent readers how they go about reading a text, and we are apt to get a variety of answers. Some will skim first and only then choose how best to proceed. Others will always read word-for-word carefully. Yet others will pick up a pen and outline the reading as they go.

Many will say it depends on the reading and their purpose. For a well-written text, they may choose one approach, for a poorly written text, another. If their purpose is mastery of the reading, they may opt for one approach, for general familiarity only, another.

Yet ask a group of typical students how they go about reading, and chances are most will report reading word-for-word or, if candid, not at all. A reason many do not read much is their assumption that word-for-word is the only way. For many students, of course, especially in this TV era, that is often a tedious and often unproductive way to read. As a result, many avoid reading.

Remedy: Especially for students expected to do a lot of reading, show them the tricks of good readers. Perhaps discuss two or three ways to read most likely to fit the readings in the class.

In a high school, for example, a teacher might simply ask students what different ways exist to read something. The alternatives might be listed on the board. A few of the options appropriate for that class might then be explained more carefully. "Different people prefer different ways of reading," the teacher might conclude. "And smart readers choose different ways for different purposes. I recommend experimenting with two or three different ways, especially if you have not tried many, so you find ones that work for you."

One middle school teacher had students ask family members what ways exist to read something and amassed a long list, including:

- Ask questions first. Then read to find answers.
- Look at the pictures and headings. Read only those parts that look interesting.
- Set a time limit. Read only to that limit, to limit your frustrations.
- Read little by little, so it is not a heavy chore.
- Aim to write a summary of the reading or of sections of it.

Another teacher asked three different students to explain three different reading approaches to the class. All students then were asked to use all three approaches twice and to log their experiences. Finally, the class discussed their logs and discovered, not surprisingly, that some reading methods worked better for some students, other methods for other students or at other times. The point was well made: No need to read everything word-for-word. It is intelligent to pick your way of reading.

I am inspired when
I play soccer!
—*Tina, first grade*

Chapter 12: Handling Testing and Grading

The grading system keeps sparking problems. Teachers say it takes up too much time, and too many students argue about their grades. Students say the system is unfair, and they do not like all those tests and pressures. And researchers point out that grades used to motivate students tends to extinguish students' intrinsic motivations for learning. Yet the old system persists. What to do? My recommendation: Don't start by making drastic changes. Major changes in grading-testing will likely be threatening to many people, raising unnecessary problems for you. Instead, start by employing strategies that more effectively *inspire* students to work hard. It will become gradually clear, then, that learning can occur without a heavy reliance on the old system of tests and grades. Changes can then be more easily managed. As you proceed, however, do your best to minimize problems associated with the existing testing-grading practices. The strategies of this chapter may help you do that. In general, they serve three purposes:

- They take the emphasis off grade-getting, which is the central concern of so many students. They put more emphasis on learning and the development of life-long learning habits.

- They reduce discouragement among those students who are slow to earn top grades, those students tempted to give up even *trying* to do well.

- They reduce the time we need to spend on testing and grading. They give us more ways to assess student progress while students are learning, so we need not spend so much time on the testing practices that do little to improve learning.

The **review test,** described in Chapter Two, is particularly valuable in this regard. With this strategy, the teacher poses a question. All students write answers at their desks. The correct answer is written on the board or announced orally. Students check their work and, if necessary, make corrections. The teacher then poses the next question, and the process continues. As teachers observe students engaging this process, they can usually tell fairly accurately how well students are doing. Student papers need not be collected to give teachers this information and, in **review tests,** are not intended to be collected. With this strategy, then, we can assess student progress while we advance our lessons.

Here are four other useful grading strategies.

Strategy 12-1   Portfolio

Ask students to keep a collection of their work, both for their own review and for the teacher's review. **Purpose:** To give students responsibility for organizing and evaluating their work.

Portfolios are simply collections of work students manage for themselves. In an elementary class, for instance, each student might have a folder which contains collected writings, worksheets and drawings. At the end of a week, each student might be asked to sort through the folder, write some **outcome sentences** based on the week's papers, star the items they feel best about, and perhaps select any they want to bring home to show families.

Portfolios develop self-management abilities. They reduce the need to test students. And they are broadly adaptable on many grade levels. They can be used as a supplement to testing or as the core evaluation plan. Dennie Palmer Wolf (1989) has suggestions for this. You may get additional ideas about ways to use a portfolio from the statement below, which I once distributed to college students beginning a teacher training program.

Self-managed evaluation process

Many college students are accustomed to asking about requirements and then going about fulfilling them. That approach does not empower learners or learning. Indeed, it rather serves passivity and uncritical obedience. This is *not* the approach our faculty intends. Our commitment is to instruct in ways that strengthen people, that expand their ability to learn intelligently and self-responsibly. We are also committed to reducing disconnection, disconnection between courses and between what is learned and what happens in real life.

A key element in our approach is the student portfolio. This is a request for you to take responsibility for building one for yourself. We recommend you build it with three purposes in mind:

- To organize and integrate the whole of your work, so you can clearly track your progress and interests.

- To reflect on your current experiences and the choices ahead, so you can maximize the amount and the relevance of your learnings.

- To keep your work in a coherent and tangible form, so your progress can be communicated to the faculty.

Portfolios are meant to be self-managed and designed. As you begin building yours, you might consider including some of the elements below.

No instrument smaller than the world is fit to measure men and women: Examinations measure examinee.

—Sir Walter Raleigh

Personal goals You could have one section of your portfolio include notes about your long- and short-run targets. You might begin by listing some. You might state goals broadly and/or with a focus only on teaching. For teaching, you might list:

- *Knowledge Goals,* what you want to understand: Why some people don't learn, what B. F. Skinner proposed, how values are developed.
- *Skill Goals,* what you want to be able to do: Get a job, handle misbehavior, avoid overwork, be appreciated, keep all students involved all the time.
- *Being Goals,* how you want to *be* as you do what you do: Be flexible, be confident, be empathic, be caring, be optimistic, be assertive.

Experience log You might include in your portfolio a log of significant experiences related to your professional growth. Perhaps list courses you took, books and other materials you read, conversations that were meaningful, experiments you tried, family events that made a difference.

Learning log You might include a method of tracking your professional development. You could base this on your learning goals. Perhaps indicate somehow which goals have been met and which new ones are emerging.

You might also include a section that logs what you were able to extract from your experiences. You might simply include an ongoing, dated list of sentences with such beginnings as:

- I learned...
- I am beginning to wonder...
- I was surprised...
- I rediscovered...
- I now better appreciate...
- I now promise to...
- I have become more skilled at...
- I'm getting clearer about...
- I uncovered a new question about...
- I reevaluated the assumption I once had about...
- I was proud of the way I...

These could be categorized in some way, such as learnings about teaching methods, psychological principles, useful references, ideas for different units of study, etc.

Supporting Items Your portfolio might also include a table of contents and examples of work you produced. Perhaps include papers you wrote, summaries of different theories that interested you, tapes of yourself teaching at different points in your program, or feedback forms from students. In many cases, you will want to have a home reservoir of materials and assemble your portable version, your *port*-folio, to share with others in whatever way is appropriate at the time. In all sections, unless the faculty directs otherwise, say as little or as much about any element as serves your best interests.

Tim was so learned, that he could name a horse in nine languages. So ignorant, that he bought a cow to ride on.

—*Benjamin Franklin*

Note this special request: Please treat your portfolio as a learning tool. Do not highlight its use as an assessment tool. Do not build a portfolio to impress the faculty. That may erase much of its power to serve you. It may even erase some of your own respect for learning and growing. You will occasionally be invited to show parts of your portfolio to the faculty. That can help them assess your work accurately. And you may occasionally be asked to create and include special items, such as a summary of your learnings to date or a list of current interests and needs. But you will never be asked to reveal parts of your portfolio you choose to keep private. If you want to impress the faculty, use your portfolio to demonstrate your sincere, steady, intelligent strivings to get the most from your learning experiences.

Strategy 12-2 Grading plan

A plan for grading that considers both professional requirements and the best interests of the students. **Purpose:** To make a balanced, comprehensive grading plan.

Most of us give grades. How might we best go about that, especially if we care not only about learning now but about living and learning in the long run? I recommend keeping in mind the limits of what is feasible, which will, of course, vary by school and our own readiness for risks, and then to consider adaptations of common practices. Adaptations some teachers have found valuable and workable:

Minimum testing After students have been in class for a few weeks, and assuming we do more than lecture, we can usually tell quite accurately who is learning much and who is learning little. We may need to look at students' **outcome statement** lists, homework papers, **portfolio** items, or other such material. But we rarely need many tests to identify the high and low learners.

If we give *occasional* tests, less to scare students into studying than to give them chances to summarize and "show their stuff" to us, we will almost certainly have enough data to scale learners into grading categories.

This is the minimum-test approach I generally recommend. It does not rely on tests alone, but on all the data available, objective and subjective. Both we and students are then free to spend more time on learning and less on testing.

Professional responsibility statement What if a student or parent comes to us and complains: "You cannot rely on subjective judgment. I want to see hard evidence that supports your grades." How can we respond?

I favor telling the truth: We want to spend more time on learning and less on grading. We use all our experiences to determine how much each student is learning. Over time we can tell about most students and, when we are unsure, we simply look for more data.

Success is not a magic ingredient that can be supplied by teachers. Building on strengths allows students to create their own success.

—Robert Martin

If that was insufficient for a parent, I might add a statement stirred by my professional dignity, such as:

> I certainly understand your concern that Ben be graded fairly. Yet, as a dedicated professional, I need to be trusted with my judgments. It would diminish my ability to teach if I had to take the time to collect and document the data everyone would like to see. I hope you will trust my competence to make my judgments. Please visit my class if you think that might reassure you that learning is taking place or that I am aware of what students are doing. And please speak to school administrators if you would like to be sure they trust me to judge my students fairly.

Being criticized is, of course, uncomfortable. It is uncomfortable even to worry about defending our grading judgments. It is tempting to avoid it, even when it means using more time and energy for evaluation than we believe best. Professionally and personally, I prefer doing the best job I can in the classroom and being prepared to call up my courage when necessary to respond to criticism. It helps me to pre-think what I might say, as by writing for myself a sample statement, and you may want to do that for yourself.

The upgrade option We can relax many students' preoccupation with grading — and get them attending that much more to learning — simply by making any individual grade earned less significant. Some teachers do this by collecting large numbers of grades. Such teachers might grade daily work, weekly tests, monthly reviews, and so on, so any one item is less critical. I find that procedure more likely to *add* attention to grading than take it away. It certainly adds to teacher noninstructional chores.

An alternative is to have fewer grades collected and to make any one less significant by allowing students to do extra work whenever they do not like the grade earned. "If you would like to improve your grade," a teacher might say, "write a contract saying what you would like to do to earn extra credit. If I okay your proposal, and you do what I judge to be quality work on your upgrade project, you will get the grade you desire."

The certain makeup Similarly, I favor telling students they can always make up missed work. I sometimes insist that the students find their own helpers or tutors, which they usually can do from within the class.

I get inspired when I'm in a game with the score tied and we have the ball.
—Chris, high school

Compared to penalizing students for work avoided or missed, it seems to me less punitive, more respectful, and more in tune with concern for the development of self-management, to allow any student to make up work missed if, of course, the student is ready and willing to do that. Is that coddling? I would not say so. Making up work missed, like doing extra work to raise a grade, is not very easy in our busy world. This is especially so when new work keeps coming up for students to complete.

Goal agreement Many students are accustomed to hearing a teacher announce course expectations, content to be covered, requirements and the like. It is possible to provide that and invite course agreement and then to ask students if they want to create some of their *own* expectations for the course:

That is what I would like you all to do. Are you willing to go along with that? How about starting this way and later looking again to see how we all feel about this course outline?

Also, I wonder if you can find any goals of your own related to the focus of this class. If you have personal goals, there is a chance we can find ways to help you reach them. You might, for example, write a personal learning contract. Or we might set up groups to help you reach your goals. Want to search for some personal goals?

If we give grades, then, and they relate to how well students have fulfilled course expectations, it is more likely that grading will proceed amicably. If our goals have become the personal goals of students, we will be more "with" the students, less outside them, judging them. We might even arrive at grades cooperatively. Most significantly perhaps, we will be teaching and advancing personally responsible learning.

Procedure agreement   Sometimes agreements can also be sought for procedures that relate to grading.

Here are several samples of what I consider excellent work. Let's study these together so my definition of excellence is clear.

As for rating your work, here is what I propose.... Any suggestions for improving that process? Willing to go along with it, at least for now, until we find something better we can agree on?

Incidentally, I do not recommend giving credit for participation in class discussions. Some students naturally speak out in class and others learn better when they can relax and just observe. It seems to me unfair, an indignity really, to tell the quiet people they must speak up or suffer a grading penalty. After all, we each have our own ways.

Strategy 12-3   Focus on learning statement

> Inform students of your intention to focus on learning, not grading, and invite their suggestions and cooperation. **Purpose:** To build a new emphasis on learning openly and respectfully.

Some teachers find it valuable to state openly to students that they intend to place the class focus more on learning, less on grading, and to discuss this carefully enough so students are not thrown by such a shift and willingly cooperate in the change.

To do this, a teacher might simply pose the question to students: What would it take for us to take some of the heat out of testing and grading and give more of our attention to serious learning? Often a more detailed approach to students works better, as in the lesson outlined below, from a junior high math teacher experienced in the approach of this book. Here are paraphrases of what she said:

If, in instructing a child you are vexed with it for want of adroitness, try, if you have never tried before, to write with your left hand, and then remember that a child is all left hand.

—*J. F. Boyse*

1. Many students are preoccupied with grades. For some it's more important to get a good grade than to learn something. How many here feel a bit like that? Who would be willing to risk sharing their thoughts? (Teacher listens, often saying something like, "Yes, I can understand that.")

2. I'd like us to take a different approach in this class. I'd like us to focus on studying and learning and to keep testing and grading in the background. This might be a difficult switch for some. It's pleasant to get a good grade, after all. And when we please our families with a good grade, everyone is happy. But there is a downside to a testing-grading focus. See if each of you can think of one or more downsides of testing and grading. Make notes for yourself and then let's see if we can make a group list on the chalkboard.

   (Writes group ideas on board:)

   - Lots of us don't get good grades.
   - Grading makes us anxious.
   - Wasting time studying for a test when we forget right away.
   - Makes some uncomfortable when they get better grades than their friends.
   - Makes some of us sick.
   - Makes some want to cheat.
   - Some are not good at taking tests.
   - Wastes a lot of class time.
   - No one learns much by taking tests.
   - It makes us feel bad when we fail.
   - Keeps our parents on our backs.
   - It makes some of us not want to come to class.

3. I do have to give grades in this class, but I'd like to take the emphasis off that. Actually, I do not need many tests to know how much each of you is learning. After a while, as I keep working with you all, I can tell. That's how I know what I need to reteach and when we can go to a new topic. I watch and listen, and you too probably can tell how much you are learning. We don't need lots of tests to tell us that.

   We may want to have a test from time to time, not because I need to be sure how much you have learned, but because a test can be a good way to pull a unit together. That won't hurt us — as long as we know tests are not the main thing. It may even help some of you keep your attention on this class work. There are lots of out-of-school pressures and temptations, after all, and pressures from other classes too. If we had *no* pressure here, some of you might not be able to resist putting all your energy elsewhere.

   Any of you fall into that category? Okay to have some but not lots of tests here?

So that in order that a man may be happy, it is necessary that he should not only be capable of his work, but be a good judge of his work.

—*John Ruskin*

4. Frankly, however, I do not want some students to feel they are better than others. I like you all. I respect you all. I know you all have lots of goodness inside you, probably more than even you yourself know right now. I do not want grades to come across as labels of more goodness and less goodness.

There is the matter of timeclocks too. Our **truth signs** remind us that we all learn some things now and some things later anyhow, so why get too anxious about it? You may zip ahead in your math learning later in the year, or next year. That sometimes happens. It is more likely to happen if you do not get discouraged when your timeclock for learning is not now and can keep at it anyhow, doing the best you can now do.

Yet, as I said, I must give grades. So here is what I propose. Think about this and if it does not feel right to you, sometime let me know privately. Then we'll talk and see if we can come up with a different plan the two of us can live with. Here is how I propose to start:

First of all, I will give a passing grade to all who show up in class very regularly and who keep doing the best they can, at least a C.

My job is to help you get into learning. If I cannot do my job well, or if your timeclock for learning is different, or if other things were more important in your life at the time, well, that's no one's fault. That's just the way things were at the time. We all might be able to do better in the future. No sense giving someone a grade lower than C and risk making anyone feel bad because of it. That will do more harm than good, I'd say, especially since the grade you get in this course will not qualify you or disqualify you for anything very important. I could not say this if this was a course in piloting airplanes!

I will give an extra good grade, which I call a B, for work that I feel is extra good.

Does that mean that B grades are better than C grades? Not necessarily. It may just mean that those getting B grades had timeclocks that allowed them to get extra good learnings. Or maybe our class methods just suited them better. No big deal.

I will give a top grade, an A, to work that is a clear step ahead of extra good work, for work that seems to me outstanding, exceptional.

Are people who get A's better people than people who get B's and C's? Who can guess why I would not say so? (Teacher occasionally refers to posted **truth signs.**)

5. Some people may have difficulty with a downgrading of grading. Others may not really *want* to de-emphasize tests and grades. They still want to view grades as very important. I can accept that. I merely want to reduce the time and energy we take away from learning in our class.

I always tell my students at the beginning of the semester, if they don't learn, it's my fault.
—*John Bowyer*

One other point. This may help you to go for a top grade without worrying that you will not succeed. And if you worry less, chances are you will learn more and enjoy math more. Here's the plan:

Get into your class work. Give it your all. Forget about grading. And then let's see after a while what grade I think best fits your learning. If you are not satisfied with that grade, I'll mark down an I, for "in progress" or leave the grade blank and explain that your work is still in progress, and I can't quite be sure yet.

Then you and I can plan what extra work would be good for you to do, so you can in fact end up earning a grade more satisfying to you. Yet take care: This will mean extra work while you have your regular work to do. But if the trouble is worth it to you, I'm willing to offer that upgrade opportunity.

6. Let's try this system for a while. If problems come up, speak to me privately or, if you think it better, let's talk about it with the whole class. I'll bet we can brainstorm and come up with a creative remedy to a problem that comes up. But for now, let's put the issue aside. I will point up errors in your work, but I won't grade papers. I won't grade homework. I won't grade class participation. I'll just react in ways that I think might help you learn better.

Some comments:

- Unlike the teacher above, some teachers are not willing to give a passing grade to students just because they come to class everyday and worked diligently at learning. I recommend such teachers simply adjust part four above to say what is required for a C grade. One can de-emphasize grading and testing while also insisting on minimum competence for a passing grade.

- I recommend that teachers who wish to conduct a discussion like the one above share their proposed approach beforehand with other teachers and, if appropriate, with administrators, asking for feedback and suggestions. It is not easy to move far from the current assumptions people carry about the importance of tests and grades. The more ideas we have about making such a move the better. And, as with any change from old habits, the more support we have the better.

I am the master of everything I can explain.

—Theodore Haecker

- Do not underemphasize the time it will take for students and parents, and us, to become comfortable with a focus shift away from grading, and toward learning. For many, good grades have become an addiction. We may need occasionally to restate our concerns and support those having trouble breaking old habits. Fortunately, since the core purpose of schooling centers more on learning than grading, truth is on our side. We are not apt to proceed for long without finding others supporting us.

- As with many issues, no grading plan is likely to satisfy everyone. A heavy grading emphasis, of course, does not satisfy some. Unfortunately, those dissatisfied by that emphasis are less likely to complain aggressively than will those who become dissatisfied when we de-emphasize grades. We do well, then, to be clear about our intentions, not naive about expecting to please everyone, and strong in our professional commitment. We will likely need to call up courage.

- This issue reminds me of the question, "Should we promote or retain failing students?" The research is clear: In the long run, retention does not help most students learn more. Moreover, retention tends to diminish self-esteem. As one who cares to serve both learning and living, I favor promotion for all as a general policy. I would, however, make an exception for particular students, for occasionally we find that a particular student is clearly better served by retention.

- Once a de-emphasis in grading is initiated, as in the lesson above, I find it best to give the issue minimum class time. The more attention we give to grades and tests, the more important and convoluted the issues become. I recommend making our best judgments and putting the topic aside. The less we talk about grading in the classroom the better. There are, after all, more worthy things to attend. Learning is one example.

Strategy 12-4 Report card plan

A plan for handling report cards that considers both professional requirements and the best interests of the students. **Purpose:** To increase consistency between report cards and key school purposes.

Report cards are often the central symbol of an evaluation system. A good report card reflects a successful academic season, not necessarily a successful learning season. A bad report card often produces new trouble on the home front, not always an experience contributing to healthy learning or living habits. What might we do to make report cards less problematical, more appropriate to a dignified learning community?

Some possibilities teachers have found useful:

- **Progress conferences** The importance of report cards is diminished, along with their potential for negative side effects, when they are augmented with other reporting procedures. Individual student-teacher dialogues are especially useful for this. Some teachers keep students busy on other tasks and set aside a few days regularly for such dialogues. A teacher might ask students to bring to the meeting notes about recent progress. The dialogue sequence might be: How has learning proceeded for you? Here's how I see it. Any ideas about what you or I might do in the future? All things considered, what grade should we list for this work?

We shall require a substantially new manner of thinking if mankind is to survive.
—Albert Einstein

- **Open visitor policy** I usually recommend that teachers invite parents and other community members to visit classes at any time, even without notice. When visitors see students busy at work, most conclude that, yes, learning is taking place, and no, no need to ask teachers to do more. Parents, then, become less concerned about report cards, and community members become more supportive of what goes on in their schools.

  I recommend announcing an open-door visitor policy: Any adults can observe at any time for as long as they like. Only if that becomes burdensome would I even add a prior-appointment request. I suggest preparing a standard sheet of "Hints for visitors" that a student committee, or the student of the day, would give to each visitor. The sheet might also include options for doing more than observing. A teacher might, for example, invite observers to offer tutoring to students who seem stuck or to participate directly in the students' learning activities.

- **Revising report cards** Sometimes the report card currently used by a school puts us in a difficult professional position. It may prompt us to communicate more discouragement than would be good for students. In terms of DESCA, it may be difficult to avoid dignity damage, to avoid sending the message: *You are a failure as a person.* Or to avoid discouraging growth of self-management, suggesting: *It matters not what you yourself say about your work.* Or to avoid fostering envy rather than class community: *Some students did far better than you.* Or to avoid narrowing down student awareness: *Only what is listed here is worth your attention.*

  It is sometimes wise to campaign for an improved report card. What kind of report card best avoids sending such messages? In general, cards more open and less restrictive, cards allowing flexible or subjective comments. Current learning and long-term living are almost always better served when teachers have more rather than fewer options for writing about a particular student's work. This is an instance in which restrictive requirements and precision are usually counterproductive.

- **Reverse report cards** Pilon (1991) once suggested initiating what might be called reverse report cards. Those would be cards, not from the teacher to the parents, but from parents to the teacher. Teachers could start by defining student behaviors they would like to promote.

Possibilities in an elementary class:
- Engages in self-initiated reading.
- Makes use of new vocabulary words when speaking.
- Handles everyday calculations willingly and accurately.
- Listens respectfully to what others say.
- Expresses ideas in artistic ways.
- Walks and speaks as someone with full dignity.
- Maintains comfortable energy flow through the whole day.
- Manages own time and materials appropriately.
- Is willing to share and participate with others.
- Lives with awareness of the things and people nearby.

What is more wonderful than the delight which the mind feels when it knows? This delight is not for anything beyond the knowing, but it is the act of knowing. It is the satisfaction of a primary instinct.

—Mark Rutherford

The teacher, then, would ask each family to be on the lookout for changes in these behaviors. Each marking period, families would be asked to send to the teacher a card saying which behaviors have progressed and, perhaps, any other noteworthy changes observed in the youngster. The teacher would then have valuable data for class planning. She would know what students are learning in ways that actually show up in real life, at least as the parents report it, and perhaps what more is needed for certain students or the whole class. This strategy might also get parents to feel as if they were full partners in the learning process.

A similar system could be set up that would ask, not parents, but each student to report on progress. "In which categories have you noticed progress?" Again, this would be valuable data for a teacher's future planning. It could also invite more student self-responsibility for progress. It could also serve well in private teacher-student progress conferences.

I lose all my good inspiration when teachers and others put me down, don't let me voice my opinion, tell me that they are right and won't debate about it, and when teachers are really stubborn.

—Adam, high school

Chapter 13: For Learning Mastery

Most students need plenty of review if they are to master subject matter. How are we to provide that review without being repetitious, even boring? Two strategies presented earlier are particularly effective:

Review test strategy

The teacher gives one question to the whole class, students write an answer at their desks, and the teacher gives the correct answer. Students check their work on each question before hearing the next question. The process continues through a series of such questions.

If single correct answers to questions exist, as with math or spelling, the teacher usually writes correct answers on the chalkboard, so student thinking is minimally disturbed by classroom talk. If answers are more complex or subjective, the teacher either gives a correct answer or invites a few students to share their notes.

A review test could be used early in a lesson, to go over prior learnings, and also at the end of a session, to go over the day's new material. No grades are given. It is to be a nonthreatening opportunity to review material actively and correct mistakes thoughtfully. The strategy also helps students appreciate that they are in fact learning, are making progress. Students typically enjoy review tests.

Choral work strategy

The teacher holds up a series of cards. Students respond to each card aloud and together. The cards could contain math facts, chemistry symbols, examples of correct language usage, names of states and their capitals, any material the teacher wants students to internalize fully.

The pace proceeds quickly enough to keep class awareness and energy high. Choral work can be repeated daily. It typically energizes a task and produces effortless memorization of material.

Here are four other useful review strategies.

Wise men learn more from fools than fools from wise men.
—Cato

Strategy 13-1   Learning pairs

Pairs of students drill each other or help each other learn something.
Purpose: To review and strengthen learnings and build interdependence.

In the **underexplain and learning pairs** strategy, previously introduced, pairs of students collaborate to learn material the teacher has deliberately underexplained.

Learning pairs can also be used for review purposes. Students might, say, drill each other on material to be memorized by using flash cards of math facts or words from spelling lists. Students might explain their understandings of material to each other and teach each other parts not understood well. Students might base such work on an outline of information or on questions from a text.

In some cases assignments to learning pairs might be made by the teacher to ensure that slower students get the best help. Or pairs can be instructed to ask other pairs for assistance. If **class tutors** were identified, they might also be called upon for assistance.

I find it useful to distinguish **learning pairs** from **sharing pairs.** The task of sharing pairs is simply to compare and share ideas, as when students share completed homework or brainstorm ideas for a problem. Learning often results from sharing pair activities, but students are not charged with the responsibility to produce it. Learning, however, is the core responsibility of **learning pairs**, and I sometimes encourage students to do their best to help each other achieve it.

Strategy 13-2   I say review

Pairs of students share what they would say about certain subject matter. **Purpose:** To review and strengthen learnings and increase student cooperation.

Some students feel pressured and become anxious when I ask them to pair up and help each other learn, say, a list of vocabulary words. They might worry that they will not learn the material fast enough or as well as their partners. This generates an anxiety that typically cuts into learning ability.

To avoid that, I often use a form of **sharing pairs,** as in this example:

> Pair up and take turns telling your partner what you would say about each of the vocabulary words.

> Let's say a boy and girl sit together and the first word is "light." The boy might start and tell what he would say "light" is. Then the girl would tell what she would say "light" is. You could even talk about differences, if you like. Then the boy might tell what he would say the next word is. And so on.

People always told me that my natural ability and good eyesight were the reasons for my success as a hitter. They never talk about practice, practice, practice!
—Ted Williams

Or, if you prefer, one of you could tell what you would say about the first two words and then the other could tell what you would say about those two words.

Go back and forth in some way that you find well for you. Share what each of you would say about each word. I'll give you a one-minute warning when it's time to stop. "Go".

Asking pairs to share what each would *say* about a word, rather than asking them to talk about the *correct* definition, usually produces a relaxed, thoughtful exchange. Students quite naturally talk about what the correct definition is. Yet the anxiety often associated with being correct is absent.

I find the **I say review** strategy often produces more learning more pleasurably than does the **learning pair** strategy, with its emphasis on mastery. This **I say review** can, of course, be used with many types of content, such as: A list of formulas. A list of people. A list of important events. A list of places. A list of scientific principles. Cards that contain key questions (What makes for a good paragraph? Estimate 250 times 9. What factors often cause wars?).

Strategy 13-3   Pass the Q&A

> Announce a question and answer. Then ask students to pass it along with one asking the question, the next answering it. **Purpose:** To emphasize a particular learning.

This can be an enjoyable way to reinforce a worthwhile learning. Used early in a class session, it also focuses and enlivens student energy.

I once heard Janet McCann addressing a first grade class: *The question today is, "Is this Black History Month?" And the answer is, "Yes, this is Black History Month."*

She then stooped and, eye level with the boy in the first seat in the first row, said, *"Is this Black History Month?"* That boy replied, *"Yes, this is Black History Month."*

The boy promptly turned to the girl behind him and asked, *"Is this Black History Month?"* That girl replied, *"Yes, this is Black History Month,"* and she then turned to the student behind her and asked, *"Is this Black History Month?"* And so it went. Each student in turn asked the question and heard the answer, down the row, passing along the Q&A.

In teaching the greatest sin is to be boring.

—J. F. Herbart

Meanwhile, the teacher started the same process with the first student in the second row, and then the third row, and remaining rows. As a result, within two or three minutes, every student said aloud the question and the answer and heard both several times.

When the last student answered, Janet McCann said, *Everyone together now, "Is this Black History Month?"* You might guess how the class responded.

What is good about this strategy?

- Students absorb knowledge effortlessly.
- The procedure raises the energy level of a class.
- It brings even restless students into a learning activity.
- It gives students a chance to practice looking others in the eyes and speaking with personal power.

A Teacher Comments

I use that strategy almost every day to get students to hear what proper language usage is. Many of them were brought up in families where proper usage was uncommon. The kids love it somehow. I use such Q&A's as, "Did he and I go? Yes, he and I went." And, "May I have permission? Yes you may." I also use it to help them memorize authors, such as, "Who wrote Moby Dick? Herman Mehlville wrote Moby Dick." I think they like the idea of never being wrong. They hear the question and answer from me and all they need do is remember it for two minutes. Actually, I find most of them remembering it long after! Repetition is the mother of remembering, or something like that.

— Junior High English Teacher

I sometimes use the Pass the Q&A strategy without an answer. I'll say in Spanish, "Turn to page 122," and have each student turn and pass the phrase down the line. I do sometimes use it with answers, to help them practice their speaking and to memorize vocabulary. For example, in Spanish I say, "If today is Monday, what is the next day? The next day is Tuesday." Then they pass that question and answer down the line."

— Ninth Grade Spanish Teacher

I learned this strategy from Grace Pilon. I've seen it used to review an old concept before going on to something new, and to insert a bit of worthwhile content that is not part of the curriculum, as in the Black History example above, and simply as a way to zip up the energy level of students who have been silent a bit too long.

Strategy 13-4 Creative reports

Students are asked to report their work in a creative manner. **Purpose:** To get student reports that actively involve those who listen.

I get inspired when something happens that makes me stand out from the crowd.

—Heath, high school

Reports of student work can sometimes be useful. However, few activities are duller than a series of oral student reports. Small group reports to the whole class and, especially, individual book reports can too quickly become boring. Generally I recommend avoiding any extended series of oral reports. Some report styles, however, can be engaging. Here are some possibilities:

One minute reports: "Plan to tell us something, in just 60 seconds, that you personally learned. We'll start each day with five such reports until all students have had a turn."

Poster or model: "Create a poster, designed in any way you choose, that somehow reflects the book you read. Or make a model you can bring to class. We'll walk around and examine each person's poster or model Friday morning."

The group skit: "Present a skit related to something we learned about. Make it interesting, perhaps funny or dramatic. All members of your group must be involved in the presentation, so design it so you all have a part to play." For students who need to practice writing skills, I will often ask them to write out their script beforehand, which gets them paying close attention to their writing and gives me a convenient way to teach proper usage correction.

Book or history report: "Every day next week, we'll start off with several of you acting out one of the persons about whom we read. Pick any person. Your job will be to wear something, a hat, badge, anything that shows something about the person. We will then guess who you are. Or you can say something that person might have said, and then we will guess. You can even team up with someone, get them to play a part, and act out a little skit showing something that person did or might have done."

Another group skit: "Have your skit show two different ways that character might have handled the situation." "Have your skit show a smart and dumb way to use percentages." "Have your skit communicate something about either the growth of plants or the death of plants."

Pantomime or puppetry: "I'd like the next report to include either some pantomime or puppets." "Or, without words, act out a principle of science." Or a country in South America. Or the key learning you took from our unit.

Compact disc cover: "Think of some song titles that might have come from those days and design a record jacket that might have shown those songs, even though they did not have records in those days."

Dramatic reading: "Read something the person wrote and, as you read it to us, think the words, be fully into it."

Mural: "I'd like each trio to produce one mural that shows different applications of what we studied."

I complained that I had no shoes, until I met a man who had no feet.

—Anonymous

Class activity: "Each pair is to get us to do something that might be fun and that relates to the topic. Ask us, for example, to draw a pineapple with our eyes closed. Or to stand up and wave like an old tree about to topple over in the wind. Or create a five-minute quiz for us that might be fun. The idea is to get us involved in your presentation in some way."

Designs: "Using only geometric figures, communicate something about the Civil War."

Collages: "This book report must be in the form of a collage. You could cut words or pictures or designs from old magazines or newspapers. You could even paste on small objects. In some creative way, aim to communicate an image or learning that you got from your book."

Short story: "Alone or with a partner, write a short story, funny or dramatic, that tells what you did and learned or that tells about people you studied. Put it in the story box with both your names on it. Include one blank sheet at the end of your story. Next month, when you have free time, pick a story from the box to read. If you have any reactions, note them on the blank sheet and include your name."

Note that the **task group, share group** strategy can also keep all students actively involved in hearing each other's work.

The intelligence is proved not by ease of learning but by understanding what we learn.
—Joseph Whitney

Chapter 14: Stimulating Thinking

Thinking is the royal road to meaningful learning. Thinking can put irrelevant facts into useful context. In addition, thinking exercises students' unique abilities to self-manage awareness and live intelligently. It is not always easy to get students to do this kind of thinking. How can we manage it?

I know of no better strategy than one previously discussed, reviewed briefly below:

- **Outcome sentences** After a discussion, lecture, story, vacation or any rich learning experience, the teacher asks students to think back and search for personal meanings for themselves.

  To make this challenge clear, a teacher might point to a posted chart showing sample phrases, such as: I learned... I rediscovered... I was surprised... I'm beginning to wonder.... The teacher might then say, "Think back over the material we just covered. See what you can get for yourself from it that is meaningful to you. Write a few sentences, perhaps starting with words like those on the chart."

  To expand thinking further and give students new ideas, a few volunteers might be invited to read aloud one of their *I sentences*. Or a whole row or section of the class might be asked to read a statement, using the **whip around, pass option** strategy. Or students might simply be asked to file their notes, perhaps in a personal **portfolio**.

Provocative questions and assignments can also generate and exercise thinking. Possibilities:

Strategy 14-1 Sort the items

> Ask students to sort through a group of items and place them in specified categories. **Purpose:** To exercise critical thinking skills.

A teacher might give students an assortment of items and ask them to sort the items in some way the teacher specifies:

> Divide the list of foods into two groups, those with high calories and those with low calories. Make pairs of synonyms from the list below. Star the prime numbers on page 34. Make a list of the carnivores illustrated.

Nobody is bored when he is trying to make something that is beautiful, or to discover something that is true.

—*William Inge*

Identify the metaphors in the story. Select the papers you wrote of which you are proud. Pile the blocks that are not yellow or red.

To heighten student interest, Pilon (1979, 1980, 1981, 1982, 1984a, 1984b, 1986, 1988) recommends materials students can physically manipulate. Here is an example of a girl completing such a task. The instructions: "Select an envelope and lay out the pieces it contains in any way that makes sense to you. Put together the cards you believe go well together."

> The girl spreads the cards from her envelope on her desk. She notices that most cards are white and contain common phrases: "In the house," "John went out," "hardly noticed." Two cards, however, are blue. One says, "Prepositional phrase." Another, "Not prepositional phrase." She puts those two cards at the top of her desk. One by one, she puts the other cards under one of those headings. When she is finished, she asks a boy nearby to check her work. The boy, following checking instructions for this task, points at random to one of the cards and asks, "Did you have a reason for putting this one here?" The girl says, "Under the tree is a prepositional phrase." The boy says, "Thank you," and makes a check on the girl's record sheet, to indicate the girl completed that task. The boy returns to his desk and the girl then puts the pieces back into the envelope and files away the envelope and her record sheet.

Pilon has created several sets of cards for such envelopes, highly effective for different academic subjects and different grade levels. There are enough envelopes, which she calls THINKERS®, so each student can do one each day of the year. They are available from The Workshop Way, Inc.

Strategy 14-2 Create groupings

> Ask students to sort items in categories they individually create.
> **Purpose:** To exercise critical thinking skills.

The sorting strategy above provides the student with the sorting criteria: Sort items by calories, put together synonyms, and so on. For a higher-level challenge, as Hilda Taba suggests, ask students to create their own sorting criteria and then to distribute the items according to the criteria created.

Examples: What groupings can you make from:

> Our spelling words. The occupations listed. The assortment of numbers I wrote on the board. The words on page 202 of the index. The states in the United States. The assorted items on my desk. The battles of the Civil War.

Education should include knowledge of what to do with it.
—Anonymous

Strategy 14-3   What's the difference

Ask students in what ways two items are different. **Purpose:** To exercise skills of discrimination and perception.

The teacher can ask students to contrast two items and identify ways they are different: Verbs and adverbs, evaporation and absorption, hills and valleys, poems and songs. The index of a textbook might be one easy source of items.

Examples in English:

- colon and semicolon
- story and joke
- Shakespeare and Hamlet

- preposition and proper name
- formal letter and informal note
- incomplete sentence and jail sentence

Examples in social studies:

- community and country
- leader and elected official
- legislation and legislator

- truce and peace
- ecology and environment
- free elections and secret ballot

Other examples:

- surprise and delight
- clock and calendar
- home and house
- temperature and heat
- fraction and decimal

- opinion and judgment and conclusion
- elephant and box of cookies
- square and rectangle
- evaporation and perspiration
- inspiration and concentration

There is more challenge when items are very similar. *What is the difference between:*

- sad and sorrowful
- yard and meter
- boil and broil

- capitalism and free enterprise
- smart and intelligent
- wet and soaked

Strategy 14-4   What's the same

Ask students what is similar about certain items. **Purpose:** To exercise skills of discrimination and perception.

If you want to see what children can do, you must stop giving them things.
—*Norman Douglas*

Students are asked to compare two or more items and state ways in which ways they are the same: "What's the same about..." Clouds and mist. Leaders and followers. Eating good food and hiking tall hills. Any of the examples in the strategy above, **what's the difference**, might work.

A harder challenge can be fashioned by making the items very unlike each other and asking students to find similarities.

What is the same about:

- one song and two zebras
- a liter and a letter
- Thursday and evaporation
- George Washington and long division
- compound interest and electricity
- newspapers and kindness

Strategy 14-5   Write a summary

Ask students to write a summary of the material. **Purpose:** To exercise comprehensive thinking skills.

The teacher might ask students to write the theme of the story in less than thirty words. Or to summarize the approach of Edison in less than fifty words. Or to draw a sketch showing how something works. Or to outline the arguments for and against slavery in 1850. Or to identify the main ideas covered so far. Or to summarize the learnings one has so far gained from a unit.

Summarizing automatically calls forth thinking. It is not possible to summarize something effectively without considering the whole of it and sorting out its significant and insignificant elements.

Strategy 14-6   Make a prediction

Ask students to think ahead and make predictions. **Purpose:** To exercise the ability to think ahead.

A teacher might ask students to predict: The approximate answer to this math problem. What the chapter is about. How the film will end. What Edison did when he kept failing.

Students might also be asked to note more than one possible outcome and then to rank them in terms of likelihood and, perhaps, personal preference:

- We talked about several ways of… (increasing awareness of world events, insulating old homes in town, changing the class seating arrangement, publishing a class newsletter, etc.) Which would you say has the best chance of working? Next best chance? Please list the ways we discussed in the order of your personal preference.

- Consider what might happen if… (the UN had the only world police force, no candy were allowed in school, we all wrote our personal letters in poetry, etc.) List the possible consequences of such an act. Then number them in order, from the most likely to the least likely to occur. Finally, star the two consequences you personally would most prefer to occur, even if they are not very likely.

As soon as you trust yourself, you will know how to live.
—Goethe

Strategy 14-7   What might explain

Ask students to think back and consider what might explain an event.
Purpose: To exercise cause and effect thinking.

The teacher asks students to think back and consider, "What happened before?" or, "What might explain this event?". Motivate students not to think ahead, as in predicting, but to consider relationships between causes and effects. For example:

What factors might have led to…
- The water boiling in that situation?
- World War II?
- Our crowded highways?
- Mark Twain being so popular?

Note: Many explanations are incomplete. We often do not know all of what caused an event. What led to the water boiling? Correct, although incomplete answers, might include "the heat under the pot," "enough time for the heat to raise the water temperature," "my intention to boil water," and "the absence of ice being added to the water."

The best answer to "why" questions is often, "I'm not entirely sure, but I would include these main factors.…"

For that reason, asking "why" invites careless thinking. It invites students to conclude events can be explained fully. That is rarely true. It is not a conclusion I want my students to carry into life. I prefer they keep open to new and more complete explanations.

For that reason, I recommend not asking simple "why" questions but rather using a more open-ended question form, such as: Can you think of reasons why… What are some of the factors that might explain… Do you have any explanations for… Why would you say… Can you identify some of the main reasons for… What might explain… See if you can discover why.…

Strategy 14-8   Solve a problem

The secret of being a bore is to tell everything.

—*Voltaire*

Ask students to solve a problem that lacks an obvious solution. **Purpose:** To exercise problem-solving skills.

The teacher challenges students to solve a problem. Students might be given more than enough data or, harder yet, not enough data. For example, a teacher might:

- Provide a page listing the eating needs of three different dogs and the costs and nutritional values of four different dog foods. The question: "What would be a good plan for feeding the three dogs at a cost of less than $100 a month? If you have reasons for your choices, tell what they are."

- Supply information about a person, real or fictional, who faces a problem, say, to get a job (or save money, eat a healthy breakfast, or stop smoking). The key question: "What else would you want to know before recommending a plan? What plan would you recommend? What problems do you predict might complicate your plan?

- Pick a real-life problem. What might be a better way to handle: Book distribution in class, attendance taking, work groups losing track of time, poverty in town, traffic congestion, excessive TV viewing.

Strategy 14-9 Brainstorm ideas

Ask students to think open-mindedly about a topic and create a list of ideas without worrying about whether any idea is reasonable or not.
Purpose: To exercise creative thinking skills.

Students in a group, small or large, might be asked to create as large a list as possible of alternatives for, say, balancing the budget, choosing a story topic, finding an effective way to read a chapter, doing mental long division, heating a home, reducing violence.

Three important guidelines for brainstorming:

- Accept all ideas without judgment. An unrealistic idea may generate a new valuable idea.

- Write all ideas as they are mentioned. Do not attempt to judge each idea as it is offered. Keep minds open during the brainstorm. Judgments are for later, when you look back over your written list.

- Generate ideas quickly. High energy and quick pace often lead to new creativity. If ideas come too fast for one person to write them, get two or more to take turns recording offerings.

Never tell people how to do things. Tell them what to do and they will surprise you with their ingenuity.
—George S. Patton

Chapter 15: Beyond Facts and Details

Some academic learnings are more important than others. Isolated facts and details, for example, have limited value. Furthermore, it is difficult to get appreciation of subject matter and to keep all students involved when we stick only to facts and details.

Fortunately, we need not do so. We now know how to weave facts and details into learnings that are more interesting, meaningful and valuable. The strategies of this chapter illustrate ways of doing so. More particularly, they help us weave together four subject matter levels: (1) facts and details, (2) concepts and generalizations, (3) applications, and (4) personal values, defined as follows:

1. **Facts and details** Specifics, names and dates, individual events, usually information and skills with limited usefulness.

   - What is the date of the Declaration of Independence? Where was it signed?
   - What is the chemical symbol for water? For sodium chloride?
   - What reason did the main character give for hiding his gun? Where did he hide it?
   - What were the four main causes of World War II? Who were our allies?
   - What is 23 multiplied by 145?

2. **Concepts and generalizations** The big ideas, information and skills more generally useful.

   - What motivates people to declare their independence? What is a declaration?
   - How are elements joined into chemical wholes? How are symbols derived?
   - How are violent acts related to frustration? What else often leads to violence?
   - What forces contribute to warfare? To international cooperation?
   - What's an efficient way to get a total amount from a group of identical amounts?

3. **Applications** Practical applications of knowledge or skills.

   - How important is political independence to people in the United States nowadays?

Nothing in education is so astonishing as the amount of ignorance it accumulates in the form of inert facts.

—Henry Adams

- How would you analyze this sample? What pollutes the air in our town?
- What kinds of violence are increasing these days? What might cause that?
- In what ways do we find conflicts in our town? What might explain it?
- What is the total of the square inches of all our desk tops?

4. **Values** Issues that likely touch on what students personally care about or feel is valuable to them. The word "you" is prominent.

- How important is independence to you? When is it hard for you to act independently?
- What elements in your life often give you personal satisfaction? Can you draw a symbol of some of those elements?
- How do you handle frustration? What would help you do better at it?
- Are there any conflicts now that bother you? Are there win-win options available?
- Can you recall occasions when you would have liked to have been able to do multiplication quickly and easily? Would you like any help in learning to do so?

Each level of subject matter makes a unique contribution to the whole of learning. The strategies below suggest how to take advantage of these levels.

Strategy 15-1 Concept-generalization focus

Select a concept or generalization and build lessons around it. **Purpose:** To bring learnings up to the level of concepts and generalizations.

We can center a unit around a big idea, a concept or generalization. In science, for example, we can center a unit on balance, evaporation, or plant growth. In art: on color, movement, or sketching. In English: on poetry, metaphor or comedy.

With this strategy, we would use facts and details to illuminate the big ideas or general skills. As a result, many students will remember the facts. They will pick them up in passing, much as we learn the names of the streets in our neighborhood by passing them repeatedly. Here are some examples:

The trouble with facts is that there are so many of them.
—Samuel Crothers

Geography: Today we will start a unit on Europe. I will occasionally use flash cards to help you connect cities with their countries. We will see a film on rivers and mountains of Europe. We will read about people from different regions. And I will ask you each to draw and label a map that shows the location of all that we study. This will bring up a lot of facts and details. Some of the facts will stick in your memory, of course, but there is no need to remember any particular fact. Aim to get the *idea* of

Europe as a region, such as where it is, what it looks like, what its people are about. As we proceed, please make a list of interesting things you learned. At the end of the unit, I'll ask you to turn in your map and to summarize your list of learnings, so I know the main things you learned about Europe and, perhaps, what interested or surprised you most.

Math: Today we will start work on percentages. Your job is to prepare a scrapbook of several kinds of percentage problems, showing how you can correctly solve each one. This will require you to understand where percentage problems occur in real life. You will have to figure out a way to solve such problems correctly. We'll explore all that and help each other. Many of you will master the process of doing percentage calculations during this unit. But that might still be tricky for some of you, so don't worry if your timeclock for mastering the calculations has not yet arrived. Practice asking someone to help you solve your problems correctly. But be sure your scrapbook shows you can identify several kinds of percentage problems and, by yourself or with help, get each correctly solved.

History: We will begin our Civil War unit. Our approach will be to look closely at the daily lives of six different people who lived during that time, some famous and some not. As we do this, you will pick up many details and facts of that war and of those times. Some of you will remember the facts, but I would like you not to aim for that. Aim rather to get a general understanding of that war, and especially how people on different sides of the issue experienced it. At the end of the unit, I'll give you some time to work with one or two others, or alone if you like, to prepare a written or oral report, or perhaps a mural, dramatic skit or model if you prefer. Your task for this final work is to show some of the key things you learned about the Civil War.

The concluding questions or summary evaluations would not focus on the facts of the lessons. They might be, for example:

- **What in general can you say about**... the three chemicals we studied so far; the misspelled words on the board; the stories we read; how plants grow; the American history leaders we discussed.

- **Classify the specifics we studied into the concepts of**... organic and inorganic chemicals; spelling exceptions and not exceptions; subjective and objective writing; the plant-growth factors of soil, light and temperature; favoring democracy and not favoring democracy.

- **Write some outcome sentences**... Reflect on our lessons and write sentences that begin with such phrases as I learned... or, I was surprised... or, I'm beginning to wonder... or, I promise... or, I believe....

Man's business here is to know for the sake of living, not to live for the sake of knowing.
—*Frederic Harrison*

- **Compare and contrast**... the three chemicals we studied with chemicals we studied before; subjective and objective writing; early and late plant growth; Lincoln and Lee.

Caution: Many students come to realize that they forget facts soon after the final exam. And that even if they remember the facts, other than for trivia games, the facts themselves are not very useful. Yet many students *assume* facts are what schooling is all about.

It is often prudent, then, to make explicit an intention that students clarify a larger issue, or advance a general skill, or grasp a basic concept, and not merely remember a batch of details. Telling students that that is our focus helps them let go of limiting assumptions about what they can get from lessons.

Strategy 15-2 Connecting subject matter to values

Connect a subject matter lesson to an issue students are likely to care about. **Purpose:** To exercise mature thinking on real-life issues and to motivate academic study.

Often it is possible to begin a unit with a values-level discussion, that is, a discussion about an issue that matters to students. Alternatively, we can end with such a discussion, as a demonstration of how academic study can connect to what matters in daily life. Examples:

On reading a story: The teacher picks a concept from a story the class will study next and starts the lesson with values-level questions he thinks will provoke student interest. Before study:

> Today we will begin a story by Clarkson. One person in the story is very optimistic, as you will see. Do you often feel optimistic? Make some notes to yourself about one or two times either you or someone you know felt very optimistic or very confident. What happened? Later I'll invite you to share some of your thoughts with a partner, or to pass if you would prefer. We'll then talk a bit about optimism, seeing what we now know about it. Then we'll read the story and see what else we can learn.

A similar discussion can be used after studying a piece of literature, to turn the reading into a personally meaningful experience. After study:

> One theme in the book we just finished was perseverance, not giving up even when the going got tough. Make some notes to yourself about times you or someone you know stuck to a task, even when that was very difficult. Then, thinking about your examples, note anything that made perseverance easier. What ideas does our story suggest for handling times like that?

On an event or person in history: A teacher might pick a concept related to an historical event or famous person and similarly connect it to value issues that personally touch students, using it either before or after study.

It often happens that I wake at night and begin to think about a serious problem and decide I must tell the pope about it. Then I wake up completely and remember that I am the pope.

— Pope John XXIII

Before: Lincoln was sometimes unsure of what to do, as our next unit will make clear. How about you? Can you identify times you remember being unsure of what to do? What would be good ways to handle such times? Let's think about this a bit now, and again after we study our unit, to see if we learn anything more about making choices when we are unsure. I will add my thoughts, too. People often must make a choice when it is not clear what is the best choice. I would like you to learn something about how best to do that.

After: As we learned, Alaska and Hawaii were the last states to be admitted to the nation, yet most residents were not unhappy about being last. How about you? Were you ever last or almost last at something? How did you feel? What would make that okay? What makes it harder when you are not in the first few?

On mathematics: Connecting mathematics to students' personal reality can also effectively motivate new study and/or add a dimension of meaning to completed study.

Before: Before we move ahead with subtraction of large numbers, I want you each to collect three examples of subtraction in real life. Use your imagination or ask family members, if you like. Then consider what would be very hard for you to subtract from your life. What would you love to get rid of?

After: Before going on to our next unit in geometry, let's spend a few minutes talking about circles in reality. We'll share ideas later, first in pairs and then as a whole class, but first make some notes about one or more of the questions I wrote on the board. What circles of things or people or ideas are important to you? What feelings, if any, have you about circles? Have you any broken circles in your life? Are there any circles you could complete for others? Can you draw a silly circle?

Three steps for building a values discussion on a subject matter lesson

1. Seek an issue that can be connected to your lesson about which students are likely to feel strongly. The connection can be very indirect. Sample issues:

money	love	jealousy
luxuries	strong personal beliefs	deception
prejudice	things I love to do	help in a strange place
honesty	hugging	crime in town
special people	smiles	cars
blind people	fear	telling the truth
growing up poor	hope	the way you look
giving up	delight	great surprise
favorite games	generosity	graceful and kind
things hard to wait for	courage	terribly disappointed
stealing	perseverance	sorrow
won a prize or honor	fury	planning ahead

Children know how to learn in more ways than we know how to teach them.
—*Ronald Edmonds*

friends	teasing	strong positive or
giving compliments	bossiness	negative feelings
someone dying	cruelty	terrible mistake
loneliness	pets	hopes for future gifts
insecurity	hobbies	stuck, not sure what
keeping a secret	being too short	can be done
wanting something	being too tall	
and not getting it	the years ahead	
understanding others'	tears and laughter	
points of view	a gift	

2. Ask questions in which the word "you" is central. Samples:

- Have **you** ever experienced something like...?
- Do **you** know someone who...?
- Have **you** ever enjoyed...?
- Have **you** ever had trouble with...?
- What might **you** do if...?
- What else might **you** do?
- What choice would make **you** feel best about yourself?
- What would **you** most want to avoid doing?

Avoid hypothetical questions that are not likely to matter much to students. Hypothetical: "How would life be different without cars?" ("Won't happen, so why should I care?") Better: "What would be hard for **you** if cars were outlawed?"

3. Structure a safe, thoughtful way to handle the questions. I often use the write-share-learn sequence (see **Action flow plan** Chapter One). And I typically offer students the option to pass on any question or any procedure. That both protects student privacy and promotes student self-management.

Three comments on values and subject matter

- These value-level considerations, used either before or after study of facts-concepts-applications, not only perk up interest but give students practice in thinking seriously about serious life issues. That is something many students sorely need. Young people will face many complex choices in their lives. They will face those choices with more balance and reason, and far less impulse and danger when they have had practice in school thinking this way.

- When taking a unit up to the personal values level of subject matter, I find little need to make the leap logical. On circles, one can leap from geometry circles to circles of friends or circles of personal habits. On rocks, one can leap from categorizing hard rocks to wondering about hard people and how best to deal with them. On long division, one can leap to divisions in our personal lives or in the school or community.

Expensive silk ties are the only ones that attract spaghetti sauce.
—Anonymous

Such leaps allow us to create powerful lessons, teach students about what is involved in good living, and keep rich variety in schoolwork. Students usually appreciate this and often grow a great deal from it. Indeed, you may find that some students profit as much from such deliberations as from any academic studies.

- We commonly assume that we should start with the fact-detail level. Start a history unit by learning the relevant names and dates. Learn grammar and spelling before writing letters. Learn the parts of the microscope before beginning to use it. There is logic in the argument. But I have come to find that logic often squeezes artistic teaching too dry.

Yet with some units and with some students, particularly students who cannot handle big ideas, it is advisable to start with facts and details, giving them success at that level. I would want, however, not to restrict myself with facts and details. Whenever I could, I would want to tag on at least a brief values discussion, to give students practice in serious thinking about serious issues. Here are examples of three teachers doing that.

Science teacher: Now that we have looked at the earth's crust, I'd like to take a few minutes to look at how people from different lands relate, or how people within one land relate when they are different from one another. Please make a note or two about how you feel when you meet someone from a foreign land or someone who is very different from you. No need to share this with anyone. Keep it private if you like. (Then) Sit with someone near you and share any thoughts you have about this that you care to share. Just a moment or so for this. (Then) Let's all discuss how we want to be with people who are different from us.

Math teacher: Now that we have finished our unit on percentages, I'd like to take a few minutes to talk about percentages in your personal life. Please start by noting an estimate of the percent of time you feel strong, capable, confident. Then note what you might do to increase that percent, if you have any ideas about that. I'll give you just a moment or two to make some notes. We'll then give you a chance to share thoughts with a partner and, finally, we'll get together and I'll mention some suggestions I find useful for people who want to spend more time as their strong, capable, confident selves.

Whatever your past has been, you have a spotless future.

—Anonymous

History teacher: Before we leave the Civil War unit, let's see if we can list on the chalkboard some ideas for talking over conflicts peaceably, resolving differences before they get into negative, hard feelings. Let's say two friends were in conflict. What kind of conflict might that be? What are some smart and not so smart ways to resolve such a conflict?

Strategy 15-3   Application projects

Help students apply learnings to real-life situations. **Purpose:** To make learning more meaningful to students.

We can often jump subject matter to the application level simply by asking students to take something learned and seek ways of applying it in real life.

Example 1   Students have just learned 8 x 3. The teacher asks for a possible real-life application.

> S: Well, if I had three families and there were eight of us in each family, that would be an example.

> T: Yes, that would fit. Who has another idea?

> S: How about we had three pizzas, each with eight slices?

> T: Yes, 8 times 3 would tell us how many slices all together. Who else would risk sharing a possible application for 8 times 3?

Example 2   Students are studying the Bill of Rights.

> The teacher says, "Take a few moments and jot down one or two rights you think are not well protected in our community. Perhaps also try to write some words for a law that would better protect those rights."

> When a few students finish writing, the teacher might announce, "One minute more," use **sharing pairs** to have students compare notes briefly and follow that by a brief discussion for whole class sharing. The discussion might conclude with an invitation to students, optional, to submit something to the class in the future, to see how many would approve a new right-protecting law.

Example 3   The teacher has talked about the wisdom of thinking before acting.

> The teacher then asks, "Is there someone in your life, perhaps a friend or relative, whom you wish would do more thinking before acting? Or are there some situations outside of school in which you yourself might wisely do more thinking before acting?"

> Students might make notes, with the caution: "No need to share any of this. Keep private anything you care to." A brief discussion might follow. The teacher might then conclude with, "In all of life, now and later, perhaps especially when you are out of school, there are advantages in pausing to think before acting. You might want to practice building that into your life. If you do something about this, please let us know sometime. If I ask what is new or good in your life, as I sometimes do at the beginning of a class, you can report some experience."

Recently, I went to a center for teenage girls where the teacher asked what they would like to discuss most. Human biology? Care for their infant? Physiology of childbirth? Family planning? The girls showed no interest. Then the teacher asked, "Would you like to discuss how to say no to your boyfriend without losing his love?" All hands shot up.

—Eunice Kennedy Shriver

Example 4 A unit has been completed.

> "Think back to something you learned. Can you imagine a practical use for what you learned?" The teacher might add, "Write or draw something that tells what applications you thought of. Work alone or together with a partner or two. Tomorrow we will share our ideas."

When students are regularly asked to apply what they learned to reality, they get into the habit of connecting learning and living and, likely, do better at both.

Strategy 15-4 What know and want to know

> Start a lesson by asking students to note what they already know or might want to know about the topic. **Purpose:** To build a unit on the knowledge and questions students bring to the topic.

I do not recall teachers ever asking me what I wanted to learn about a topic. Had I been asked, I might have thought about it and uncovered a curiosity or two. And if I heard my classmates' curiosities, it is very likely I would have found something I wanted to learn. As it was, many of my classmates and I sat quite passively through our lessons, taking what we got, like it or not, with our curious minds gradually drying up for lack of exercise.

From Donna Ogle I learned a teacher can take a different path:

> We will begin a unit on the Congress today. What are some things you already know about the U. S. Congress? Let's brainstorm. I'd like two newsprint writers to come up and take turns writing down all the ideas that come up, true or otherwise. Who will start us off? We want a list of things you already know about the U. S. Congress.

When the class seems ready to move on:

> We'll leave that list posted for a while. Now let's start another list. What are some things you would *like* to know about the U. S. Congress? What are some things you are curious about or concerned about? Be creative and open-minded. Who will start our brainstorming?

If a child doesn't learn the way you teach, teach the way the child learns.

—Anonymous

If the teacher suspects a thin list will result, prudence recommends priming the pump with some teacher comments:

> For example, you may wonder how to meet with your congressperson. Or how you can *become* one. Or how much it costs to get elected. Or you may wonder if representatives really read citizen letters. Or if it makes any difference. Or why we have so many representatives in Congress. Or about scandals. Or what adults in town think of the present Congress and what the Congress should do. Any of those questions interest anyone here?

The particular questions students list at the outset do not limit the learnings that will eventually result. The teacher can add any content deemed necessary. The lists are simply a starting point to open minds to the unit.

Once the lists are formed, the teacher has several options.

Option 1 Leave the lists posted for future reference.

A teacher could simply proceed with instruction as usual, taking advantage of the fact that students will now probably be more motivated to dig into the unit. The teacher would also have the advantage of knowing what the class already knows and what interests them, which might help in planning instruction. At the end of the unit, then, the teacher might say:

> Looking back on our study, I'd like you to take some time and review the things you learned and do five things. (1) Make a list of your key learnings. Then compare your list with the posters we made the first day. (2) Did you learn that something you originally thought was true was not exactly as you first understood it? (3) Did you learn anything very new? (4) What now would you say are the three or four most important things you know about the U. S. Congress? (5) Do you now have some questions you still wonder about? We'll share that in pairs and then use a **whip around** to sample the whole group's ideas.

Option 2 Update the lists as the unit proceeds.

Gradually the lists could be revised and augmented so that, at the end of the unit, they represent what is then best known and what is yet of interest to some class members. One fourth-grade class used those lists interestingly. The teacher asked a committee to reproduce the original two lists and the final two lists and then invited students to take them home, to show families the kinds of learnings that had occurred.

Option 3 Turn the lists into cooperative learning activities.

A teacher could have students who have overlapping interests get together and study further, using a convenient form of cooperative learning or, in the words of Sharan and Sharan (1989/1990), a "group investigation model."

> I'd like you to design your own study now, based on what interests you. Although you could work alone, I'd prefer that you work with one or two others. I prefer that no group be more than three because it is hard to keep active and involved when there are four or more people in one group. Let's see if we have any common interests. Who can say what they would like to investigate? Speak up if you have an idea, and then we'll see who might be interested in that same general idea.

Alternatively, a chart could be formed with students signing up for topics. Or the teacher could form trios arbitrarily, by having a class of thirty count off by tens. Or the teacher could announce:

Nothing saddens me so much as witnessing brilliant young intellects addressing enormous efforts to trivial problems.

—Solomon Snyder

I'd like you to get into trios now, sitting with people with whom you have not worked recently. Get to know some new friends better. (The teacher helps out as needed until groups are formed.) Now before I tell you about deadlines and what product I'd like each group to produce, I'd like you to talk over some possibilities for your group investigation. What might be fun or important to do or learn more about?

When teachers have topics suitable for this strategy, it usually leads to rich learning experiences. When students participate in shaping the focus of study, their dignity flowers. Energy levels go up. Self-management comes alive. Community feelings grow. And awareness is sharpened.

Strategy 15-5 Concept charts

Maintain a classroom chart of important concepts studied. Occasionally refer to the chart to refresh awareness of items on it. **Purpose:** To keep key concepts fresh and alive.

Imagine walking into a classroom and seeing this sign on the wall:

Friendship
Courage
Equality of opportunity
Loyalty
Kindness
Self-control of impulses
Integrity
Whole self
Striving and accepting
Candor
Supportive behavior
Intrusive behavior

There are three things that I get inspired by when I'm at school or even at home. First, is beautiful art work. The next thing that inspires me is the animals. The way they live their lives. Finally, the thing that inspires me is outdoor nature. The beauty of it.

—Bambi, sixth grade

You ask about it and the teacher explains, "I call that a **concept chart.** Whenever an important idea comes up in class, I write it on that chart. I refer to those ideas from time to time, when they naturally come up in class. I sometimes include important names, even symbols I want students to remember. But mainly I include concepts I want students to internalize and that are unlikely to be completely understood the first time they come up in lessons. It helps me keep key ideas fresh and active."

Concept charts provide handy reminders for everyone, and facilitate learning in layers, not lumps. They serve visual learners especially well.

Sample concept charts: Key formulas covered in class so far. Special vocabulary words. Historical events of note. Authors studied. Correct language usage phrases. Tricky spelling words.

Chapter 16: For a Community of Learners

Although many of the other strategies in this book will naturally lead to a healthful class climate, additional strategies speed and ease that development. Here are four.

Strategy 16-1   Good living target

Inspire students to consider what they can do to live and work well together and occasionally urge them to keep moving in that direction.
Purpose: To inspire students to take some of the responsibility for creating a cooperative learning community.

How can we get students to become an effective community of learners? One way is to set that as a class goal and to help students circle in on it. We each must do this in our own way of course, but here is one possibility.

Mrs. Jones announces to her class: "From now on I would like us to aim to become a classroom that practices good living as well as good learning. I want us to get along together, to help one another, to be supportive of each other. I want us to work together as a healthy, happy, cooperative community of learners. I want us all to *like* being here in class each day."

Such an announcement might be made the first day of school. Or it could be made after a class has been underway, to signal a new era. "So far we've focused on learning," a teacher might say. "From now on, I want us also to be aware of *how* we learn. I want us to target on being a class that not only learns a lot, but does it in ways that are good for us. I want each of us to feel stronger, more open, more creative, more confident from being here. I do not want learning to go on in ways that make anyone feel weaker, or more resistant, or less confident."

It is only with the heart that one can see rightly; what is essential is invisible to the eye.

—Antoine de Saint-Exupery

That announcement would be especially valuable for students not expecting a class to be concerned with more than the amount of subject matter learned. It opens students to a new expectation and the power of expectation makes a difference. When students expect that the group will work in ways that are good for everyone, they will help bring that about.

Perhaps ask one or two students to create a visual representation of that target, something to hang on the wall that pictures what the class is aiming for, something that can remind students that they want to become a kindly, cooperative community.

Once the class accepts such a good living target it can be used in many ways. You might appoint a committee to make periodic assessments and give reports to the class. You might also make your own assessments, perhaps:

Raise awareness when "misses" show up "I hear grumbling about the assignment. Grumbling does not seem to fit into a group that is working happily and positively. I wonder how we can do better."

Be honestly appreciative when the target is hit "This group is really working well together. I especially like the way we are helping one another, keeping our procedures working so smoothly, and going out of our way to assist those who might feel left out. Thank you for all that. I appreciate it very much."

Writes a fourth grade teacher:

I put a line across the chalk board and wrote at one end, "Teasing. Students left out." I said some classrooms have students who do not work together nicely and asked for their examples of what else might sometime show up in such a class.

Then I wrote at the other end of the line, "Reaching out to help. Smiles and honest compliments." I said that some classrooms live together happily and asked for some other examples of behavior showing that.

Then I asked the class what it would take to move us toward the "good living" end of the continuum. We brainstormed a list. Finally I wrote a "one" at one end of the line and a "ten" at the other end and told the class sometime I would ask them what number from one to ten they felt was the current climate.

Since I did that, the students are much more aware of what they can do to get along happily. I'm hoping this good living target, as you call it, will get internalized and they will be aware that they can do something, now and later, as adults in their families, to get along well with each other. A good number of my students have no clue that people don't have to scratch and squable, that they can choose to get along better.

Strategy 16-2 Cooperative planning

Announce a topic or problem and ask students to help you think about the best ways to deal with it. **Purpose:** To communicate teacher respect for student thoughts and to cultivate a cooperative class climate.

A free society is one where it is safe to be unpopular.
—Adlai Stevenson

Few of us react positively to bossy people. When people push us, our instinct is to push back or to step aside. On the other hand, when people reach out to us, when they invite us to join in an activity, when they ask if we are willing to join in, we are likely to be nonresistant, ready at least to consider cooperating. This recommends such strategies as **lesson agreements**, in which the teacher begins a class by outlining what is ahead and asking students if that seems agreeable to them.

Three similar invitations help build a positive community climate:

- **Course agreement** The teacher invites acceptance not of one lesson but of a long-term plan.

  "Rather than touch on all the topics in the book, I would like us to handle a few topics with depth and care. Here are the topics I recommend.... Any reactions to that suggestion? Can we agree at least to start off in this way?"

  This is not to be an invitation to anarchy or to doing nothing. The teacher is to remain firmly in control. It is simply an invitation to new and better ideas and to a spirit of responsible cooperation.

- **Cooperative planning** In some cases it is wise to involve students in the construction of the plan. If the teacher and students can agree, the resulting plan typically provides high levels of student commitment and motivation.

  "How shall we handle this next unit? Let's brainstorm and make a list of some options. Then let's see if we can agree on how best to proceed."

- **Cooperative problem solving** The class might also be asked to cooperate in solving a class problem.

  "Let's brainstorm a list of ways we might do better at getting all our papers handed in on time. How about two volunteers write on the board all the ideas we can come up with. Later we'll sift through the list and see if we can agree on something worth trying."

Strategy 16-3 Community living lessons

Include lessons and activities that help students appreciate what is involved in living as a cooperative classroom community. **Purpose:** To advance appreciation of what a cooperative classroom community requires.

Fewer discipline problems will erupt when groups see themselves as cooperative, live-and-let-live communities. We do well, then, to create lessons and activities that teach them about working as a team, accepting one another, respecting one another and the teacher. Some ideas:

I get inspired when I see small children learn new things.

—Kim, high school

- Perhaps refer to the sign introduced in the **truth signs** strategy, **It's intelligent to ask for help. No one need do it all alone.** "That's part of living happily together," we might say. Perhaps remind students what a natural neighborhood looks like. One person drives a bus. Another paints a house. A third walks home carrying groceries. Each person is doing different things, yet all with a common, live-and-let-live attitude.

• Two new signs that might be posted:

> **We can aim to be a group that is all for one and one for all.**

> **We can accept and support one another. We need not ignore or reject anyone.**

• Consider connecting this issue to the following American principles:

Democratic government Authority resting in the people. Collective decision making. Government of the people, by the people, for the people. No arbitrary laws or cruel punishments. Laws based on open-minded discussions. A balance of powers to limit misuse of power. Each citizen sharing in group responsibilities. Respect for the common good. One nation with liberty and justice for all.

Individual freedom Freedom to speak one's mind. Being free of unnecessary duties and controls. The right to life, liberty and the pursuit of happiness. Equal opportunity. Individual differences. The Declaration of Independence. The Bill of Rights. Acceptance of others. Searching for better ways. Free enterprise. Each citizen managing his own life.

We advance these principles, of course, when we practice living them in the classroom. We thus prepare students for mature citizenship roles. We can remind students of these two American principles, perhaps concluding with the challenge: "Let's learn how we can live and learn well together here, each with the right to manage his or her own work, each with the responsibility to avoid interfering with others' rights, and each with the opportunity and responsibility to play a respected part in the group as a whole."

• To communicate the meaning of a healthful community, one teacher had students wear name tags the first week so all would get to know one another more quickly. He also talked about teamwork in sports and in factories. He said he wanted his class to learn to work together as a "Great Team." That particular class decided to give itself a class name, to exchange phone numbers so people could call if they needed help with homework, to set up a hospitality committee to welcome new class members, and to have occasional class outings on weekends.

Look well into thyself; there is a source of strength which will always spring up if thou wilt always look there.
—*Marcus Aurelius*

• Another teacher began the school year with the phrase, "One for all and all for one," challenging her class to be stouthearted enough to keep working for that class spirit, even when it was tough to do so.

Later on she used two quotes to start a discussion on what a community classroom might be:

> The circle is a sacred symbol of life.... Individual parts within the circle connect with every other. What happens to one, or what one part does, affects all within the circle.
>
> — Native American Driving Hawk Sneve

> He drew a circle to shut me out.
> Heretic, rebel, a thing to flout.
> But love and I had the wit to win.
> We drew a circle that took him in.
>
> — Edwin Markham, in "Outwitted"

In some way, then, perhaps making use of images of a smoothly functioning family, a friendly neighborhood, effective teamwork, or basic principles of our society, we might aim to inspire students to become a mutually supportive and respectful community of learners. Because this is not a familiar goal for many students, from time to time we must remind them of this ideal.

How do class rules fit this strategy?

We do well to remember our purpose. We care about advancing both current academic learning and long-term dignified living. Our priority is not to control everything students do. Our aim is not to prevent behavior problems from ever coming up. We do not, of course, want unnecessary problems. We certainly do not want to generate misbehavior. Yet some problems can be valuable for teaching students what in reality is involved in living the good life. This impinges on how we view class rules and, indeed, if we want them at all.

The **intelligence call up** strategy reduces the need for a set of rules. Using this strategy, rather than relying on rules, we remind students that they are intelligent beings, smart enough to make informed, appropriate choices, just as they do everyday at home and on the street. This strategy has us frequently saying: "Think through the situation you face. What are all your options? What would be the smart thing to do? What comes to you when you use your brain power? You will see what's best. You will see what makes the most sense. Let's live together here as one supportive, intelligent community."

Put young people in the best possible conditions for nature to do its work.

—Florence Nightingale

The intent here is to teach students how they can handle problems, as they will need to handle them as mature citizens. Some teachers, however, still feel the need for specific rules or, as I would prefer to call them, behavior guidelines. If so, I recommend the second of these two approaches:

- Ms. A: We will need certain rules of behavior in our class if we are to work effectively. Perhaps rules about speaking out or disturbing others or getting work in on time. What rules do you think we will need here? Let's discuss this and brainstorm a list. (Afterward) Now which rules on our list are most important? How shall we handle those who violate rules? What would be appropriate consequences for such violations? How will we remember these rules and their consequences?

- Ms. B: I want us to get along well together. I want us to live and learn together much like a healthy community or family, with respectful give and take. I want us to help one another when that is appropriate. And leave others alone when we judge that is the wise thing to do. Some guidelines might help us become such a community. Perhaps, "Honestly yet respectfully, let someone know when he or she is bothering you." One guideline I personally need is, "Do not leave the room without a hall pass." What other guidelines might we consider? (Afterward) How can we keep to these guidelines and avoid slipping off them? How should we react when people make mistakes, as all humans do?

Both teachers might end up with behavior guidelines: Raise hands before speaking. No hitting or running. And so on. But the second teacher is likely to elicit more goodness and cooperation from students. And, since cultivating goodness and cooperation is a concern to us, we can use our discipline plan to further our purposes. A discipline plan, then, need not be an unfortunate necessity. It can be a valuable tool both to prevent problems and to advance mature living.

Even in classes that can use rules, I recommend announcing early on that our intent is for the class to learn to live together as a productive, happy community. Talking much like Mrs. B. above, we would announce that we intend to see a classroom here in which we all get along well together, respect one another, lend a hand when needed, let people be when we judge that the better choice. That, of course, is the purpose of the **good living target** strategy.

Strategy 16-4 Easing student distress

> Model someone who reaches out to ease class members in distress.
> **Purpose:** To reach out kindly to students who are upset and model healthful community living.

When we are teaching we may notice that a student is distressed. The student might be suffering from a family disturbance, or from the loss of a pet. A student may be suffering from a humiliation from peers, or lingering pains from a test failure.

How can teachers reassure such students, ease their pain, or otherwise help them get past distress and back into confident studies?

1. **I'm with you** Sometimes we can say something that communicates to students that they are not alone, that we are with them.

> "I think I understand how you feel, Michael."

The best and deepest moral training is that which one gets by having to enter into proper relations with others.... Present educational systems, so far as they destroy or neglect this unity, render it difficult or impossible to get any genuine, regular moral training.

—John Dewey

"Shantal, the same kind of thing happened to me once. I can appreciate what you're going through."

"I see the hurt in your eyes, Todd. And I hurt with you."

2. **Take your time**   It might be appropriate to reassure students that the distress need not be diminished or dismissed. They can take the time they need to live through it.

"Take your time with it. No need to rush back into your class work. We'll somehow help you catch up."

"No need to pretend you don't feel what you feel. Is there any way I can make it easier for you while you are here in school?"

3. **You are not unworthy**   Perhaps reassure students that their experience does not diminish them in your eyes. In some way, tell students what they experience has nothing to do with their essential dignity and worth.

"You may have failed at something. But I still care for you. And I always will. Your essential goodness is not touched."

"It's okay to feel what you are feeling. You are no less strong or worthy for it. Lots of us have had to suffer the same thing."

4. **Want to talk about it?**   Perhaps gently invite them to share their experience. Some might be willing to share with the whole class, and it might be good for all if they did.

"Would you like to tell the class, or some of them, about what's going on? Or would you like to have me tell them? It might be good for them to know."

"Lots of us have experienced a loved one dying. I wonder if you would mind my talking about this issue with the class, not mentioning you or your situation. Then, if you choose, you could tell them about what happened to you. But perhaps such a discussion is best put off for a while. Have you any thoughts about this?"

Some students get sufficient emotional support from family members and comments such as these might not be too valuable. But that is not so for all students. For some students, words such as those above can prevent a permanent crack in confidence or faith. Indeed, in discussing this with teachers, I often hear a comment such as, "Yes, I myself would be less of a person today if one teacher had not once reached out in ways like that."

The secret of life is...
Oops, I can't tell you.
It's a secret.
— Anonymous

Chapter 17: Inspiring Personal Growth

It is difficult to build a positive class climate when students generally feel negative or approach class work apathetically. Many strategies already presented counteract such tendencies and naturally cultivate a healthy interdependence, for example:

- Ask a friend
- Choral work
- Cushioning
- I'm with yous
- Paired reading

- Sharing pairs
- Truth signs
- Honest I appreciates
- DESCA challenges
- Support groups
- Tutor training

Here are seven strategies particularly effective in releasing students' positive powers and supporting the development of a dignified learning community.

17-1   Whole self lesson

A lesson to teach students how to accept themselves and others and how to open up more of their good selves. **Purpose:** To teach students how to live more often as their preferred selves.

The **whole self lesson** helps students, as well as their teachers, to be accepting of themselves, even when they are not being their best selves. Here is an example of that lesson. It is in a form I used recently when working with a group of teachers. You might consider each segment in this lesson as if you were in that teacher group. That will probably best prepare you to craft a version of the lesson for your own students.

Water finds its level; the swallows fly south in winter; children learn.

—Leo Tolstoy

A whole self lesson with adults

1. **My Open Self** First, let me talk a bit about myself. I am a person who, as I see it, includes several selves.

   For example, I am sometimes my easy-going, open-minded, flexible self. That is a self I have inside me these days, for these are fairly good days in my house and, if the winds are just right, I can be that self. I call that my *open* self. We are all different however. Consider your open selfhood for a moment. On a piece of scrap paper, make a note of one or two qualities that show up for you when you are your open self. (After a pause:) Anyone willing to share what comes up for you when you are in your open self?

2. **My Narrow Self** At other times I am much more self-centered, narrow-minded, irritable, tight. I do not feel at all easy and flexible. I call that my *narrow* self. Alas, I can also be that way nowadays. How about you? Make a private note about what comes up for you when you feel tight, small, narrowed down. Anyone willing to share something you wrote?

3. **Four of Our Selves** Check the line below. I've put four of my selves on it and a few qualities that describe each. I first noted one of my *former* selves. That's a self that showed up for me when I was much younger and rarely shows up nowadays. I suspect it lies dormant inside me. I hope it stays dormant.

   Then I included notes on my current narrow and open selves. Finally, I added what feels like a *possible* self, a self that is not now available to me but that I sense exists deep inside me someplace. A self that might, and then again might not, emerge as an available self. I occasionally get a hint that it is a possible self for me.

A FORMER SELF	MY CURRENT NARROW SELF	MY CURRENT OPEN SELF	A POSSIBLE FUTURE SELF
Lonely, withdrawn, passive, not confident, suspicious.	Self-centered, narrow-minded, resistant, picky, insensitive, abrupt, irritable, confused.	Easy-going, open-minded, relaxed, generous, flexible, humorous, accepting.	Peaceful, loving, content with whatever comes up in daily life.

   Try drawing a line like that for yourself. Or, I should say, for your *selves*. You can skip the inclusion of your former and possible selves, if you like. It is most important that you write notes describing your current narrow and open selves. See what turns up for you. (Discussion as appropriate.)

4. **Narrow Selfhood Inevitable** Most of us feel more comfortable when we are our open selves than when we are our narrow selves. Should we regret it when our narrow selves show up? Is that unfortunate? Wouldn't it be far better for us to learn how to live always as our open selves?

   Try it if you like. But you may find it is not possible. Toothaches occur. A disappointment shows up. We look in a mirror and don't like what we see. It rains at the wrong time. Lots of things happen that get us feeling off balance, tight, uncomfortable, not at all our open, balanced selves. As I see it, humans naturally experience both narrowed and open selves. It is part of the human condition. Events show up that throw us. No way of escaping it. That make sense in your experience.

5. **Open Selfhood Evolves** Furthermore, I do not believe we can expect to have one open self for an entire life. Rarely is a child's open self the same as his or her adult's open self. Even as an adult, if I were my current open self

The man who goes alone can start today; but he who travels with another must wait till that other is ready.

—Henry David Thoreau

for a very long time, and that has never happened, chances are I would not be satisfied until I became something different, something larger, something in the direction of my possible self. Soon enough, my open self would no longer feel so complete to me. Perhaps that is what maturity is all about. It seems to be related to the idea of becoming the best we can be, or developing our full potential.

6. **Accepting The Inevitable**   I do not believe humans are meant to live only in their open selves. We have both narrowed and open selves and humans naturally spend time in each. Makes no sense, then, for me to try to live only as my open self. I have to remind myself of that from time to time because I have a tendency to get down on myself when I am my narrowed, tight self and not my good open self.

I also do not believe humans outgrow their current selfhood and move to a new selfhood before the time is right for that growth. A child cannot be an adult before the time for that arrives. An acorn cannot become an oak at any old time. It makes no sense, then, for me to regret that I have not yet become my possible self, the self I sense I might someday be. I have to remind myself of that from time to time because I have a tendency to get down on myself when I am not as good as I sense I might, someday become.

As you might imagine, I sometimes need to say to myself: The sun does not rise before sunrise. Things are what they are. Me too. I am not yet better than I now am. Furthermore, I am not always as good as I sometimes can be. Sometimes I get into my tight, narrow self. No sense getting down on myself for that.

How are you at accepting yourself when you remain in your current stage of selfhood? If you do not accept yourself, you might notice that you are being your narrow self. So the most general question is: How well do you accept yourself when you are being your narrow self? (Discussion.)

7. **Practicing Acceptance**   I would like our classrooms to make it as easy as possible for students to accept themselves, even when they are not being their best selves. The reason is simple: When people are not accepting of themselves, they have two problems rather than only one.

The first problem we have is not being as good as we might be, that is, not fully ready to use all the best we have in us. Imagine yourself being your narrow self. Can you see that you would not likely be expressing what is best for you and those around you? So, that's our first problem. Being in a state in which the best in us is not easily available.

If we accept ourselves at that time, that's one problem and we can work on it. Let's say I am angry, so angry I cannot think too clearly. If that is my only problem, I can say this too will pass, ups and downs come, and I might even be able to do something to make it pass more quickly. Say something positive to myself. Walk among the trees. Think of my wife's lovely ways. Whatever.

It is while you are patiently toiling at the little tasks of life that the meaning and shape of the great whole of life shines down on you.

—Phillips Brooks

But if we do *not* accept ourselves, we have a second problem. So I, for example, might not only feel angry, but also feel guilt, frustration, or self-blame, feeling I should not be angry. I don't want to be angry. I want not to be what I am. Makes it *harder* to keep going. Certainly harder to think clearly about what's going on and what I might do next. Indeed, it is being down on ourselves for being down that is often the larger problem.

In truth, when we do not accept ourselves, when a narrow self quality shows up, as sooner or later it will, we are rejecting a part of ourselves. If that becomes habitual, it leads to all kinds of ills, both mental and physical. It is not empowering to reject a part of oneself.

I recommend we practice accepting ourselves as fallible human beings. We make mistakes. Events happen. Moods change. For one reason or another, from time to time we find ourselves in our uncomfortable, narrow selfhood. That's just the way life works.

When I have slipped, and when I notice it, I like to say, "Well, there I go again. I'm being my narrow self. But no sense getting down on myself for that. Time to move on!" Sometimes I find it useful to say that aloud, sometimes to the people around me. Such an admission makes it easier for me to avoid getting stuck in a deeper slump.

How about you? What works to help you accept yourself when you notice you are your narrow self? If you have trouble, remember Mark Twain's explanation of why you are less than perfect. "Man," he said, "was made at the end of the week's work, when God was tired."

8. **All Of Me** Let me now talk about my whole self. No mystery here. It is all of me. If I were to return to the line above where I listed my selves and put a circle around what are now my narrow and open selves, the circle would represent my current whole self. For good or ill, that's me. Want more clearly to know yourself? Simply return to your own assortment of selves and put a circle around all of them.

When sages tell us, "Know thyself," I believe they want us to know the parts in our circle. When sages tell us, "Accept yourself," I think they want us to accept our whole self. And when my own father told me, as he often did, "Be yourself; don't put on airs," I think he was giving me the same message. What do you think?

9. **Opening The Open Self** You might give these ideas a test. See if they serve you in some way. Here are two experiments I recommend.

This above all: To thine own self be true....
—*William Shakespeare*

- First, try calling up your open self sometime when you believe it might be especially useful to you. You might wait for an important appointment. Or you might wait for the next time a tricky choice comes up. Or you might pick a time when you want to do several things and will not be sure what to do first. Or perhaps you will *not* want to do something, yet feel pressure to do it. Or perhaps there will be nothing you want to do and you will be unsure what to do about *that.* Or perhaps some pattern or habit of yours you dislike will show up and you will wonder how to handle it.

When such an occasion shows up, pause and say to yourself, "How would my open self handle this situation?" Or, "What would my open self want me to do?" You may have to ask yourself the question several times, until you get the hang of it. If you repeat the activity, you might even log the results of each event and see if you can learn something from the trend.

• Or try calling up your whole self the next time you feel off, tight, or anxious. Perhaps say to yourself, "Now wait a minute. I am now being my narrow self. I can see that. But that is not *all* of me. I am sometimes other than the way I am now. Let me not forget that."

See what happens. Again, you might find it useful to log any results that show up. I should add that if you never again feel your tight, anxious or narrow self, no need to worry about this second experiment. Or worry about much else, I suspect.

A whole self lesson with students

Here's how a third-grade teacher reported presenting the whole self lesson to her class.

1. Whole class *5 minutes* Individual writing *2 minutes*	I told the class about my own open and narrow selves. (I didn't talk about my former self or my possible self. I was not sure their concept of time could handle that.) I made two circles on the board, filled in several qualities of my open and narrow selves in each, and then asked students to fill in two circles for themselves.
2. Whole class *2 minutes* Individual writing *2 minutes*	I asked for three volunteers to read any one of their open and narrow self qualities. Almost all volunteered, so I called on five students. Then I asked all to sit in pairs and either to share some of their notes or talk about what I said about myself. I didn't want to force talk if some wanted to keep things private. All seemed to go at this with good energy.
3. Whole class *5 minutes*	I then talked about its OK when we are our narrow selves, how narrowness happens to me (they laughed) and how it happens to everyone. I asked if some would tell when *they* became their narrow selves. Tests and scolding were the winners. This produced lots of comments all could identify with and lots of good natured smiles all around. They all seemed to recognize their common humanity.

Our heads are round so that our thinking can change direction.
—*Francis Picabia*

4. Whole class
   List created
   4 minutes

Next I asked them what helped them become their open selves when they felt "off" and we made a list on the board: Playing with friends, hugs from Mom, etc. These students seem to have a much clearer perspective on life than many adults. I believe this step opened up new ideas to some students.

5. Whole class
   Speak-write
   5 minutes

I told them I wanted to explain more about this. I said I would talk and, when I paused, I wanted them to think and make notes. I gave three mini-lectures on the whole self. I started by drawing one large circle around my two circles and labeled that my whole self. Then I talked about how I and people we studied in history had whole selves, and how each student has a whole self. I ended by recommending they appreciate their whole selves, especially when they feel like a failure or when someone treats them badly. "We all have narrow self times." But as humans, I said, we also have open self times. We are whole human beings.

6. Individual writing
   2 minutes

   Whip around
   10 or 11 minutes

After they made their last notes, I had them think back on all we had talked about so far. I pointed to the **outcome sentence** beginnings I have posted and asked each to write one or two **outcome sentences.** After a minute or two, I asked if anyone would share something they had written, and almost all hands went up, so I used the **whip around** and had all either read one or say, "I pass." No one passed!

In Summary

The lesson led to many new ideas for them. Several said they better understood their parents and why parents sometimes seemed upset. Two said they wanted to take the lesson home, to see what others in the family thought were their narrow and open selves. Several students referred to their "bad selves." I just suggested they call it their "narrow" selves, and they seemed to do that afterwards. Later that day, I heard one boy say to another, "I was my open self on the playground, wasn't I?" They seemed to get it. I'll follow up in some way, although I haven't decided how yet. As I think about it now, I will invite all students to ask their open selves for advice next time they have a choice to make.

We must not only give what we have; we must also give what we are.

—Cardinal Joseph Mercier

Some follow-up possibilities

After the **whole self lesson** has settled in the class, it is natural for students to talk about their open, narrow and whole selves. These words become powerful tools in growing appreciation for oneself and others; appreciation, too, of the magnificence of life in general. One teacher put up a new sign to keep the whole self lesson alive:

> **We can accept our narrow selves, become our open selves, and in that way be our whole selves.**

A Teacher Comments

"It's a running, lighthearted gag now. Since I taught that lesson, when I or a student is 'off' someone is apt to suggest the person is stuck in narrowed selfhood. Almost always when that suggestion is voiced, everyone, including me, the person who most often is 'off,' relaxes, even smiles. Not bad at all."

—College Teacher

"I know they learned it because I hear things like this, 'I'm my open self today, so I should do well,' and, 'Be your whole self, man; don't get down on yourself.'"

—High School Physical Education Teacher

"Students now use being in narrow selfhood as an excuse, as I can't do good work today because I'm my narrow self.... It's not that they didn't give excuses before. But although they talk more about narrow selves, they <u>act</u> more like open selves, so I am happy to say something is working."

—Sixth Grade Teacher

Strategy 17-2 Personal challenges

Inspire students to activate their best intentions. **Purpose:** To encourage students to overcome personal obstacles.

All fine compliments.
All the good wishes.
Will never replace
Help with the dishes.
—Anonymous

Teachers give *assignments*. Students tend to hear them as obligations and experience them as burdens. Teachers can also offer *challenges*. Students are more apt to experience these as stimulating and uplifting. No rewards are needed for challenges. Daring to face them is its own reward. The **learning challenges** strategy offers academic examples. Yet challenges need not be restricted to academics. Students might even design their own.

Over this holiday, I'd like each of you to consider picking some challenge for yourself, not easy but not impossible, and to dare to meet it. Possibilities: Cutting down on TV. Eating better. Talking out something honestly with someone. What others might be possible? Who can think of another challenge someone might undertake?

Let us know Monday if you accepted this special project and, if so, how things worked out. Take a few minutes now in your groups to talk over what you might do. Those for whom this is not a good idea, please volunteer to be cheerleaders for the people in your support group who work at challenges. You might phone them a few times. Do whatever you think makes sense. As our sign says, "We can support one another. No one need be all alone." Be generous with support. It's much easier to win big when we have cheerleaders to cheer us on!

Challenges spur the development of important life skills, including perseverance, wise self-management and often collaboration and communication. Some of the most valuable challenges revolve around the critical issue of self-acceptance. Such challenges assist students in learning when and how to be self-accepting. Here are two samples of challenges that build on the **whole self lesson** strategy.

Narrow self challenges

- I would like to challenge you to make notes on how your narrow self shows up for you. Don't worry about the fact that your narrow self has emerged. If you are as human as the rest of us, you can be sure it will sometimes emerge. When it does, just note *how* it shows up for you. Specifically note exactly where in your body you feel it. Perhaps see if you can associate your feelings with a particular color or shape, too.

  If you accept this challenge and make notes, you can look back and see if there are any interesting patterns. The idea of this challenge is to become more aware of how exactly your narrow self comes to you. It might help you to better understand yourself.

- Another challenge is to experiment with different things you can do when your narrow self emerges. Perhaps experiment with different things you can say to yourself. Or things you can do or stop doing. See what actions have different results.

Open self challenges are a bit different. Two possibilities:

- This challenge is to risk expanding your open self. You might start by noticing how open your open self is. Where its present limits are. Or see how good or generous or flexible you are when you are your open self. Then take a step ahead. Risk being somewhat more open, or good, or generous, or flexible, or whatever comes to you when you are in your open self. For this challenge, you just want to stay aware of times your open self shows up and then consider risking being a little more open. Do not

No man is free who is not a master of himself.

—Epictetus

try to force your open self to show up. Using force that way tends to toss us in the direction of our narrow selves. Just wait and watch, experiment with opening more in some way, and then perhaps draw or write something about your experiences.

- How about accepting a challenge to find ways to get to be your open self more often, or for longer periods? If you accept this challenge, you can experiment and see what works for you. Certainly consider being fully accepting of your narrow self when it shows up. The more fully you are accepting of all of life at any moment, the more open you can expect to become. But experiment on your own and perhaps report what, if anything, works to get you more time in your open self.

Some students might want to undertake a longer-term personal challenge, perhaps to break a bad habit or start a new one: Eating better, holding one's temper, overcoming habits of procrastination. Students usually need support and planning if they are to succeed at such challenges. A strategy for that, the **self-management contract**, is in Chapter 20.

Strategy 17-3   Power inspirations

Comments that inspire students to activate their personal power.
Purpose: To inspire students to develop important personal strengths.

- "Say it as if you mean it," says a teacher to a student who just spoke with low energy.

- *"Stand up tall with a backbone,"* says a teacher to a class lounging sloppily in the hall.

  These are examples of teachers trying to trigger a release of students' positive power. All humans have such powers — to speak up, stand tall, remain committed, act with courage. Yet many students are not often asked to find those powers and shine them out in their realities. Rather than give students a lecture on this, or sometimes in addition to a lecture, I like to issue challenges to do it.

- *"In your sharing pairs, practice looking your partners straight in the eye. Practice being your whole, certain self!"*

- *"Read aloud to your partner with power, quiet power so you don't disturb others, but with full intention, full breath."*

- *"Practice speaking up for yourself this weekend. Practice living with full integrity."*

- *"Please reach to tell the truth in our class. As long as you do not intend to hurt someone, in which case you might do better to keep it to yourself, say what you feel, believe and mean. Even if it's unpopular, tell the truth."*

It will pass if it's partial, not if it's whole.
—Anonymous

• *"When you do something this weekend, aim to put yourself fully into it. Don't let yourself do it halfway. Practice doing things full out and let us know how it went."*

Reminders I find many students needing repeated inspirations if they are to learn the skill of accepting their narrow selfhood.

• *"You are down on yourself. I can understand that. We all get down on ourselves sometimes. Accept that reality. Are you willing to do that now?"*

I also like to remind students that a whole self is available to them:

• *"Next time you have doubts about yourself, call up your whole self. Remember what your whole self is all about. Open yourself into that selfhood. See if that helps you move ahead with assurance."*

• *"Not sure what to do? Even after you talk with others, are you still not sure? Call up your whole self. Set yourself in that self. And then trust your own wisdom. Trust that you will know what to do or, perhaps, know that the best thing to do now is nothing. Practice building confidence in your own wisdom."*

• *"Next time you cannot accept someone or feel yourself rejecting someone, open yourself into your whole self. See if that makes it easier for you to be the way you want to be."*

Personal Power Chart Some teachers like to discuss the positive powers of humans as a prelude to comments such as these. One teacher posts a chart and points to it from time to time. Some ideas for such a chart:

As a Human You Have Power to:

- Speak up for yourself.
- Tell the truth.
- Stand by a friend.
- Apologize after causing hurt.
- Do a good deed.
- Say it as if you mean it.
- Stop what you are doing.
- Change your mind.
- Do what you need to do.
- Pull yourself together.
- Open your mind.
- Defend each other.
- Call on your courage.
- Think for yourself.
- Say "No" when you must.
- Say "Yes" and mean it.
- Go for the gold.
- Accept whatever you get.
- Make choices.
- Be yourself.

There is as much difference between us and ourselves as between us and others.
—Michel de Montaigne

I especially recommend challenging students to express themselves with confidence and spirit. I call these **power inspirations**. I do not recommend they be issued when teachers do not sense they will invite and encourage strength. Also, I do not want to *pressure* students to be strong. I do not want to deny the needs of students to grow by their own timeclocks, live their own lives.

Strategy 17-4   Be choice

A lesson to teach students how they can more often be the way they want to be. **Purpose:** To help students expand their power of choice so it includes beingness.

Be choices are different than *do* choices. Very often we consider what we should do. Should I phone Pat? Should I go shopping? Should I do this now or later or not at all? Some days we make a detailed to-do list. Those are what I call *do* choices. We choose what we will do.

Less often do we make *be* choices. Yet we can make be choices as often as do choices. If I go shopping, for example, there are several ways I can *be* while I am shopping. I can be efficient, aiming to get in and out of the store quickly. I can be friendly, taking time to smile at open faces. I can be adventurous, on the lookout for new foods to try, new corners to explore, new people to meet. When I go shopping, there are many ways I can be and I can *choose* which of those ways to be: Efficient, friendly, adventurous, thrifty or whatever. I can even choose to be without a be choice. That is, I can choose to be spontaneous, open to whatever shows up. That's what I call making a be choice.

Be choices sometimes make all the difference in the world. Let's say, for example, that I choose to phone Ashley. That's what I will *do*. And let's say Ashley is a tricky person for me to talk to. It might be well for me to pause and consider how I want to *be* during the call. Do I want to be my accepting, listening self? My assertive, straight-talking self? My open-minded, flexible self? There are several ways I can be when speaking to Ashley. And if I deliberately choose a way to be, it is much more likely that I will, in fact, be that way. Which might make a difference in the outcome of the conversation.

When we use the **be choice** strategy, then, we pause and choose how we want to be in the time ahead. I usually use it when I make my lesson plans. On the top right corner, I write how I want to be as I teach that lesson. Often I'll write, "Be flexible, tuned into students." Another common one for me: "Be clear and brief." Sometimes: "Be energetic and upbeat." It depends on what I sense the students best need for that lesson. I also like to teach the be choice to students.

Teaching the be choice

What a wonderful life I've had! I only wished I'd realized it sooner.

—Colette

When I teach this to students, I start by distinguishing between do and be choices, much as I did above. I make the distinction by offering examples of my own do and be choices. Then I might say:

> Let's try making a be choice here. In a moment, I will ask you to look around the room for, perhaps, ten seconds. As you look around, please be your ordinary self, just as you might look around the room if I were busy and you had nothing else to do. No talking, just looking around. Start now.

Thank you. Now let's do that again, but this time I want you to write a be choice before you look. Let me give two suggestions. Perhaps choose to be your curious self. Be on the lookout for something new or interesting. Most of us have curiosity inside us; so, if you like, you can look around as your curious self.

Or perhaps choose to be your careful self, looking closely at details, not letting your eyes slide past something too quickly. Really looking into whatever your eyes see.

So choose now which way you would like to be, curious, or careful, or some other way, if you like, and write your personal be choice on a piece of scrap paper. Writing a be choice makes the choice more certain inside ourselves. (Pause.) Okay, please look around now, being the way you wrote you would be.

After asking students to share any differences between the two look-arounds, I might then say:

Please write on your scrap paper how you want to be for the rest of the lesson today. You cannot always choose what you can do, here or anyplace. But you can always choose how you want to be. In class now, for example, you might choose to be relaxed, or intelligent, or careful, or happy. What are other ways a person could be in a class like this? (I simply hear their ideas.)

Choose any way you want to be and write it down now. Writing it usually plants it more solidly, certainly in awareness. If we have time, I'll ask you later if that be choice made any difference for you today.

I might follow that experiment with:

In general, I would recommend you experiment with be choices. After school, for example, you might pause and ask yourself how you want to be when you walk in the door at home. Or, whenever you see some friends ahead, you might pause and choose how you want to be as you meet your friends. Want to be your cooperative self? Your leadership self? Your energetic self? Experiment with be choices in whatever seems interesting to you. Perhaps next time I'll ask if someone would be willing to share their experiences.

I also like to talk about using be choices when a conflict arises.

An example from a lesson The labor union conflict we studied ended with no real winners. How could it have been handled differently? Notice how both parties took a win-lose position. Both were full of conflict, were oppositional, antagonistic. What do you think would have happened if one or both sides paused and made a different choice? If, instead of being full of conflict, they chose to be open, that is, to come at the problem seeking a resolution both might agree on?

Life is like riding a bicycle. You don't fall off unless you stop pedaling.
—*Claude Pepper*

An example from a real-life situation About the fight you two had yesterday, as I understand it, each of you thought you were right, the other was wrong. And both of you were stubborn, insistent. Let's imagine one or both of you paused before things got too bad and made a different be choice. Let's say you chose not to be stubborn but, say, to be open about the argument: You chose to be open-minded and to try to see the whole picture. And let's say you asked someone to sit with the two of you to help you talk about the argument and better understand the whole picture. Can you see how that might have prevented some of the worst of what happened yesterday? Can you see how someone in a conflict could, in fact, pause and choose not to be conflicting, but to be open-minded? Tomorrow, I'd like to role play such a situation with the whole class. You two can play yourselves in the skit, or we can get others to play the parts and you can watch. We'll talk more about this kind of be choice tomorrow. I'm telling you now to give you time to think about this beforehand.

If I had already taught the **whole self lesson**, so my students would understand the words, I would likely include in one of the discussions above:

> You can choose to be your open self if you like. Of course, you may not remain your open self even if you choose it. For you also have a narrow self. That's also part of you. But if you *choose* to be your open self, chances are you will more often or more fully *be* that way than if you made no choice at all. Experiment and see.

It is particularly effective for teachers to model someone who makes be choices as well as do choices. Writing personal be choices on daily lesson plans is one way a teacher can do this. Making deliberate be choices is especially valuable when teaching difficult classes, as discussed in the **teacher balance step** strategy in Chapter 18.

Strategy 17-5 Validations

> Show all students, including those who upset you, that you see them as worthy human beings. **Purpose:** To help students appreciate themselves.

Inspiration is experiencing the power of nature in a bumble bee, the fragrance of a gardenia, and the echoes of silence on a mountain's peak.

—Kelley Shull

Someone may smile warmly at us in passing, for no special reason, just because he or she is happy. It can be heartwarming. We can get the same experience from an unanticipated little gift, or someone taking the time to listen to our very ordinary ramblings.

Such events can strengthen the feeling inside us that we are valid human beings, that our existence is worthwhile, that we matter even when we do nothing special. We might call such messages **validations**. They validate our very existence.

Compare such messages with praise. "Good job!" someone may say. That might strengthen the certainty that we are successful, competent or respected. But it often is a *conditional* worth, conditional on our doing good jobs. It does not necessarily strengthen our certainty that we are worthwhile even when we do not do good jobs. It does not help us accept ourselves just because we are the human we then happen to be.

Many students could use more validations. Many believe they are worthwhile only if they succeed or please others. They are not so sure they have *inherent* worth, unconditional worth, just because they exist. And that self-doubt makes it difficult for them to relax with themselves, to learn with quiet confidence, to live with inner strength.

How can a teacher give such validations? Here are some possibilities:

- Respond to work that students do or answers that students give without praise and rewards, but with, for example, **honest I appreciates, I'm with yous or honest delights.**

- **Smile** on students, even when they do nothing to deserve it, and do it equally for all students, including those who most irritate you. Perhaps challenge yourself and make a plan to give all students such a smile at least once a day.

- Provide all students with unanticipated little **treats** or special events, being sure to say something like, "It's for no special reason. Not because you worked hard or behaved well. But just because I enjoy having you in class. Just because I like you. Thank you for being yourselves."

- Give them such **messages** even when you do not give treats. Use the power of language. The words themselves become the treat. To one student: "I sure like seeing you" or, "Your eyes sparkle today, John." To the whole class: "This is a fun group" or, "So good to see you all after the weekend."

- Simply but profoundly, be very **polite** to all students. Be sure to say "thanks" often, and "please," and "I appreciate." The value of politeness is probably rooted in the human satisfactions that come from being treated as an inherently worthwhile person.

- Give all students some warm **eye contact**, and let it linger a bit, perhaps when they turn in papers or walk through the door.

- Find ways to **show interest** in student ideas, feelings, concerns. One way I do it is with the **new or goods** strategy, as when I start a class by asking, "Anything new or good in your lives?"

The **star of the day** strategy, below, is particularly validating of a student's worth.

Being ignorant is not so much a shame, as being unwilling to learn.
—*Benjamin Franklin*

Strategy 17-6   Star of the day

> Each student has a turn to be the star of that day, with whatever special responsibilities or privileges might be appropriate. **Purpose:** To give every student a regular validating reminder.

I find that students in many elementary school classes deeply appreciate a chance to be the star of the day. For this, I recommend a simple rotation plan, of course, with every student on the list. The day might start with yesterday's star introducing the star of today. That student might then stand and take a bow, getting a cheer from the class.

Any special tasks for the day, then, might be assigned to that star; Running errands. Helping with attendance. Passing out papers. Being always first to be called upon when volunteering an answer. Yet what students get to do is less significant than how they get to feel. And how they get to feel is, once every thirty days, *important*.

By the way, some teachers have a Student of the Week, but I prefer to give everyone a turn more often. For some students waiting a month to feel important is waiting an eternity.

Strategy 17-7   Sensible risk taking

> Teacher reminds students of risk-taking possibilities, allowing students to advance their risk-taking abilities according to their own timeclocks. **Purpose**: To help students learn how and when to take risks.

"We can learn more and do more when we're willing to risk." So says one of the signs recommended by the **truth signs** strategy. But risking is risky. Learning how and when to call up one's courage and act in the face of feelings of risk is not easily mastered. Many students are not even able to risk *learning* activities, often fearing they will not do as well as their friends, or not be successful, or not satisfy a parent's demand for excellence.

How do we help students learn how to handle the risks of learning and, perhaps more crucial, the risks of life after class? In general, I recommend occasionally reminding students of how risks call for courage and, when appropriate, inviting them to practice intelligent risk-taking. Some possibilities:

I get inspired when my boyfriend and I go roller-skating.

—Kim, high school

1. Consider using a **risk reminder** when inviting students to participate in discussions. Rather than, "How many are willing to share an answer?" occasionally say, "How many are willing to *risk* sharing an answer?" Raise awareness that risks might be involved.

   Perhaps add **cushioning**. "Would it be okay if some choose *not* to risk sharing right now?" "Sure," students might say, "How come?" you might ask. Someone might answer, "We each have our own ways and timeclocks. Besides, some of us may need more time now to think about all this."

2. Connect topics being studied to risk and courage. If, for example, a person in a story, or in a history lesson, or in a current event took a risk or backed away from a risk, a teacher might ask:

- Did the person take a wise risk, a foolish risk or what? What makes a risk wise? What makes a risk foolish? What could that person have done to make the choice wiser?

- Given the current state of your maturity, what would you likely have done if you were in that person's situation? What would you have been most proud of doing?

- Have you ever actually been in a situation like that? How did you handle it? How would you like to be able to handle it if it ever shows up again?

3. Make occasional time for extended courage and risk-taking discussions. I especially like to ask students to make private notes about questions like those below and, afterwards, to share their thoughts with others.

- Some risks would be foolish to undertake. Yet some risks, like making a speech in class or jumping off a diving board, can *feel* dangerous but not be dangerous at all. Can you think of other examples? It has been said that a wise risk is one that offers benefits but not serious dangers. Do you agree? How can you tell if a situation that feels risky is really dangerous or not?

- When we face something that makes us anxious, we can call up our courage and act. Courage can be defined as the quality we have that allows us to act even when the action *feels* risky. Can you give examples of when you felt you acted with courage? Any ideas about how you could more fully get in touch with your courage?

- Timid people are reluctant to take the risks many other people readily take. Yet many of us are timid in some situations, but not in others. Are there situations in which you tend to be timid? Are there situations in which you tend to act recklessly, taking foolish risks?

- An impulsive act is different from a courageous act. When we are aware and have time to notice dangers ahead, and we act anyhow, we use our courage. An impulsive act does not require the use of our courage. Are there situations in which you typically act impulsively? Courageously? Do you think animals can act courageously?

- A hero is someone willing to walk straight into the center of what feels most dangerous. Often the hero feels he *must* do that, that something inside him *insists* he do it, even when others think it is extremely foolish. Do you know of any people who acted that way? Is that being extremely foolish, courageous, very aware of inner drives, or what?

Success is not something that can be measured or worn on a watch or hung on the wall. It is not esteem of colleagues or the admiration of the community.... Success is a certain knowledge that you have become yourself, the person you were always meant to be.

—George Sheehan

4. Direct the **new or goods** strategy occasionally toward courage. In addition to asking, "Anything new or good in your life?" sometimes ask, "Anyone had an occasion in which courage was called for?" If so, "Were you able to call up your courage and act? How did it work out? How did it feel to be able to face a risk and act with courage?" Perhaps even make a formal announcement of what might be called "courage reports" or "risk reports":

> From now on, let's have individual courage reports from time to time. Please let us know whenever an occasion arises when it feels very risky to act, in school or out of school. I call these courage reports. Let me know whenever you are willing to offer such a report. Your experiences can help others learn something about courage. You may also be inspiring to us. It's one way we can help each other in this class.

5. Invite students to write notes about their risk experiences and give them to you privately. I sometime use a "thought box" for this. I put a box on my desk and announce that this is my Thought Box. I invite students at anytime to put in thoughts, feelings or experiences they would be willing to share with me.

"I like to know each of you as well as I can," I may say. "I will read all notes. If you add your name to your note, and if I have a reaction to what you say and time to write it, I will write that reaction and return your note to you. But you can use the Thought Box just to let me know what's on your mind, what's new in your life, what suggestions you have for our class, or anything else. You can even use it to show me pictures you drew."

All virtue lies in individual action, in inward energy, in self-determination. There is no moral worth in being swept away by a crowd, even toward the best objective.

—*William Channing*

Chapter 18: Maintaining Our Own Balance

This chapter offers strategies we teachers can use to maintain our own good balance in the classroom, obviously a critical issue if the group climate is to remain one of good balance.

Strategy 18-1   DESCA checkups

Check yourself occasionally to see how you are doing at serving student dignity, energy, self-management, community and awareness. **Purpose:** To keep from drifting off track.

It's easy to get lost in the business of daily teaching and forget our larger purposes. I find it helpful to make a plan to keep visions fresh and sharp. Here are specific recommendations for teachers who want to keep on a track that serves dignity, energy, self-management, community and awareness. (DESCA)

- **Give yourself DESCA ratings** Keep a copy of the DESCA scales handy. Scan them often. Make the image of a DESCA classroom vivid for yourself. Perhaps make a drawing of your personal image of a DESCA classroom.

  Then make a commitment to rate your lessons, not to give yourself credits or demerits, but to refresh and sharpen your memory of the five scales. It will also jog your creativity, and help you be alert to ways in which you might do better.

  Make a schedule to rate your lessons regularly, perhaps every day the first week of each month. Let the repetition of the procedure gradually lead to an internalization of the full possibilities of DESCA.

  Incidentally, you could do your initial ratings on a lesson you watch *others* teach. Regularly rating others' teaching lessons seems to work almost as well in terms of internalizing DESCA possibilities, and is less likely to trigger anxieties connected with not yet being a perfect teacher. If your timeclock for accepting your less-than-perfect self says "not now," it might be smart to start with this method of internalizing DESCA.

Others will treat you with the amount of respect you feel you deserve.

—Marie Hackett

- **Ask for student perspectives** Occasionally ask your students for feedback on how they view your lessons. You might use the DESCA scales or the DESCA questionnaire. One teacher introduced the procedure this way, "As you know, I want this class to embark on a new path, a path that leads to more DESCA for all. And I want to know from time to time how each of you sees the class."

  I sometimes put a pair of students in charge of this feedback-gathering process and ask them to run the process the first week of every month. I can then forget about it, more or less.

Rather than using a form of the DESCA scales to collect this feedback, some teachers post the DESCA scales and invite students to put notes on the teacher's desk whenever they have suggestions for improving some aspect of those five dimensions.

- **Ask supervisors to check your DESCA ratings** Do you have supervisors who must observe your class and give you feedback? Suggest the DESCA Scales. Many supervisors prefer rating classrooms on criteria teachers care about. Give them a copy to use when they need to assess your classroom.

Some supervisors would appreciate a copy of the DESCA scales for another reason: They are open to ideas for what measures teaching excellence. If you believe DESCA might contribute, they might be happy to consider it when assessing other teachers as well.

Strategy 18-2 Teacher balance step

Take steps to keep a comfortable personal balance and, when it is lost, to regain your balance. **Purpose:** To keep yourself together enough so you can teach effectively.

Teachers get thrown off balance, especially from excessive pressures and difficult student groups. What helps us keep our balance? One strategy is the **be choice**. It is my favorite strategy for marshaling my confidence and avoiding projecting anxiety and irritation. I decide how I want to be and write that be choice in the top corner of my lesson plan. I often write, "Be confident and caring." I want to bring neither anxiety nor irritation with me to class.

But no matter what I write, I find I teach with relatively high confidence. Why? The be choice seems to help me shine out my best self. It also helps me teach as someone who knows himself. Indeed, when I make a be choice, I am someone who *chooses* the self he wants to be.

In any case, I know the be choice helps me project a positive personal power. In terms of building and maintaining a cooperative class climate, that is significant. Teachers who project positive personal powers clearly have fewer discipline problems and inspire more goodwill. You might want to play with this strategy. See if you can get it to help you circle in on the selfhood you want to place in front of your students and to help you avoid losing your balance in the classroom.

First say to yourself what you would be; and then do what you have to do.
—Epictetus

What can we do when we lose balance? We each have our own methods. Go for a walk. Talk to a friend. Buy a new pair of shoes. But we can also notice that our lost balance has put us into a narrowed-down selfhood. With that notice can come acceptance. We can say, "That sometimes happens, and not only to me, to everyone. I've lost it, and here I am settled in my frazzled narrow self. Might as well accept that reality." With that acceptance, you will discover, comes an openness. And that openness often brings out one's open, secure, imaginative, capable self. Which brings us into balance. If the **be choice** is my favorite step to avoid imbalance, the narrow self-acceptance step is my favorite for escaping it.

The open self choice for handling misbehavior

I mentioned that the **be choice** helps prevent discipline problems. It also helps when handling the problems not prevented. For a moment, imagine a mother scolding a boy who has just messed up the kitchen, and not for the first time. This mother has lost it.

> How many times do I have to tell you! You are impossible! This is the hundredth time you messed up my kitchen. Get out of here! I'll tell you one thing: You'll be sorry you did this!

There were lots of "you" statements in that outburst. What is the likely outcome? If the boy were a withdrawn, vulnerable type, we might expect him to experience hurt and an urge to withdraw. If he were an outgoing, assertive type, we might find urges to resist welling up.

In contrast, picture the mother doling out a scolding while, somehow, remaining in touch with her larger, open self. This mother has not entirely lost it. Her outburst has lots of "I" statements.

> I can't take this anymore! I want you to know how impossible this is for me! I need order in the kitchen. Even more, I need respect for my property. I don't know what to do anymore! I can tell you one thing now: We must do something about this situation!

This scolding will likely communicate less bitterness, less blame. It rather communicates a mother unable to tolerate messy kitchens any longer, suffering an overflow of frustration.

What is the likely outcome of that second scolding? If that boy were withdrawn, vulnerable, we might predict an identification with the mother's plight and an urge to be kind. If he were more outward and assertive, I would not be surprised to hear a spontaneous apology and an offer to help with the cleanup. (For more on I statements, see **honest I statements**, Chapter 19.)

The moral of the story: How we are being makes a difference. When we are our whole selves, the selves that have access to our good, wise, strong, open qualities, we will likely handle problems with more personal balance. We will more likely react to problems in ways that will not generate negative side effects, like resistance, defensiveness, rebellion, retaliation. We will most likely produce positive outcomes.

There is another way of looking at how our being prevents problems. You may have noticed that some teachers, from day one, have very few problems. Students naturally offer them respect and cooperation. And it does not matter whether those teachers are strict or lenient. Either a strict or lenient teacher

A child becomes an adult when he realizes he has a right not only to be right but also to be wrong.

—Thomas Szasz

could have few problems. Either could also have many problems. The surface style of the teacher is not what makes the difference. Have you noticed that a coach can be a stiff taskmaster or a pure sweetheart and produce cooperative, winning teams?

What does make the difference? The extent to which teachers are perceived by students as caring and confident, as opposed to defensive and vulnerable. Teachers who generate the winning climate are those who students sense are in touch with their strengths, ready to handle whatever comes up, and who are positive, who are honestly caring about the well-being of their students.

Put another way, strict or lenient, easy or hard, loud or quiet, passionately expressive or thoughtfully reserved — all these are less important than what *motivates* the behavior. The healthiest motives, I would say, are those that flow when we stand as an open self, open to the best wisdom, passion and care inside us. The **be choice** can be used to move to that self. It is the self most likely to elicit student cooperation and respect.

In short, it's not only what we do that counts. It's also how we approach what we do. What approach has the best payoff? The approach, I would say, that has us being our best selves. A sign mentioned earlier speaks to this:

> **We can accept our narrow selves, become our open selves, and in that way be our whole selves.**

Can teachers who do not now readily communicate such care and confidence learn to do so? Yes, although usually not quickly. And not simply by wishing it were so. But we can learn it, little by little, in part by getting our nonprofessional lives working well, whatever that might entail, and in part by practicing being open to and accepting of our narrow selves.

Strategy 18-3 Self-accepting monologue

Remind yourself that you cannot expect to behave perfectly at all times. **Purpose:** To maintain peace of mind.

I'm inspired when I fish.
—Brock, second grade

Let's say, for example, you are not in the habit of making I statements. You may prefer to make I statements, but chances are sometimes you will notice that, again, you failed. Perhaps you fell back into a habit of complain and blame: "Why did you do that?" "You should know better than that." "You have to stop that." You, you, you.

Ugh, you say to yourself, why do I not say, "**I** can't understand why that behavior continues." "**I** thought we had that handled." "**I** need that to stop."

What now? When we fail at this or any other preferred strategy, I recommend a firm self-accepting monologue, which might go like this:

> Okay, I did it. It would have been better for students if I had made an I statement or, if that was out of reach, made a silent, note-only response and waited until I was more prepared. But I didn't. Again, I snapped out.
>
> Should I focus on my inadequacies? No. I do not want to focus on my weaknesses. I am not yet perfect. Might as well accept that. No sense in rejecting the part of me that is imperfect. Should I focus on the past act? No use. The question is: What, if anything, do I want to do next time such a situation arises? So let's see, what can I do next time?

I want students to look at their inappropriate act without guilt, without resignation, without dismay. I want them to think about what happened and learn from it. I do not want them stuck in discouraging memories or obsessed by personal imperfections. I want them confident about doing better. Ditto for us all.

Incidentally, I very much like sharing this strategy with students. Sometimes I tell students how I used a **self-accepting monologue**, pretty much telling what I said to myself and why. This teaches a valuable life skill by modeling. Sometimes I explain the strategy to students. I then ask if any of them have already talked that way to themselves and how it worked out. Finally, I invite students to experiment with self-accepting monologues and, if appropriate, to let us know sometime if it helped them in some way.

Strategy 18-4   Reality-acceptance monologue

> Take a moment to remind yourself that not all bothersome behavior can be eliminated. **Purpose:** To maintain peace of mind.

Judy Kupsky tells of a third-grade boy who was keeping her awake nights:

> He was wired with high energy and no self-control. Nothing anyone could think to do had any effect. He kept calling out, moving about, bothering people around him, messing up the class. It was driving me crazy. The harder I tried to stop his disruptions, the worse it got. Finally I gave up trying to change him. Like my stringy hair, I realized there was nothing to do but live with it as best I could. He just was not going to change. After I gave up, I realized the other students were not nearly as bothered as I was. Now, somehow, I don't expect him to change, and I don't fight it, and things are not nearly so bad. Fighting with it was the worst part. Now I have more energy to live with it.

Have patience with all things, but chiefly have patience with yourself.

—Saint Francis de Sales

Somehow we assume bothersome behavior should always be eliminated. When we run across a bothersome student whom we are unable to change, we can easily become stuck in double frustration. He is clearly irritating to us. We are stuck in a struggle we are not winning. We then have two problems instead of one. Instead of just suffering the student's antics, we must also suffer the frustration of being unable to win the change-him game.

When we suffer that way, it often helps to remind ourselves that, like all humans, we have limited powers. We cannot always get things to turn out the way we want. We might as well accept realities we cannot change and move on from there. This might be done with a monologue, somewhat like this:

> I realize I was assuming I could get him (or her, or them) to change. It looks like that won't happen, at least not now. No sense in continuing to fight that reality. Might as well accept it. Let me just deal with the reality as best as I can now and stop worrying about trying to change it.

I suspect that most students have less difficulty adjusting to bothersome students than do teachers because students do not assume they can change others. For them, it's more a matter of how to best minimize the difficulties. To them, it is not an overblown issue.

Strategy 18-5   Teacher talk chart

Keep handy a list of comments to make that are preferred and not preferred. **Purpose:** To keep from drifting off the track you prefer.

Little things pile up to make big differences. The kinds of comments teachers make accumulate over the weeks, often with lasting impact. Elsewhere in the book I note several comments that, I would say, bring out the best from students:

Cushioning statements, to relax anxieties, ease full participation
Power inspirations, to spur students to express their full powers
Intelligence call ups, to get students to exercise their minds
I'm with yous, to communicate togetherness
Plain corrects and incorrects, to inform with dignity for all
Praise and rewards for all, to cheer on everyone equally
Honest delights, to model spontaneous joy
Learning challenges, to spark commitments to learning
Inspiring statements, to call forth spirited action
Risk reminders, to awaken possibilities of intelligent courage
Easing student distress, to be understanding to a student in pain
Validations, to say, "I appreciate you just the way you are"
Calm reminders, to remind the forgetful, with dignity for all
Authority statements, to disapprove as the authority without
    stirring emotions
Honest I statements, to model truth telling

Everyone who remembers his own educational experience remembers teachers, not methods and techniques. The teacher is the kingpin of the educational system. He makes and breaks programs.
—Sidney Hook

Some comments, in contrast, often slow the growth of a healthy class climate. I would so categorize:

> **Any questions?** — which tempts us to re-explain and over-explain and frustrate students who have heard enough.
> **Didn't I tell you?** — or other rhetorical questions with a sarcastic bite
> **Look at how nicely row two has lined up** — used less in appreciation of row two than to manipulate students in other rows
> **Great job!** — when said to only some students, or when students hear it as exaggerated puffery

Make your own charts: Comments I want to make more often, and comments I want to avoid making. We all have different habits and inclinations, so such charts need to be personally appropriate. They can be handy lists to keep visible as we go through our days. They can help us check our progress and circle closer to the teaching style we prefer.

Strategy 18-6 Priority assertion

> Notice when you feel overburdened and then back off to see the whole picture and make plans in line with your priorities. **Purpose:** To avoid frustrating yourself unduly.

Overburden is a common experience of teachers today. There are too many things to do, too many pressures, too little time. Such burden often comes when we accumulate and cannot eliminate, something that results when we lack a basis for saying "No" to any demand. We feel pressured to do it all.

"It's crazy in my school," says a math teacher. "We have all these students with all these problems. No parent support. They are getting ready to add special education students in my classes. They ask me to go to all these committee meetings, write all these reports, write lesson plans a week in advance. And I must now waste time preparing students for those blooming state tests!"

The central remedy is twofold. First, a professional criterion for judging what is most important, because the reality for most of us is that we *cannot* do it all. And, second, the courage to tell the truth, that is, to tell others that we, as professionals, must sometimes make priorities and choose *not* to do it all.

Until you can have a heart for your own failings and suffering, you won't do very well having a heart for other people's. Yet it requires courage to hear yourself in pain, and to observe your pain with respect, understanding, caring and fairness.
—Tom Rusk

I suggest we make such judgments in terms of what best contributes to both current learning and long-term healthful living or, more concretely, what serves DESCA. If an act advances student dignity, energy, self-management, community and awareness, I say we are safe in concluding it is important for today's students facing today's world. We would do well to give it high priority. Additional demands or opportunities that allow us to get better DESCA scores are to be welcomed. Actions that do not help DESCA can be tagged low priority. Those that reduce DESCA scores can be set aside as counterproductive.

Keeping teacher pressures in reasonable bounds this way is basic to maximizing a classroom's efficiency and teacher impact. Without such a process, we are apt to spin and lunge, burning ourselves out in the process.

Then, many of us would do well to practice saying no. Too often we want to do everything for everyone, and we sink under impossible burdens. How does one learn to say no to a request, even a demand, we judge non-vital? I know of no easy method. I do know some teachers have undertaken the personal challenge to learn to do better at saying no and report they do so. Hints from their experiences:

- Start with easier risks. But do start. Don't delay. Practice saying aloud something like, "I would like to be able to do what you ask, but it would be better for me not to even try to do so. I must learn to get better balance in my life. Please forgive me for saying, sorry, but no. It's hard for me to say that, but I now feel the need to risk it. Can you see my point of view?"

- Ask someone to support you. Tell someone you need to make space in your life and you are cutting down your commitments. Suggest the person ask you from time to time how you are doing, as a reminder, as an encouragement to take better control over your life.

- Post a note on your refrigerator: "I can't take care of others very well if I do not also take care of myself."

- Be patient with yourself. When you make no progress, accept that fact. After all, we each learn in our own ways, by our own timeclocks.

Strategy 18-7 Respecting your own stage

> Remind yourself that teachers go through stages of development, and it is unwise to expect more of yourself than is now appropriate. **Purpose:** To avoid the frustrations and disillusionment that may come from unrealistic expectations.

Are you an experienced teacher? If so, the strategies of this book will probably help you expand your instructional repertoire. Are you a beginning teacher? If so, these strategies should help you move through the stages most teachers experience. Yet you would be wise not to expect yourself to skip a stage or do too much too quickly. Consider these three common teacher stages:

1. **Pleasing others** Beginners often start with a mind set on mastering job requirements, getting accepted and, especially, pleasing those in authority. They want students to like them. They want parents to like them. And they want whoever is in authority to like them, at least enough to offer a permanent job. Some teachers call this the "survival" stage.

Ideals are like stars — you will not succeed in touching them with your hands but, like the seafaring man on the desert of waters, you choose them as your guides and, following them, you reach your destiny.

—Carl Schurz

2. **Teaching the subject matter** After some experience, particularly after teachers get tenure, many shift their focus. They worry less about pleasing people, more about getting students to learn the subject matter they were hired to teach. Such teachers are willing to confront students, push them to work hard, even to confront parents: "I believe your son would do better if he did not watch so much TV." Teachers at this stage often feel it very important to cover the subject matter.

3. **Teaching beyond subject matter** After teaching some time at level two, many teachers notice that no matter what they do, some students never learn much subject matter. Furthermore, they may notice that many of the students who do learn it promptly forget it, often within days of exams. More discouraging yet, the teachers may come to see that the students who do not forget what they learned hardly ever use much of what they learned. How often, after all, are adults asked to find the area of a parallelogram or name the battles of the Civil War?

Such observations lead teachers to reevaluate the importance of subject matter. Typically, then, they become less worried about covering subject matter, more willing to give class time to other matters, for example, to the events that excite or worry students. And they become less willing to push students to learn the class subject matter, regardless of the cost in anguish to the student or frustration to the teacher. Such teachers typically open their concerns beyond subject matter to show respect for good living as well as good learning.

Those teachers open to stage three teaching are, of course, most likely to be ready to run a classroom that produces good academic learning and inspires advances in DESCA.

If you are a beginner, you will almost certainly start at stage one, and you might merely aim to use the strategies of this book mainly to help you manage all you must manage. The strategies will almost certainly help you do that. You may find it wise to hold the running of a fully inspiring classroom as a future target. Guard against expecting so much from yourself that you invite disillusionment.

What is learned in high school, or for that matter anywhere at all, depends far less on what is taught than on what one actually experiences in the place.

—Edgar Friedenberg

If you have recently moved into stage two, similarly, you may find it wise to allow yourself to be where you are as long as you need to be there. Many of this book's strategies will help you teach your subject matter effectively. That is one of their purposes. Yet, I do not want to suggest in this book that everyone must do more than be a superior subject-matter teacher.

The message here is clear, "Respect your own timeclocks." Know that you can use these strategies to uplevel your teaching relatively rapidly. You can certainly use them to avoid getting stuck in any level longer than necessary.

If you are one of the few beginners willing to risk starting with a level three focus, know that these strategies can make success easier and more likely. You might even discover, as others have, that you will not displease others by being a level three teacher. You might find many people absolutely delighted that you can teach in inspiring ways. You will also discover that you will not slight subject matter mastery by becoming a level three teacher. In fact, I know of no better way to involve students with subject matter than a way that is inspiring to them.

The future is uncertain. Human aggressiveness may indeed overtake us all. But what have we got to lose by choosing kindness and civility?

— Peter Gay

Chapter 19: For Routine Misbehavior

When it comes to student misbehavior, prevention is clearly the best remedy. It is the easiest and quickest. Fortunately, according to reports from teachers, the high-involvement strategies of earlier chapters go far toward such prevention. But not always far enough. Teachers typically report that once those instruction strategies are underway, far fewer discipline problems show up, and those that do are much easier to handle. But misbehavior rarely vanishes. And, early on, before the benefits of the strategies take hold, misbehavior may not even diminish. If you would like prompt behavior improvement in your class, then, it is wise to be prepared. What preparation is best?

1. **Collect new ideas** Collect new discipline strategies to augment those you already know. Some strategies of this and the following chapter are possibilities. This chapter contains strategies for handling everyday behavior problems, the ones we face most often and solve most readily. Many teachers will need nothing more than the strategies in this chapter. The following chapter focuses on strategies for more pesky cases, the kinds of problems teachers stew about long after the school day has ended.

2. **Make a plan for action** Most teachers do well to make a plan of action. When it comes to improving discipline, it is unwise to rely on improvisation. We do not want to vacillate and backtrack. Perhaps start your plan by listing the kinds of problems you will face. Then group those problems and for each category list strategies you would be willing to try. If you take the time to be specific and clear you will be able to proceed with maximum confidence. Significantly, teacher confidence is a large part of effective discipline.

   No need to include only strategies from this book, of course. Your plan must be right for you and your reality. I would recommend, however, you choose strategies that work without leading to further problems. Some approaches to discipline fail that test.

Habit is habit, and not to be flung out of the window by any man, but coaxed downstairs a step at a time.

—Mark Twain

3. **Step beyond the quick fix** Some approaches to discipline solve one problem and aggravate another. Let's say Billy was disturbing me by talking to a neighbor. I could threaten Billy with a punishment ("One more time young man and I will ...") or embarrass him with a reprimand ("Is your head so dense I must tell you again?"). That will often get him to stop his side talk. But too often it will also prompt him to resent me, even to want to retaliate someday. It can also get him to withdraw from future learning, at least until the smart of my comment settles. It might even reinforce any

feelings he carries that he is not a worthwhile person. Furthermore, it is not particularly pleasant to me to spend my teaching days issuing threats or generating embarrassment.

I could respond with less threat and embarrassment, perhaps by saying nothing and simply writing Billy's name on the chalkboard, as a reminder to him and others that I noticed an infraction of class rules and punishment is now at hand. But even that cool warning has significant side effects, especially in the way it suggests that the worst part was getting caught, not acting inappropriately. It's a suggestion that, when repeated often enough, buries students' growth toward self-responsibility.

Fortunately, strategies exist that allow us to handle Billy's side talk without those side effects. We might call on the **intelligence call up** discussed in Chapter 8, and say quietly to Billy, "Try to control that side talk, Billy. You're smart enough to find a way to do it!" Or call on a strategy discussed below, the **authority statement**, and say without negative emotions, "I need you to be quiet now, Billy." Another strategy below, **redirect student energy**, might have us redirect Billy's attention: "Billy, would you read the next problem aloud to the class?"

Those of us who teach must control misbehavior, but some ways of doing so are better than others. We sought strategies for this collection that are least likely to cause future problems and, in line with the inspiring approach, most likely to teach valuable lessons about self-management and dignified living.

4. **Stay in charge** If you are now teaching and plan to improve your discipline style, it's usually wise to start small. Do not discard all your current discipline procedures. You do not want to allow those students always ready to test the limits to get too far out of hand. It's the wisdom of those who tell us not to smile until Christmas. It's far easier to advance from orderliness than chaos.

   Rather start by investing most of your energy in getting students more actively, productively involved each day, thereby reducing student frustration and time for misbehavior. Use the strategies of the earlier chapters for this. As you do so, make your discipline plan and gradually add some of the strategies of this and the following chapter.

5. **Be inspired and inspiring** In addition, as you go call on your inner confidence. Know you have new strength and insight available, all humans do. Step out expecting that you will be able to draw up those resources if and when you need them.

   Conceptually, the key is learning to expand beyond relying only on your authority and your power to manage rewards and punishments. We can use authority and we can use rewards and punishments. But they are insufficient for the growing need inside today's students to learn how to live with balanced, intelligent, workable self-responsibility.

Discipline is not a simple device for securing superficial peace in the classroom; it is the morality of the classroom as a small society.

—Emile Durkheim

Said another way, the inspiring approach of this book steps beyond a reliance on extrinsic motivations. It aims to inspire healthful *intrinsic* motives. When that is our perspective, we might even make use of punishment. For example, in the situation above with Billy, I might in fact punish Billy. But if I did so I would want Billy to sense clearly that I am punishing him not for me, because *I* am angry or because *I* need quiet, but because of *him*, because I care about him and his future, because I trust he can grow toward self-responsible maturity and, for him and for now, I believe a punishment might spur him to step to it.

When it comes to discipline or any other teacher chore, as mentioned in the book's Overview chapter, we can keep viewing every student, as we can in fact keep viewing ourselves, as being born into this world with innate DESCA. All humans carry essential Dignity. Natural energy. Instincts to self-manage. Longings for community. And open awareness. In the case of discipline, we can ignore those qualities or we can manage students in ways that inspire their development. The strategies of this and the following chapter suggest in concrete terms how you might go about testing the inspiring approach.

Confidentially...

- Please do not push yourself too hard, too fast, if this inspiration approach is new for you. Furthermore, create your own path forward. Stay true to yourself. We all learn in our own ways, and by our own timeclocks.

- And please do not get discouraged at errors or failings. It's okay to make mistakes. That is the way we learn, of course.

- Finally, consider a memory exercise. Recall those times when you could not go outside without an adult, or could not read a whole sentence, or did not know how to drive a car, or were not able to do something else important to you, and then, after you grew a bit more, or after someone showed you how, you were able to do it. What was impossible may well have become second nature to you. You might also recall some anxiety about letting go of the old and moving on to the new, for risks often show up when we face something new. Those memories may remind you that when you are willing, you can go past risks, and in time move into new levels of living. It's useful to remember that any of us can, of course, do more and learn more when we are willing to risk.

Educate your children to self-control and you have done much to abolish both misery from their future lives and crimes from the society.

—Daniel Webster

Strategy 19-1   Authority statement

A simple, direct statement of the teacher's authority. **Purpose:** To employ authority without hostility, and to show students how a person can express authority respectfully and reasonably.

No doubt about it, we teachers have both the authority and responsibility to keep student behavior within bounds. And sometimes that requires us to disapprove of what students are doing. The trick is to deliver such disapproval in ways that are respectful — respectful both of ourselves and of students.

I want us to accept our responsibility and communicate our authority easily, comfortably, firmly, but never harshly:

- When I say, **"No, you may not leave now,"** I do not want the student to hear, *"You should know better than to ask,"* or, *"What a silly question,"* or, *"Do not bother me with such questions."*

  I do not want the student to feel stupid, or slighted or put down. I want the student to hear my statement simply as a fact, the responsible adult's position.

- When I say, **"That's just too much for me,"** I do not want to sound apologetic or weak. And I do not want the student to think I'm saying, *"You should not want to act the way you are acting."*

  I simply intend to say that I have limits. I, too, am a human being. Too much talk or rattling or whatever is going on is in fact too much for me. Furthermore, I want the student to hear in my tone, *"I know you are willing to make that reasonable adjustment to my reality, for that's what people do when they live together as a community."*

- When I say, **"We do not do that here,"** I do not want the student to feel chastised, just informed. I do not want resentment, just clarity.

  I do not want him to think I'm really saying, *"You should have known better than that."*   I prefer that the student hear my statement as, *"You did not understand this, so I'm giving you the information."*

- When I say, **"No, that's not correct. The answer is Washington,"** I do not want the student to think, *"Too bad. I was hoping I was right."*

  I much prefer the student to think, *"Oh, I see. Washington is the answer. I'll remember that for the future."*

- When I put **a finger to my lips** to signal someone to shush, I do not want the student to feel guilty or bad or irresponsible.

  I want the student simply to think, *"Oops, I should stop talking. The teacher is reminding me of what I already know myself."*

Make the work interesting and the discipline will take care of itself.
—*E. B. White*

- When I say, **"Sit down this very minute. Take control of those impulses,"** I do not want the student to feel I am being hostile and punitive or that the student is a defective or uncontrollable person.

  I want the student simply to notice that I am taking charge at a time when self-control has temporarily failed in some important way, that I am doing what is necessary to protect the welfare of all. I want the student to feel that I am on the side of safety and learning, not against him or anyone else.

The simple authority statement is similar to what Ginott (1972) calls a sane authority message. Ginott says it would be insane for a teacher to belittle a student who has lost self-control or to suggest a student should not be feeling what he or she is in fact feeling.

<u>Insane</u>	<u>Sane</u>
You two stop talking. You have no consideration for those who are working.	This is a quiet time. We need it to be absolutely silent.
You have no right to be angry. You know the rules. You must wait your turn.	I know you are upset. The rules sometimes work out that way. But now I really need you to wait your turn.

Three guidelines for authority statements

1. **No hostility**   In general, I recommend disapproving statements be emotionally neutral, like a red traffic light. A red light does not communicate criticism or malice. It does not blame or sting. It just gives a signal to stop. I recommend authority statements be similarly straight and simple, similarly unemotional, noncritical. They are to stir up no more antagonism than necessary.

   Sometimes we can even exert our authority with a playful touch.

   - When a student is fussing about in a way that is too distracting, I might simply pause for a split second and glance his way, with a wink or smile.

   - Or try a joke: "Let me finish this please. I've been waiting all weekend to give this speech."

   - Or simply keep talking and walk near the student, or touch him warmly on the shoulder. Not a sting, a touch of care.

2. **No hesitancy**   I find it best to make authority statements promptly and cleanly, not hesitantly or apologetically. I want students to see me as strong enough to speak forthrightly, not needing to apologize for my responsibilities. And I want students to see themselves as strong, too. I want each student sensing, "He clearly sees me as strong and smart enough to take straight talk."

Every misbehaving child is discouraged and needs continuous encouragement, just as a plant needs water and sunshine.
—*Rudolf Dreikurs*

3. Not unnecessarily   Personally, I tend to voice disapproval more often than is necessary. I like a smooth-running classroom and am often too quick to respond to bumps in the proceedings. A boy may be walking aimlessly about the classroom. Very likely something in me would jump up ready to disapprove. Yet saying nothing might be the better choice. The boy might soon enough get back to work. Or he might not be disturbing others more than they can easily handle.

Even if it is not easy for other students, it might be better to remain quiet. The other students might then need to call up extra concentration power. Or some of their peer-conflict-resolution power. There is some advantage to give students the opportunity to stretch in these ways.

When I too quickly solve problems of healthy community living in the classroom, it sends a signal that I do not trust students to handle those events on their own. That assumption sets up dependency expectations. Students might then expect me to handle all group behavior problems, probably slowing the development of self-responsibility. For all these reasons, I want to avoid intervening unnecessarily.

Body language can help   Body language can also be used to make a simple authority statement. Here is an example suggested by Fredric Jones:

1. Sam and Jim are talking while the teacher explains fractions to the class. The teacher makes eye contact, pauses momentarily, and then continues with the explanation. If Sam and Jim continue to talk...

2. The teacher pauses again, makes eye contact, and shakes his or her head slightly but emphatically, perhaps giving a fleeting palm-out signal. If Sam and Jim continue talking...

3. The teacher calmly walks over and stands near Sam and Jim while explaining, and perhaps increases student involvement by saying, "Now all work this problem on your scratch papers." If Sam and Jim still keep talking to each other...

4. The teacher makes eye contact with each and calmly says, "Jim, Sam, I need you to stop talking right now." (Adapted from Charles, 1992, p. 84.)

Brief explanations can help   Many teachers find it wise to include a brief explanation with a disapproval.

- Please do not touch that material now, Dennis. I'll need it later for my demonstration.

- I want no one here ever teasing anyone in this school. I'm the kind of teacher who gets very upset when I hear others being put down in any way.

Hate the sin, love the sinner.
—Mohandas Gandhi

A brief explanation highlights the reasonableness of authority statements. It makes them sound less arbitrary, easier to accept. Long explanations, however, are to be avoided. Long explanations suggest that we do not trust students to understand, or do not expect them to accept our authority. Such suggestions are often viewed as a teacher failing to respect students, a view that does not serve easy authority.

Also note, explanations are best when they are maximally truthful and personal. Compare:

> Teacher A: Everyone must have work in by Wednesday at 3 p.m. I cannot get my evaluations in on time if any work comes in after that.

> Teacher B: Everyone must have work in by Wednesday at 3 p.m. It is difficult for me to handle the papers and budget my time if work comes in after that.

Teacher B's authority, I would say, is apt to be easier to accept. Students are more apt to believe that it is "difficult" to handle the paperwork than to believe that it "cannot" be done.

Another example in which Teacher B's words are likely to be heard as being more truthful and personal:

> Teacher A: No running in the halls. It's a school safety rule, and I must enforce it. People who run in halls get hurt. So watch yourself and never run in any hallway.

> Teacher B: No running in the halls. It's a school rule. More important to me, I do not want to see you or anyone else hurt. Running in halls too often results in serious injury. If you see others running, please ask them to walk fast if they are in a hurry and to avoid injuries.

Motivation is critical Explanations are especially valuable when the motive of the teacher is not clear to students. The motive, as I see it, is at the heart of effective classroom limits. Let me explain.

You may have noticed that some of the teachers who are very strict are fully respected by students, often very much appreciated by them. Similarly, some of the teachers who are very lenient are fully respected by students and, again, often very much appreciated.

On the other hand, you may have noticed that some of the teachers who are very strict are not respected at all. They might even be highly resented. Similarly, some teachers who are very lenient are not respected at all. It is in this sense that I see it relatively unimportant whether a teacher runs a tight ship or a loose farm. What then is important?

I believe it is important that students are not constrained in too small a space, so the ship is not too tight. I want students to have enough space so they feel they can express at least some of their talents and initiatives. It is also important, I believe, that boundaries are not so wide as to be invisible to

There is nothing in the world that will take the chip off of one's shoulder like a feeling of success.
—Thomas Wolfe

students, so students experience neither the safety nor the guidance that boundaries can provide. In short, I believe the central issue is the extent to which students perceive boundaries as being for the good of all, for the students and the teacher, rather than being imposed by the teacher in any self-serving or uncaring way.

Explanations can often clear up student misunderstandings about this. If students see limits as too tight, explanations can make it clear that, say, I the teacher really need those limits now so I can best teach you, or you need these limits now even though you may not fully appreciate it. The message: I am doing the best I can to care for you. Similarly, if students feel a need for more guidance or security, explanations can communicate, for example, I the teacher do not feel comfortable in being more controlling than this right now, or you may feel insecure but you need to learn to manage your own life, and this freedom can help you to do it. The message again: I am doing the best I can to care for you.

Our motives, then, are critical. As long as we are not too controlling or too lenient, authority tends to be accepted, even appreciated, when students know our intention is to do what is best for them.

Strategy 19-2 Redirect student energy

Turning the attention of a misbehaving student to something that is not disturbing. **Purpose:** To dissolve misbehavior without generating negativity.

Jack keeps tapping his pencil, making loud noises. The cool **authority statement** strategy might have us walk over to Jack while talking to the class and touch the arm holding the pencil. If that does not stop the noise, we might take the pencil from him, perhaps with a smile, commenting, "Take your pencil from my desk later, when you feel more settled."

The **redirect student energy** strategy might have us getting Jack more involved in the lesson, as by asking him a question. Or we might ask Jack to help emphasize a key point: "Jack, say to the whole class clearly — *One percent is always equal to one-hundredth.*

That is, we do not focus on what is wrong. We avoid calling attention to misbehavior. Rather, we use our creativity to redirect the student's energy to something less disturbing, letting the misbehavior evaporate.

- John keeps giving his opinions to a neighbor during class discussion. "John, please write a note of any comments you have about this issue. Later I'd like you to share them all with me."

- A student is strolling about distracting quiet reading time. "Bob, please fetch me that dictionary from the back before you sit down and read."

I lose all my good inspiration when someone gets me angry or when I forget what inspired me to begin with.

—Lee, high school

- Two students are arguing too heatedly. "You two seem excited. Let's try some mental arithmetic. Val, make a guess which is larger, a third of a hundred or two dozen. Tess, do you agree? Here's one for you: What is five times thirteen? Take a moment and work it out on paper, both of you, and see if you are correct." You expect the students will soon forget much of the heat of their earlier argument.

The intent here is to keep behavior in reasonable bounds without generating negativity. Indeed, redirecting student attention in this way often communicates your respect for them, an appreciation that although they might not yet be able to manage themselves well enough, they need not lose dignity because of it. The **calm reminder** strategy, following, has a similar impact.

Strategy 19-3   Calm reminder

A reminder of what a teacher wants that does not communicate disrespect of students. **Purpose:** To keep class proceedings running smoothly without generating negativity.

Even well-intentioned students forget what I've required. It is a truth I sometimes forget. And when I do forget it, I am apt to resent having to restate the requirement. Yet sometimes a calm restatement is the best choice. To preserve student dignity, it is certainly better than a response that might bite or diminish, such as, "Were you paying attention the first time I said it?" or, "Didn't I explain that already?"

- "Nick, I'd like you to notice if the hall pass is on the hook before asking about it."

- "Tom, when our hands go up, it's the signal to end small group talk."

Rather than complain or fuss, I will sometimes just explain the procedure again, as if I had never said it before. No blame. Just a simple restatement. The unspoken message: "I guess this did not register in your memory." No big deal.

I do not, however, always remind students of procedures. It takes a judgment about what is best in a particular situation. See the **once principle** for a strategy that aims to eliminate unnecessary reminders.

The art of being wise is the art of knowing what to overlook.
—*William James*

Strategy 19-4   Next time message

A non-blaming reminder of what a teacher wants next time. **Purpose:** To correct students' behavior without discouraging them.

Moorman and Moorman (1989) suggest that when a correction is needed we focus on next time, not this time. We invite guilt in the room by focusing on what went wrong.

- "Nick, next time remember to put your paper in the box."

- "Kim, next time please ask before you use my pencil."

Next time messages are best delivered matter-of-factly. When I use them, I do not intend my tone to communicate, "You should know better." I do not want to focus on what is already done. I simply intend to remind students of what would be the ideal behavior for next time.

Strategy 19-5   Check yourself message

Directing students to check what they have done, offered with the expectation students will then notice corrections needed. **Purpose:** To remind students to practice managing themselves intelligently and self-responsibly.

- "Check yourself to see if the words are lined up properly on your paper."

- "Check to see if your notebook contains all five items."

Moorman also recommends check-yourself messages when students can use a reminder. The intention is to avoid criticism and to imply, "I know when you check you will see what to do. You are smart enough." Check yourself messages build. Intelligent self-reliance is served.

Strategy 19-6   Silent response

Making a mental note of a misbehavior and leaving until later the consideration of what, if anything, is to be done about it. **Purpose:** To give students room to solve their own problems. Also, to avoid a hasty, inappropriate response.

A student fails to bring in the required notebook. Chats with a neighbor while the teacher talks. Neglects to do work assigned. Or makes a smart-aleck remark.

Pilon (1988), and reinforcement theory generally, says sometimes the best response is a silent response, a response to oneself that says, "A problem here. Let me note it now and see, later, if something need be done and, if so, what."

Sometimes later attention is, in fact, needed. Yet the problem may disappear on its own. That is especially likely if the class climate is increasingly becoming kindly and supportive and there is a growing respect for the teacher who, by responding silently to misbehavior, demonstrates a balance and self-confidence that inspires a respectful response from students.

We keep looking today for an objective way out of the crisis of excessive objectivity. We need something different, something larger.

—Vaclav Havel

Responding to misbehavior by only making a mental note, not by doing anything overtly, is not the response of a timid teacher. It is that of a secure teacher, or at least a teacher strong and wise enough to pretend security until sufficient security does emerge.

Never for danger   I would not, however, recommend responding silently in two cases. First, whenever physical danger is involved: A book is tossed across the room. A fight between students is more than playful. When physical danger exists, more than silence is called for.

Second, when danger to the teacher's mental health exists. We all have our sore spots, where incidents call forth the furies in us, furies quite beyond our control. It is better in the long run, for us and for our students, not to suppress those furies, not to bury insistent anger, not to amass lingering resentments. It is not even good for our physical health. See the **honest I statement** for a strategy for such situations.

Why respond silently?   Why should we ever respond only by making a mental note to ourselves? After all, some experts tell us to act and act immediately in the face of misbehavior, before things get worse. Some thoughts:

1. As noted, many problems disappear on their own. No sense in using our energy to respond immediately to every incident, or to respond when the problem is not dangerous and might well solve itself or be solved by student-initiated self-responsibility. Yet I do not recommend a slight response when our motive is to avoid the discomfort of facing the problem. Students sniff such timidity. Some tend to take advantage of it. It's probably better to call on something like the **authority statement** strategy.

2. The silent response models an adult with personal security, someone unworried that one incident will destroy the group climate. It can be reassuring and educational for students to have such a leader. In addition, it can be strengthening to our own peace and security, partly because as we practice going with the flow, we learn how to live that way.

3. The silent response communicates a confidence and trust in our students, a confidence that they can and will learn to self-manage behavior, that they do not need to be babied, told what is right and what is wrong, at every turn, always told what to do and what not to do. The silent response strengthens the power of positive expectations.

4. The silent response gives us the space to choose what response will produce the best long-term impact, whereas an immediate, more impulsive response will more likely aggravate our problems. It is the wisdom of counting to ten before responding to an upset.

5. Furthermore, an immediate response to a student who has just misbehaved adds awareness and energy to misbehavior. We often do better to turn awareness and energy toward the behavior we desire in the classroom, to accent the positive, rather than to add attention to acts we prefer to see forgotten.

6. This is especially important in terms of any concern for student dignity and growth in self-management. When a student act is singled out for a teacher response, very often a student with questionable self-worth experiences a

Life is like playing a violin in public and learning the instrument as one goes on.
—*Samuel Butler*

further weakening of self-worth. Very often the student feels inside, "I was bad," not "The act was bad." Rarely does the student feel, "Perhaps I can learn something valuable about how to behave in the future."

Final note

Withholding an immediate overt response does not equal no response at any time. I might note a behavior problem and, then, the next day teach or re-teach a lesson to some or all of the class. For example, if I see too much aimless walking about, I might role play walking in class with efficient purpose and dignity, without criticizing any students for prior behaviors.

In general, I prefer to intervene minimally. I believe in leaving enough space so students can practice and learn self-discipline. That requires that I remember to ignore minor disturbances. Which actually makes things a lot easier on me. It also reduces the number of student retaliations in my classroom, for it reduces the number of times I heap criticism on students who are tempted to pay me back whenever they feel diminished. No action is often the best action.

> **A Teacher Comments**
>
> *I like the silent response. I use it all the time. If I had to react to each and every little disturbance, both the students and I would go crazy. My first reaction is to ignore a problem. If I reacted every time someone disturbed the class, I bet some students would only mess up more frequently and get pleasure out of that.*
>
> —Junior High Teacher
>
> *Ginger was repeatedly late to my class, but only a few seconds late. At first it bothered me. Then I sensed Ginger was playing an independence game, that her style was not to go along with authority figures. She was bright enough so her lateness was not serious and it was not prompting others to be late, so I decided to ignore the issue and let her live her life in her way. Interestingly, when her lateness stopped bothering me, Ginger stopped being late. Odd, eh?*
>
> —High School Teacher

Strategy 19-7   Clock focus

> Students stand and watch the second hand of a clock rotate one, two or three times, as they choose. They then sit and resume work. **Purpose:** To settle restless energies. Also to grow student concentration power.

I get inspired when a teacher makes the class laugh.
—"Slim," high school

Sometimes an elementary school class will get restless or too edgy, especially during long stretches of individual work. At such times, I might announce, "Clock focus please." Here's a teacher explaining this procedure the first day of school:

When I call, "Clock focus," here is what you do. You stand, relax, and then watch the second hand on the wall clock. Practice your focus power. Just watch closely as the second hand moves around the circle. You can watch for one full circle, or two, or three full circles, depending on how much focus power you want to practice. This develops your ability to concentrate. It's also useful for settling yourself. Incidentally, you can do this anytime, whenever you want to settle your energies, in school or at home.

Let's try it all together now. Stand and do a clock focus for at least one full circle now and, whenever you are ready, sit and resume your individual work. We will practice this again later, but let's do it now and afterwards talk about how it went. Clock focus please!

This is another strategy I learned from Pilon (1988). I especially like it because it helps students learn to manage their energies and focus their attention at the same time it settles a class. It also develops concentration power. I suspect students like it for another reason: It gives them a chance to stand and stretch and take a break from brain work.

Strategy 19-8   Visitor chair

Without communicating any displeasure, the teacher asks a student to sit in a chair near the teacher as "time out." **Purpose:** To keep disruptive students near the teacher until they can manage their own behavior.

When young students are working individually one will sometimes talk too loudly or tease others or otherwise be disruptive. Often that problem will soon enough disappear, and a **silent response** is the best response. However, if the incident is seriously disruptive, or if it continues, the use of the "visitor's chair," a strategy I learned from Pilon (1988), might be in order. It might be introduced the first few days of the year like this:

Sometimes, class, when we are scattered around the room, one or another of us is apt to lose our composure, talk too loudly or somehow disturb others. When you notice you did something like that, put on the brakes quickly. Just stop it. No one is perfect. We all have impulses that can prompt us disturb others. Be aware when that happens to you and stop it. That's practicing intelligent self-management.

Admitting error clears the score and proves you wiser than before.
—Arthur Guiterman

If someone near you is disturbing others, and you see the person is not aware enough, or not self-managing enough at that time to stop it quickly, hold out a hand like this (flat, parallel to the ground), to signal them it's time to settle down. That might help them become aware and settle down. Let's help each other that way. As one of our class signs says, we can accept and support one another.

If I notice settling down is not coming right away, I may go over to you, or ask one of our classmates to go to you, and say quietly, "Visitor's chair."

Your job then is to come sit in a chair near me, wherever I happen to be in the room, until you settle down, at which time you may go back to your place.

You may want to do some clock focusing while in the visitor's chair. Or, if I am working with a group, I might invite you to work along with us. In any case, you may go back to your own place whenever you conclude you can be properly self-managing again. No need to ask my permission. All of you are intelligent enough to know when you can do that.

Note that when I want someone to come sit nearby in a visitor's chair I do not call out the student's name, "Charles! Visitor's chair please." Such a public announcement often grates on pride, denting dignity, inviting resentment. Either I go over and speak to the student quietly or send a messenger over with instructions, "Speak very quietly to Charles and ask him to come here."

If a student is not being dangerous to self or others and not being seriously disruptive to other students, I prefer a **silent response**. It is often the case that I am more annoyed by Charles than are other students. The lesson they might need to learn is how to keep working when all is not perfectly calm and peaceful about them.

Strategy 19-9   Honest I statements

An honest expression of personal needs and feelings, avoiding comments about what "you" did or "you" failed to do. **Purpose:** To communicate honestly without blaming, without generating defensiveness or guilt. Also, to model a valuable interpersonal skill.

Communication theory teaches us that "I" statements have a very different impact than "you" statements.

I statements	You statements
I hate it when I get interrupted! That makes me feel like what I say is unimportant.	You keep interrupting me! You have no respect for what I say. Stop doing that.
I'm angry at having to say the same thing three times! It's very frustrating to me.	I wish you would listen to me! You did not hear me the first two times I explained.

The greatest evil that can befall man is that he should come to think evil of himself.
—Goethe

"I" statements often lead to mutual understanding. "You" statements often suggest blame and lead to arguments, resistance, social isolation, resentment and retaliation.

I statements get students to understand the impact their behaviors are having on others. They help students see the consequences of their acts in very personal terms, terms they can understand deeply and clearly.

I statements, therefore, are effective in showing students natural consequences of misbehavior. They minimize the chances that students will feel resentful or feel urges to withdraw or retaliate. They maximize chances that students will want to cooperate and be supportive. It's smart, then, for most of us to become practiced in making I statements when misbehavior shows up.

A lesson for students It is usually also smart to teach students to make such statements. Here is one teacher doing so:

> If a classmate does something that is disturbing to you, you might want to tell the person what exactly it is that is disturbing. Maybe the classmate was not aware of the impact of the behavior. You might say something like, "The tapping on your desk is really annoying to me right now. Maybe you didn't know that."
>
> If you absolutely *need* them to stop, tell the truth, tell them you need it. Learn to make what I call "honest I statements." Say something like, "I really need more quiet to concentrate and do my work."
>
> I call that an **honest I statement.** That is a statement that is *honest.* It says how you really feel or what you really want. And the focus is on *I,* what *I* feel, what *I* want — not on the other person, not on what *you* are doing or what *you* need to stop doing. "You" statements get people feeling criticized and put down. We don't want that in our classroom.
>
> I'd like this to be a class in which we are honest about our needs and in which we do our best to help people get what they need. In the long run, we will all get along better and appreciate each other's real needs if we learn to make **honest I statements.** We may not always be able to *do* what others want, but we can always respect others, and use our intelligence, and choose what we think is best to do.
>
> Let me role play how this might go. I'll be a student now. I might say to a classmate, "What you are doing is bothering me. It's hard for me now to do what I'm trying to do." That would be an **honest I statement** if it were true, if it was really hard for me to do what I wanted to do.
>
> Notice that I put the emphasis on what *I* want or need, not on what the other was doing. I don't want to risk putting others down or to treat them with less than full dignity. Blame often does that. **Honest I statements** make it easier for other people to understand our situation without feeling blamed.
>
> Let's pretend for a minute. Imagine someone was messing up your work. Imagine some way that was happening. Then write a sentence or two that would be, first, honest and, second, that would not so much blame or complain but would be an *I* statement, that would talk about your own feelings or wants or needs.
>
> Try it. Then we'll see if someone will risk reading what they wrote. We can then work together, aiming to get all the potential blame out of each statement. Let's practice this a few times.

Some cause happiness wherever they go, others whenever they go.
—Oscar Wilde

Expanding language awareness Ginott (1972) talks about a special advantage of using eloquence and variety when expressing feelings. We can enrich student vocabulary and refine their emotional awareness when we use such language as, "I am feeling indignant," or, "I am chagrined," or, "I feel bewildered and confused about what is best to do next."

Perhaps make a list of emotional words valuable for your students to appreciate more fully. You might then review the list from time to time so the words are readily available if and when a chance to use one comes up. Possibilities: Guilty, sorrowful, panicky, anguished, remorseful, suspicious, infuriated, depressed, awkward, fearful, anxious, glum, gloomy, ecstatic, irritated, manipulated, conflicted, regretful.

Strategy 19-10   Apologizing

An honest teacher apology, modeling respectful social behavior. **Purpose:** To model behavior healthy for mature relationships and to reduce guilt in the classroom.

It's strange how often apologies are avoided. The strong feel they should never admit being wrong. The weak feel they are always admitting they are wrong. Yet an apology is almost always healthful for all concerned, especially when it is a clean, caring, honest "I statement": *I did something that was hurtful to you and I am sorry about that.*

I find it very valuable to make such apologies in classrooms. "I'm sorry," I might say, "that I nagged so much yesterday about neatness. I wish I hadn't done that. Now for today's lesson...." Just a simple statement, without elaboration or discussion, I find often works wonders.

I also like to encourage students to learn the art of apologizing. Once I did this with a high school class somewhat like this:

> Class, I'd like to see us apologize when we make a mistake and hurt someone. As you will probably see, I will apologize from time to time. Sometimes I get too impatient, or too irritable, or too tired, or too something. And I snap at someone or, sometimes, snap at the whole class. I may not realize that until later. Yet I like to come back and say I'm sorry once I get better perspective.
>
> For example, I once snapped at a student and the next day said, "I'm sorry I got so angry and talked so irritably yesterday. No one deserves such treatment. I hope I didn't hurt your feelings. I don't want to hurt you or anybody else. It's just that sometimes I am unable to do better. I'm sorry if I hurt you."
>
> Sometimes I may say that to a whole class. And you, too, might apologize sometimes. It clears the air. It often dissolves guilt. It helps keep a group running smoothly. And usually makes us all feel a bit closer.

It gives one a sense of freedom to know that anyone in this world can really do a deliberately courageous act.

—Henrik Ibsen

To give us a bit of practice now, imagine you have made a mistake and acted in a way that was not your best self. Maybe start by imagining what you could say or do that might be hurtful to someone. Then write possible words you might say, maybe the next day, to that person. After a few moments, I'll ask you to share your ideas with a partner. Maybe someone would be willing to role play such talk for us all. Let's see what we can learn about phrasing apologies.

Such a lesson is often unnecessary. I find that simply by modeling the apology, that is, simply by giving voice to apologies in the classroom when I do something about which I'm sorry, students pick up on the strategy and begin to apologize to each other more often. And I find that contributing substantially to a healthy class community, whatever the age of the students.

A Teacher Comments

Nowadays I go out of my way to apologize to my little tikes. Some of them only know scolding and, too often, beatings. I doubt if some of them ever in their whole lives heard an apology from an adult. It seems to be catching. Little Timmy the other day got angry and blasted some blocks that messed up others. Another boy was ready to hit back but Timmy said, "I'm sorry I did that," and immediately all seemed to have been forgotten.

—Preschool Teacher

Strategy 19-11 Waiting place

A place where a student can conveniently wait until the teacher has time for a private conversation. **Purpose:** To provide a structure that allows a student to be alone briefly and then in private dialogue with the teacher.

Some classrooms of younger students profit from having a special spot designated as a waiting place.

Girls and boys, sometimes I find it useful to speak to a student privately, to tell about a prize earned or to give some personal advice. And sometimes I'll be too busy to do it right away. I'll want you to wait for me, so we can talk privately when I have a moment.

For our waiting place, I'd like to use that corner, right near the door. Let's call that our waiting place. To demonstrate, Victor, will you please go to the waiting place? A little farther back, Victor. Yes, that's the spot.

From now on, whenever I ask you to please go to the waiting place, please stand over there and wait for me. You might do a clock focus while waiting. I'll try not to be too long. Then we can talk privately and you can go back to your work.

I get inspired when I see a beautiful newborn and I'm totally amazed at how perfect they are.

—*Jessica, high school*

Soon after introducing this strategy, it might be wise to ask a student to wait in that waiting place. It's wise, too, to have such initial uses not involve disciplinary events. It might be used, for example, when we want to send a message home with one child or to give a private compliment to someone.

Subsequently, it can be used whenever it would be valuable to have a student disengage briefly from his activities while the teacher is busy elsewhere. Or we might use it to give time for a student to settle restless energies. Or as a place to wait until we can conveniently offer, say, a **calm reminder**, **next time message** or **apology.** Or as a place to wait safely when we have made a **silent response** and feel the need to do more but, at the moment, are unsure what is best.

The greatest opportunity is where you are. Do not despise your own place and hour. Every place is under the stars, every place is the center of the world.

—*John Burroughs*

Chapter 20: Other Discipline Strategies

When the discipline strategies in Chapter 19 are combined with satisfying instruction, most misbehavior tends to vanish. But not all misbehavior. Many teachers find additional strategies necessary. Here are several consistent with this inspiration approach. They allow us to handle our problems without diminishing student dignity, or dampening constructive energy, discouraging self-management, fracturing class community or slowing the growth of open-minded awareness.

Strategy 20-1   Broken record

Repeating a statement that a student seems not to be respecting.
Purpose: To persist in asserting authority without arguing with students.

Canter (1976) suggests what he calls the broken record technique:

> T: Jimmy, we do not fight in this room. I want you never to fight here again. I never want anyone hurt.
>
> Jimmy: Bryan started it. He hit me first.
>
> T: That might well be. I didn't see. But we do not fight in this room. Please remember that.
>
> Jimmy: Well, Bryan started it.
>
> T: Perhaps so. I'll watch in the future. Yet remember that we do not ever fight in this room.

Children need love, especially when they do not deserve it.

—Harold Hulbert

This broken record strategy is especially effective, says Canter, when students do not seem to acknowledge your original statement. Two Canter cautions however, reported by Charles (1992):

(1) When you repeat your original statement, preface it by a comment showing you heard what the student said, e.g., "That might well be. Yet I'd like everyone to hold side comments until I'm through talking." Or, "I understand your feeling. However I need you to stay in your seat."

(2) Repeat your statement a maximum of three times. Do not slip into a verbal power struggle with an obstinate student. If a student is not agreeable after three re-statements, simply put the issue aside, go on to something else and consider later what, if anything, might be the wise next step.

Strategy 20-2 Person-to-person dialogue

Talking with a student privately, relying mostly on **honest I state-ments. Purpose:** To advance mutual understanding between the teacher and student.

A person-to-person dialogue is a private talk between teacher and student. It is meant to be free of blame, rancor, argumentation. Its aim is mutual understanding.

Carla has been disrupting the class by persistently talking to her neighbors. Yesterday the teacher tried a **simple authority statement**: "I need you to be quiet during lessons. I find your talk to nearby students quite distracting." No luck. Today Carla keeps up her distractions, if anything more defiantly. The teacher asks Carla to talk with her in the hall while the rest of the students are busy at desk work.

> T: Carla, I must admit your talking is getting to me. I find it very hard to take. (Teacher pauses)
>
> Carla: (Looks down, watches feet silently)
>
> T: I'm not sure what to do, Carla. The situation is beginning to feel serious to me.
>
> C: Well, stop picking on me.
>
> T: (Mildly) Seems like I'm picking on you.
>
> C: Sure. You never look at others in the class who are also talking. Others talk just as much as I do.
>
> T: (Wanting to communicate that she understood what was said) The other students seem to talk as much as you.
>
> C: Yeah. Right. (Carla seems to have nothing more to say)
>
> T: I don't want to pick on you. Or anyone else. I want to be fair to all my students.
>
> C: Then stop picking on me!
>
> T: I'll try to watch that, Carla. I'm sorry if I did that. I wonder, though, if that will solve my problem. I mean, I'm still worried that you will talk to your neighbors during the lessons, distracting me and other students. (Teacher pauses, not wanting to make this into a lecture)
>
> C: Well, then, stop picking on me.
>
> T: Yes, I'll try to make sure I don't do that. (Pauses)
>
> C: Can I go now?
>
> T: (Uncertainly) Maybe we've talked enough for now. I guess you understand that it bothers me a lot when you talk to neighbors during

The savage in man is never quite eradicated.

—Henry David Thoreau

lessons. And I understand that you don't want to be picked on. So let's leave it like that.

That conversation may not have accomplished much. But it probably did nothing to make the situation worse, as it might have if Carla felt dislike or rejection from the teacher. And there is a possibility that the respect the teacher demonstrated for Carla will get Carla feeling more cooperative, more willing to curb her distracting talk in the future. In fact, such dialogues often do have that effect. They can solve quite serious problems.

It is not always easy to engage a disruptive student in such conversations. The chief danger is that the student will feel blamed and, as a result, will become defensive and resistant to future efforts.

To avoid that problem, I try not to assume the conversation will solve the problem. I choose a more modest target: An increase in mutual understanding. I aim to talk in a way that communicates no one is to blame. It is simply that a conflict exists between two sets of needs. In the above example, it is between Carla's need to talk and the teacher's need for no talk.

A person-to-person dialogue can aim to bring such different needs to the surface. We can expect, then, that often people's kindness and cooperative instincts will motivate an appropriate change of behavior.

I do not recommend persisting if a conversation gets bogged down or keeps getting off track. I might simply disengage with a comment such as, "I don't know where to go from here. I'd like to put this conversation on the shelf for now and think about it more. Maybe we should talk together another time."

Guidelines

Here are four guidelines for **person-to-person dialogues:**

1. **Make honest I statements about what is inside you** Avoid focusing on what the student does or does not do. Aim to be truthful about your thoughts and, especially, feelings. Risk communicating your ideals, anxieties, frustrations, needs, fears. Help the student see that you, too, are a real feeling human being.

2. **Defer to the student** Pause often. When the student wants to speak, stop and allow it. Don't make mini-lectures. Help the student see that you want to understand.

I now perceive one immense omission in my Psychology — the deepest principle of human nature is the craving to be appreciated.
—William James

3. **Every time the student speaks, show you heard** Perhaps pause for time to digest the words. Summarize what the student said. Repeat a few of the words the student used. Or just show attentiveness by nodding.

4. **Avoid asking questions** Questions ("Why did you do that?" "Did you not know I was bothered?") often make students feel controlled, manipulated, defensive. Questions in disciplinary situations tend to result in students feeling inferior and accused. That reaction can be avoided by turning questions into statements: "I'd like to know if you had a reason for what you did." "I wonder if you knew I was bothered by what you were doing."

Strategy 20-3   Self-management contract

A discussion with a misbehaving student that starts with a **person-to person dialogue**, is followed by brainstorming a written list of possible next steps, aiming to produce a written agreement on exactly what is to be done next. **Purpose:** To solve a discipline problem in a way that grows self-responsibility and is win-win for all. Also, to show students how interpersonal conflicts might be resolved peacefully.

The **self-management contract,** as I call this strategy, is similar to what some people call contingency management or contingency contracting. As I use it, the process begins with a step very similar to the **person-to- person dialogue** above. It extends much further, however. As an example, consider this teacher:

> T: Billy, I asked you to talk with me because your restlessness in class is really getting to me. I see you talking out of turn and generally bothering the people around you. It is certainly distracting to me. I get the feeling you don't care to listen to my lessons. Today I even sensed, and I may be wrong, that you *enjoy* disturbing my lessons, as if you get pleasure out of it. Sometimes I even feel as if I'm being teased. That gives me very uncomfortable feelings. And I'm frustrated about what to do. I wonder if you can tell me anything about this.

That is in the style of an **honest I statement.** It is STEP ONE in this **self-management contract** strategy: *The teacher makes an **honest I statement** of feelings, thoughts or needs.*

THE SELF-MANAGEMENT CONTRACT

Step One: Makes an honest I statement of feelings, thoughts or needs.

Risk being as truthful as possible.
Defer to the student. Give the student space.
Every time the students speaks, listen and show you heard.
Avoid asking questions. If necessary, say what you need.

Step Two: Start a brainstorm list of possible things to do.

Get paper and list the first action mentioned, and everyone thereafter.
Avoid judging any idea, yours or the student's.
Seek more than three ideas, even if some are goofy.

Step Three: Seek agreement about which acts to try.

Start by saying which ideas you might accept. Mark them on the list.
Ask student for acceptable ones.
See if both can agree on next steps.
Follow up on agreements. Show you care.

When a person praises punishment, nine times out of ten this means he is prepared to administer it rather than submit to it.

—Anonymous

Often Step One is sufficient. The key is to be honest and show the student that you, too, are a person with feelings and needs. Often a student will respond to such an honest statement more or less apologetically and, thereafter, behave more or less satisfactorily.

But not always. Here is how the discussion with Billy might proceed when Step One was not sufficient.

> Billy: It's not always my fault. Tim does the same thing and you don't notice him!
>
> Teacher: I see. I understand, Billy. It seems like I'm ignoring Tim. Yet I want to talk about my concerns with your self-management now. I wonder if you would be willing to practice better self- control.
>
> Billy (after a pause, with the teacher simply waiting): I'm not that bad. What do you want me to do anyway?
>
> Teacher: Well, I guess the main thing that bothers me is the way you move about and distract me and, I suspect, distract others during a lesson. I really need you to practice controlling that better.
>
> Billy: I'm just kinda restless. I like to move. Tim does the same thing and others, too, and you never pick on them.
>
> Teacher: Perhaps, yet I wonder if you would be willing to consider making a plan to control yourself better.
>
> Billy: What do you mean?
>
> Teacher: Well, let's brainstorm a minute. Let's list some things you *might* do that could help you better handle your restlessness during lessons. Let's just imagine wildly and list some ideas for now. Later we can go back and see if any of the ideas are worth a try. For example, you might put a reminder sign on your desk, maybe saying, "Relax." I'll write that on this paper as number one. (Pause as teacher writes) *1. Reminder sign on desk.* Or maybe you could ask a neighbor to signal you every time you get restless and don't notice it yourself, so you could pull yourself together and settle down. I'll list that as idea two: *2. Ask neighbor to remind me.* Any ideas you can think of?
>
> Billy: Nah. Tim needs to be here too, you know.
>
> Teacher: I might have to talk to Tim sometime, but now, let me think. For three, you could talk this issue over with a friend, tell a friend how I said that behavior was bothering me. See if that turns up any good ideas. I'll write here, *3. Talk it over with friend.* Any other possibilities come to mind?
>
> Billy: Nah. I guess I could walk around some. That might help.

Grant me the serenity to accept the things I cannot change, the courage to change the things I can, and the wisdom to know the difference.

—*Serenity Prayer*

Teacher: That's an idea. (Writes) *4. Walk around.* (Long pause) I could perhaps make up a special signal for you when I need you to settle down, like touch my left ear.

Billy: Nah. I don't want any special signals. Tim and some others need that too, you know.

Teacher: OK. But now we're just brainstorming, and we want to write *all* ideas we can dream up. Later we can see if we both agree some are worth trying. Let me write that so I don't forget it: *5. Special signal to settle down.*

Billy: I could quit this class.

Teacher. That's another idea. (Writes) *6. Quit this class.* Any other ideas?

Billy: Nah.

That was STEP TWO of this strategy: *The teacher starts a brainstorm list of possible actions to improve the situation.* All ideas are to be accepted. And — this is critical — all ideas are to be written.

In the process, all student comments are to be acknowledged. We might paraphrase student comments or say we understand, much like the teacher above did when the student mentioned Tim. The students must know we listen to them, as we want to be listened to. We give students plenty of time to talk. We do not make mini-lectures. We pause often.

We avoid asking questions, too. Instead we make statements. We do not ask, "What can you do about your restlessness?" We certainly do not ask such a question as, "Don't you know better than to keep behaving that way?" We rather state what is on our minds: "I wonder if you have any ideas about what you can do." Or, "If you have any ideas please let me know." When we turn our questions into statements, and then pause so students have room to respond or not, as they choose, we reduce student defensiveness and, more importantly, we keep demonstrating that we respect students' power to manage their lives.

After the brainstorming list, STEP THREE is often needed: *The teacher and student seek agreement on a specific action plan.*

Teacher: Maybe we will think of more ideas to write down later, but let's see if we both agree that any ideas on this list are worth trying. Let's look at this sheet together. I'd be willing to go along with numbers one and three. (Teacher puts a check mark by those.) And I guess I'd go along with number two. (Checking that, too.) Any of those you would agree to go along with?

Billy: I'd agree to try one, maybe. And four.

Teacher: Well, we both agree on number one, reminder sign on desk. Let's try that for a few days. Maybe we can think of some other ideas

There will never be saint without a past of mistakes, never a sinner without possible sainthood.

—Gururaj

to try later. But, for number one, let's be real specific now and work out the details.

Follow-up Several follow-up discussions will sometimes be called for. These might reinforce or adjust the action plan. Follow-ups are especially appropriate for students who have unusual difficulty in managing emotions or impulses, or who have learned not to expect respectful treatment from teachers, or who are accustomed only to rewards and punishments and do not respect their potentials for learning to self-manage their lives intelligently. Here is a sample follow-up, not complaining but holding the student to respect his agreement:

Teacher: I did not see a sign on your desk today.

Billy: I can't find it. Maybe the cleaning people threw it away.

Teacher: Billy, we agreed you would keep a reminder sign on your desk.

Billy: I know, but it got lost.

Teacher: What was our agreement?

Billy: Okay, okay, I'll make a new one. You sure are pushy!

Teacher: (Ignoring the implied insult) Thanks, Billy. See you later.

Why bother Is it worth the time to go through this process? From a narrow, selfish viewpoint, it certainly is. A self-management contract often prevents much storm and stress later on. From a larger, more fundamental perspective, it can be the best means to teach a difficult student an especially meaningful lesson: At least one adult knows that he can learn to live as an intelligent, self-managing citizen and, furthermore, one adult cares enough to take the time to help him do that. It is, for some students, a sobering, heartening lesson.

Guaranteed Does agreement on a plan always emerge? Do students always follow through? No and no. Yet many teachers find that the process itself drains the heat from problems. Many problems cease being serious. Why? Perhaps because the process helps us to better understand the student and, therefore, better able either to accept the behavior or find new ways of handling it. Perhaps because the student now better understands or appreciates our concern, catches our respect for him, and has a new willingness to go along with us.

The smart man solves a problem. The wise man prevents it.

—Albert Einstein

Insist How strongly may we press a student to control impulses? Strongly enough, I would say, to communicate that we trust he can do it, that we have faith in him, that he is not hopeless, a bad person, that he can change if and when he chooses to do so. But not so strongly that we communicate he must do so and do it now, whether his timeclock is ready or not, whether he chooses to or not, as if his dignity and readiness for self-management were of no moment. I want to take care not to get into a power struggle with students. I do not want to break their wills. I would rather wait for another time, another opportunity.

Strategy 20-4   Whole class problem solving

Asking students to brainstorm a list of possible solutions to a class problem and then seeking agreement on what options are best for all concerned. **Purpose:** To get maximum input for solutions to a problem and maximum commitment to chosen actions. Also, to model a mature problem-resolution strategy.

The above **self-management contract** steps can be applied to whole class issues: What to do when too many students are late? How to handle cliques that dampen class spirit? What can we do when the heating system fails to keep the class warm enough? Can we do something to help the students who are falling behind?

A **whole-class problem-solving** episode might go like this:

> Class, before we get started today I'd like to talk about the problem we've been having with class supplies. As I once mentioned, I do not like waste. I wonder if we could brainstorm possible ways to handle this better. Can I get two volunteers to write ideas on the board? Okay, you two, take turns writing all the ideas we come up with. Later, we'll go through the list. I'll see which ones I can live with. And we'll see which ones all of you can live with. Our goal will be to create something that works for all of us. But now let's be imaginative and see how many possible ideas, oddball or serious, we can list that might help us with this issue.

I find several good things about this strategy. It tends to uncover more solutions than a teacher alone can dream up. It elicits student cooperation in the solution of the problem. It strengthens a feeling of class as community. And it models an intelligent way to solve social problems, a skill many adults could well use.

Strategy 20-5   Conflict resolution lesson

A lesson to teach students how to talk honestly about a conflict and, if talk alone does not ease the problem, how to brainstorm a list of possible solutions. **Purpose**: To teach students how to solve problems in a nondestructive, mutually respectful way.

Some of the elements of the strategies above can be used to teach students how to handle their own conflicts. A first-grade teacher reports:

> Let's say someone kept messing up your toys. Or kept teasing you or otherwise made you angry. What could you do? You could scream or hit or cry. But there is a more intelligent way to react.
>
> Let's say a boy, we'll call him Jimmy, keeps pushing in front of the line. And let's say you get very angry at that. You might go up to him and

To me inspiration is the planting of a seed that flowers into action.

—Greg Matthews

say, "Jimmy, I don't like it when you don't wait your turn. I get mad when you push ahead in the line."

You might say that after Jimmy pushed into line. Or if that was not a good time to talk, you might wait until later. "Jimmy," you might say, "I want you to know that when you push ahead in line like you do at the water fountain, I don't like it. It makes me mad."

You do not have to do more than that. Just tell Jimmy the truth about how you feel. Maybe Jimmy did not know he was causing such bad feelings. Maybe he would be willing to cooperate better if he knew that people were getting upset.

That's a healthy way to settle conflicts. What you do is make what we call **honest I statements.** We simply tell the person honestly how we feel. The idea is not to hurt the other person or make him or her angry. Just to get the feelings out, so the other person knows, and so we do not have to keep bad feelings locked inside us.

Let's try a little acting of a situation. Let's say someone took your pencil and did not give it back. And that made you angry. Who would be willing to play a person like that? Thank you Nikki. Who would be willing to act out the person who took the pencil? Okay, Paula, you stand there. Nikki, over there so we can all hear. Now imagine she has your pencil, Nikki, go over to her and simply tell her the truth about how you are feeling.

Several trials might be valuable. And a follow-up role playing another day might be wise. Especially valuable are follow-up questions: "Who can remember what I said about a healthy way to handle conflicts when they come up?" Or, "Who can tell me what I mean by an honest I statement?" Or, "Anyone use an honest I statement in the last few days? Willing to tell us about it?"

I like showing students that I, too, am a feeling human being. One way I do that is to give examples from my own life, perhaps when introducing this **conflict resolution model,** or perhaps as a review.

How you perceive yourself determines what you think you are able to do and that in turn determines what you will try.

—Arthur Combs

I used an **honest I statement** with my neighbor the other day. In their house, they play music too loudly and too late into the night, and we can hear it. It is sometimes hard to sleep. I mentioned it to them last week, just telling them that we were having trouble with the loud music. I asked them if they would mind turning it down. But nothing changed, and I was getting very upset.

So I called them and said, "Mr. Jones (which is not the real name), I am getting very upset over here. When I hear music from your house, my blood pressure zooms up high. My family is getting upset with me because I am getting too nervous, and I just wanted you to know how serious a problem that is for me."

That's all I said. It was an **honest I statement.** The neighbor said he'd try to keep the sound lower, and it seems as if it's lower, but it's too soon to tell. An **honest I statement** does not always solve a conflict between people. But it's a lot easier and safer than fighting or suffering endlessly. I wanted to share that example from my own life.

A Teacher Comments

*I was not sure what to expect, but I thought I'd try teaching my second graders the **honest I statement** way to resolve conflicts. We talked about conflicts in life and about fighting and war and laws against hurting others and even the United Nations. Then I said they themselves have conflicts, and we role played a situation in which a brother kept changing the TV channel and the sister was getting angry. Instead of hitting or complaining to a parent, the sister, quite coolly I thought, said how she felt to the brother. I asked the students to guess how the brother felt when he heard that. The class concluded that the brother would have felt a lot worse if he had gotten into trouble with his parents. Anyhow, the next day one boy said he used an honest I statement when an uncle changed the TV channel while he was watching a program he was allowed to watch. He said it worked! And I think a girl on the playground used it the other day, but I'm not sure about that. I'll bet there will be fewer arguments and fights in this group.*

—Second Grade Teacher

*We began using our detention room for lessons on good living. Last week I had the best lesson in a long time. I taught them how to make **honest I statements** when they were in conflict with each other and how to negotiate differences when honest talk alone didn't solve the problem. I used a three-step model: (1) **Person-to-person dialogue** on the conflict. (2) If the conflict remains, write a brainstormed list of possible resolutions. (3) Go back over the list and try to agree on resolutions to try. As we talked about this and role played this model, it was clear to me that no one in the room (there were about 15) had any idea conflicts among themselves could be resolved in nondestructive ways.*

—High School Counselor

*I made a chart for my classroom called, "Intelligent Conflict Resolution Steps." It was very similar to the chart you had in the pages on **self-management contract**. My chart included the same three steps, slightly reworded. I hesitated about including in step two, as you do, the suggestion that students actually get paper and write brainstormed ideas. But I find unless they write ideas they start arguing about each one right away. When they write, it's easier for them to know they can come back to an idea and discuss it later. So I left writing in and told the class, when I taught them the steps, that it's very helpful but not always necessary. I still have the chart in my room and I refer to it from time to time. Little by little many seem to be understanding, but it's not easy in this community. Violence is the name of the game here.*

—Sixth grade teacher

Women with double first names usually know how to make terrific peach cobbler.

—Anonymous

Strategy 20-6   Dramatic distraction

> Dramatically turning student attention away from problem behavior, as by getting students to talk or posing a surprising question. **Purpose**: To keep problems from getting worse. Also to give time for the positive energies of students to come forth.

This strategy resembles the **redirect energy** strategy, but is much more forceful.

Example One: A teacher is confronting two boys fighting. The teacher does not touch either but speaks loudly, authoritatively, insistently to both.

> Kevin, put that hand down. Move over there. Right there! Eric, sit down right where you are. Sit right down! Kevin, in a minute I will ask you what's behind this. First, Eric, I want you to tell me what's going on!

Blame, threat, whine, complaint, groan, or words to that effect, says Eric. Then Kevin does the same. But no matter. Teachers who intervene with a force of personality often get fighters to pause long enough to allow a verbal venting to begin. I call that a **dramatic distraction,** for it began by distracting students from the battle at hand.

Often it would not matter at all what the students said about the fight. When people get off balance enough to fight, they can rarely explain what is going on in anything close to balance. What's important here is that the teacher gets the students to shift hostile energies from punches to words. It is unnecessary to apportion blame. In fact, in the long run, it is counterproductive. After the teacher senses enough energy has gone out of the fight, she might merely announce:

> Okay, both of you. Get back to your work. We do not want people here acting out angry feelings like that. We all get upset. But intelligent human beings learn to manage upsets so they do not do serious damage. Both of you, pull yourselves together. We want to live together here as one community. Now move on.

Example Two: Here is an example I learned from watching one of Pilon's Workshop Way teachers. She came across two students fighting in the hall, neither of which she knew by name.

> "You," says the teacher, facing one boy. "Count backwards from 100 by 2's. Go!" Mumbled responses.

> "You," she says, turning to face the other boy. "Count by 3's, starting with 10. Go!"

These odd commands, probably coupled with something inside the students that preferred to end the fight if they could only do so without losing face, did the job. The fight stopped and the teacher sent the students on their way. It's another example of a teacher using a dramatic distraction.

School is not preparation for life, school is life.
—John Dewey

Example Three: A group of six-year-olds brought Sarah to the principal's office.

> "She was stamping on our feet, hard," several students complained.

> "I see," said the principal. "Well, Sarah, would you like to apologize to these boys and girls?"

> "No," insists Sarah, head down, eyes hard.

> "Well, boys and girls, Sarah is not ready to apologize now. Maybe another day. Before you all go back, who can count from two to twelve by two's? Anyone?"

The principal can be said to have ended that conflict by distracting students. Perhaps he assumed the time was not right for a more healthful healing or a long-term remedy. In any case, it is noteworthy that the principal did not agree that Sarah did wrong or say something like, "We do not want people to be hurt like that, Sarah. Please do not do that again." Such a statement would likely have not registered meaningfully.

Incidentally, that incident occurred in one of Grace Pilon's Workshop Way schools and, in talking about it, Pilon (1988) says:

> Students *do* have common sense. They do know what's right. And they *know* they know what's right. Scolding, even frowning sends a very different message. It tells them I do not believe they know what's right. I never want to get students to doubt themselves that way.

In the incident with Sarah, the principal probably avoided adding to Sarah's negative self-concept. Sarah may even have learned that a responsible adult trusts her to know right from wrong and appreciates that, for one reason or another, she is just unable now to behave in ways that reflect her intrinsic goodness. If so, it will likely be a deeply inspiring lesson. Later on, of course, the principal might think about what else might be done to help Sarah toward better self-discipline. There is no reason why all problems must be solved in one visit to the principal's office.

Strategy 20-7 Cool-quick-certain control

Forcefully taking control and managing a problem situation. **Purpose**: To protect the safety of all.

Sometimes I forget there are those who are always near me and always caring about me. I will thank them for their reassuring love.
—Claudia Boysen

Occasionally we will face a student as out of control as a wild animal. In a preschool class, Stephen jumps and runs about wildly, heeding for only a split second, the teacher's loud insistence that he sit down. In junior high, Mary is antagonistic. Ask her to lower her voice and she sneers bitterly. Ask her to stop poking Sarah and she gives one harder poke and *then* sneers.

What might we do?

- **Be cool**   Do not show hostility. Act as unemotionally as possible.

> Do not resent the behavior. Treat students out of control as they are — out of control — not as persons deliberately planning hurt. As we do not blame a crying infant with a pained stomach, we do not blame students thrashing without self-control. Besides, blame invites resentment, making future interactions harder. Blame also invites self-condemnation, a hardening of any belief that "I am not a good person." We simply take action, as coolly as possible, as we might if a car were rolling with the brake off.

- **Be quick**   Act quickly. Do not hesitate. You can later change your behavior.

> If the student has exceeded safe limits, act promptly, even if you are unsure your limits are fair. You can always later apologize, which might bring you and the student closer. And you can always later expand limits, if you realize your limits were unreasonable. You cannot tighten limits without inviting resentment, making future interactions harder. Do not show ambivalence; act promptly. Do not communicate that what is clearly unacceptable might be allowed.

- **Be certain**   Act with confidence. Communicate no doubt that you mean what you say and be specific and clear. Request specific actions.

> "Sit down here now." "Put both hands in your lap now." Do not ask for emotional changes: "Control your temper." "Explain your motives." Such requests are difficult for students to fulfill. Ask for a physical act: "Sit in this chair by me." "Stand up and come with me." Or use a **dramatic distraction:** "Count backwards by three's from 57." "Do you remember the name of the capital of New York State?" Do not nag, whine, or scold. Do not punish or otherwise add to the pain in the student. Be the controlling force the student now lacks. Act to stop the behavior.

There is an art to this, of course, an art we will likely best demonstrate when we are being our confident selves. There is art, too, in deciding what is dangerous and what, no matter how uncomfortable it makes us feel, is really not dangerous. I know of no simple guideline for this. Some behaviors are clearly serious enough to require immediate teacher intervention. I would put in this category any behavior that endangers the physical safety of anyone.

One great, strong unselfish soul in every community could actually redeem the world.
—Elbert Hubbard

Some behaviors, however, might best be handled later, in cooler times, perhaps with a special lesson to the class, or with a lesson for only some students. I would put in this category acts that are not dangerous and might later lead to important learnings about how life best works in a community. Examples would be students leaving a mess on the floor and students failing to follow class routines.

Our personal boundaries will, of course, shift as we change, as students change, and as different groups show different needs and maturity levels. We may also choose to accept certain limits or rules because they are demanded by administrators or parents, not by us. I would, however, not recommend doing so if, as sometimes happens, we receive requests that we professionally judge not to be in the best interests of our students. All in all, we must draw our own limits. The core criterion question I use: What will best serve the current and long-term interests of us all?

Strategy 20-8   Calamity procedure

Rapidly, forcefully, calling out questions and directing students to write answers to them. **Purpose:** To regain control of a classroom that has slipped into bedlam.

Sometimes a whole class can use a dramatic distraction. For such times, Pilon (1988) calls them calamities, she recommends we have on hand several sets of questions we can use to capture students' attention. As an example, imagine a teacher has just walked into a room of bedlam. She speaks forcefully, with certainty:

> Everyone. Take out a piece of scrap paper and write the number one. (Very short pause.) Look in your English text, on page 45. Write the last three words on that page.

Short pause and teacher writes on chalkboard: *1. Under the stars.* No discussion. No worry most students have not yet moved to find their texts. The teacher assumes students will follow and moves right along.

> Write the number two. On page 26. Write the four-word subheading in the middle of the page.

Teacher pauses briefly and writes on the board: *2. No one ever knows.* Again, no discussion and fast forward.

> Write the number three. On page 104. Write the first three words of the first full paragraph.

And so it goes. Rapid-fire directions to students to: Write the next question number. Find the page called out. Hunt for and then write the material indicated.

> Write number four. Page 35. Write the caption under the picture.
> Write number five. Page 190. Write the names of two people mentioned in the second full paragraph.
> Write number six. Page 12. Write the first word on that page that rhymes with "river."
> Write number seven. The title page. Write the full name of the author.
> Write number eight. Page 87. Write the place where whales were hunted in 1911.
> Write number nine. Back pages of the book. Write true or false: There is no index in the book.
> Write number ten. Page 122. Write the full name of the man pictured on the opposite page.

I lose all my good inspiration when my mom and dad fite.
—Sara, third grade

After calling out each question, the teacher pauses a beat and then writes the correct answer on the board. The tone is firm enough to catch up some students at the outset and, as the procedure goes on and there is less for other students to do, more and more students join in. Students see that simply by paying attention and moving smartly they can write correct answers, experience success. By the time ten questions are finished, the teacher can expect the class to be somewhat settled, fairly balanced, ready to move on. "Fine," the teacher might say at the end. "Please put that away and let's begin our review of yesterday's work."

No criticism. No complaints. Just a quick-pace procedure to catch up the energies of the class in something they can successfully handle.

Pilon suggests that ten questions be used, for it sometimes takes that many for the teacher to secure the involvement of the whole class. It seems to me that if the questions are interesting enough, fewer than ten might do the trick. Consider:

> Write your name in very fancy letters on the top of a piece of paper.
> On the left side of the page list one person and three things that whistle.
> On the right side list four things you would never find on the moon.
> In the center draw a picture of yourself jumping about on the moon.
> When finished fold your paper five times and write your name on an outside fold.

A single question might even do it, if it served to capture and hold student attention.

A Teacher Comments

The room was in an uproar when I came in and I didn't even know why. But I knew I had to do something, so I yelled, "Everyone sit down and start writing pairs of rhyming words. Go!" I called that out a few times because that class liked inventing simple rhymes; and as some students actually began doing it, which surprised me, actually, I went over to some students I thought might begin writing next if I looked them straight in the eye. Finally I was able to get all but one girl sitting and at least thinking about writing. She was furious with another girl for flirting with her boyfriend.
> —Bruce Maskow, Special Education Teacher

Let us endeavor so to live that when we come to die even the undertaker will be sorry.

—Mark Twain

Strategy 20-9   Temporary removal

Instructing a student to leave the group temporarily. **Purpose:** To give a teacher temporary relief from a problem situation.

It is sometimes appropriate to ask a student to leave the room or sit in the back, yet I recommend that as a last-resort measure. I recommend it also as only a temporary measure. I find that neither the student expelled from the group nor the class as a whole is likely to get long-term benefit from it. Sometimes, however, there seems to be no choice. A student can get too far out of control, too likely to injure himself or others, or simply too upsetting to me.

My aim, when I separate a student from peers, is to find a way to get the student back as soon as possible. "I wish I knew what to do," I have said to a student I had earlier sent from class. I continued somewhat like this:

> I want you to be with all of us in the class. Yet I cannot accept these disturbances. I will think about what we can do to get you back in the center of things. Please, you do the same. If you are certain you can come back comfortably, maybe for a short time, let me know. I once had a student who came in and then, before he knew he would lose his self-control, went back away from the group again. It was a self-managed system. Let me know if you want to try that. I'll talk to you later and see where we go from here. Let me say again I'm sorry I can't now think of a better way to handle this situation. I wish I knew some way you could be in with the group without my worrying about disturbances.

This is the kind of statement I would like to hear if I were that student. It might even inspire me to turn over a new leaf.

Important here is what part of the teacher is being expressed. Is the teacher being punitive, hostile? Or manipulative, self-serving? If so, I would not predict long-term positive results. Or is the teacher being honestly regretful and uncertain about what to do? Or perhaps being her open self, being honestly caring for the student? If so, long-term positive results are certainly possible.

Sometimes a long pattern of serious disruptive behavior exists, and the student is best put in a special class. I believe the priority of such classes, again, should be helping students get back into the community of the whole. I would not want to separate such students from the class any longer than necessary. I would want to move them back into the mainstream as soon as possible. I side with those who believe separation is inherently unfair.

Most of us believe in trying to make other people happy only if they can be happy in ways which we approve.
—Robert S. Lynd

A Teacher Comments

We have a signal. When I point to a student and say, "Out please," he knows it's time to stand outside the door. He also knows I am not intending to punish him. It's not a punishment for misbehavior. I often tell the class that we have no punishments here, that I do not believe punishment helps people in the long run. I therefore say "Out" coolly, without any scold in my voice. The student then stands outside and knows that he can come back in the room anytime he thinks he has himself under control. I told the class, "You are all intelligent persons and able to know when it will be all right for you to return to your work." Students seem to appreciate my respect of their intelligence. That's the only way I use "time out," and it works very well for me

—Special Education Teacher

Strategy 20-10 Positive parent schedule

A schedule that makes it easy to send home positive messages to all parents. **Purpose:** To improve family support for younger students. Also to model a person spreading good will.

Some teachers make a schedule to feed positive comments to families about their children. One teacher, the second weekend after school has opened, manages to phone every family with a quick message, something like this:

> Mrs. Jones, this is Bill Schmidt, Tom's teacher, and I want to take a few seconds to let you know I am delighted with how Tom has been participating in our class. I don't have time now to get into details, but you can certainly be very proud of your son. Please say hello to him for me. Goodbye.

"I've learned to expect," says the teacher, "that the parent will soon ask Tom what on earth he did that was so good. And that Tom will himself wonder. Often students ask me on Monday, before they find out that I called every family. I just say that I want parents to appreciate their children, which some parents fail fully to do, and in fact that I am   delighted with how each of you has been handling the class so far. I don't make more of it than that and it works just fine."

Other teachers address a postcard to each family, watch for a specific act they appreciate, note it on the card and send it out, being sure to get all the cards sent before each month ends.

> Just a card to say I appreciated the way (child's name) reached out to help someone without a partner today.

Any average teacher can fail a student. Teachers who never anchor themselves in mediocrity will always make the poor student good and the good student superior.

—Marva N. Collins

Other sample phrases:

... comes on time every day ready to work. Shows real responsibility.
... had a beautiful happy smile when he walked in this morning.
... is willing to risk sharing his answer even when he might be wrong.
... Helped clean up today. Very helpful.

Teachers who want students to be happy in their classrooms might well help students be happy in their homes.

A Teacher Comments

I started phoning, a few each weekend, but didn't get through a lot. Besides some of my students have no phone or maybe I have the wrong numbers. I tried postcards, writing just one card a day, hoping that would work, but I don't think all of my parents read or maybe the mail doesn't always get delivered. I probably should risk going out to the apartments, but frankly I'm scared. Then I came up with the idea of having older students help me. I have a regular team now. I kind of dictate a message and their job is to deliver it, saying Mrs. Sheridan told me to tell you Jimmy did real fine in spelling today, or something like that. Some helpers phone but most make visits and deliver messages in person. EVERYBODY likes it!

—Third grade teacher

Strategy 20-11 Diagnosing student motivations

Considering what might be motivating a misbehaving student and, when appropriate, making a plan to ease the problem. **Purpose**: To handle underlying reasons for misbehavior.

Occasionally we can discover what is fueling the behavior of persistently troublesome students. And sometimes that discovery is helpful. Here, for example, are three such motives highlighted by Dreikurs (1968):

ATTENTION Some students thirst for attention from others. They want to be heard, noticed, recognized. They sometimes talk a lot and loudly, or ask bothersome questions, or move about intrusively. A few much prefer negative attention to no attention at all and will cause trouble until they get sufficiently noticed. **Annoyance** is a signal; when a teacher feels annoyed by a student, it is often because that student is driven to get attention.

How to ease a drive for attention? Not by forcing the student to be quiet; that rarely helps. Temporarily try: **Redirect student energy. Clock focus. Visitors chair. Waiting place.**

In the long run, aim to help the student get more healthful experiences of being noticed, perhaps through support groups, many learning pairs, and cooperative

It may well be that the greatest tragedy of this period of social transition is not the glaring noisiness of the so-called bad people, but the appalling silence of the so-called good people.

—Martin Luther King

learning activities. I also suggest responding to needy students before they call for attention, perhaps using one of the comments included in the **teacher talk chart**.

Also, I would look for chances to help these students grow in preventative self-control, as by using i**ntelligence call ups** and, especially, **self-management contracts** and by teaching them how to make **be choices**.

I might also seek ways to get such students more healthful attention, as by tutoring younger students or joining out-of-school group activities. In some cases, a home situation can be modified to help, as when students are too often alone at home.

> **POWER** Some troublesome students are driven by a need to exert control. Such students may be motivated by needs for personal freedom, perhaps to be free of close supervision. Often the motive will flow from an irrational fear that harm might result if they do not control matters, as if an inner voice were saying: "If I'm not in charge, I don't know what will happen." Students who carry a strong power force often resist teachers. They are sometimes furiously defiant. **Threat** is a signal; when a teacher feels threatened by a student, it is often because the student has a drive for power.

How to ease such a drive inside students? Usually not by engaging in a power struggle; that rarely helps. When incidents occur, rather aim to defuse passions, as by using cooling-off periods, **dramatic distractions**, **temporary removal**, the **clock focus** or the **visitor chair**.

In the long run, I recommend aiming to help students feel safe, as by (1) using classroom procedures that are steady and secure, (2) including reminders about your own good intentions, (3) using the **whole self lesson** to explain why all people sometimes act in nonpreferred ways and why it is wise to accept such actions, and (4) referring frequently to classroom **truth signs**, especially the sign about timeclocks.

It is also wise to aim to strengthen students' appreciation for the need to learn self-control. For this consider **honest I statements, intelligence call ups**, lessons on community living, respectful reminders and **self-management contracts.**

Consider also healthful ways for the student to vent needs for power, as by conducting recreation activities, tutoring slower students and engaging in appropriate sports or hobbies. In some cases the power of the whole class can be healthfully marshaled, as by **whole class problem solving**: How can we help our students grow in self-management?

Occasionally a home situation can be modified to help the student, as when parents mistakenly assume punishments are helping the child, or when they severely restrict a child.

The Sufis advise us to speak only after our words have managed to pass through three gates. At the first gate, we ask ourselves, "Are these words true?" If so, we let them pass on; if not back they go. At the second gate we ask, "Are they necessary?" At the last gate, we ask, Are they kind?"
—Eknath Easwaran

REVENGE Some students seem intent on doing harm. They may damage property or tease others. Sometimes it seems as if they are paying the world back for pains they once experienced, and sometimes those pains can be identified. Yet sometimes no cause for destructive impulses can be found. **Hurt** is a signal; when a teacher feels hurt by a student, it is often because that student is motivated by revenge.

How can we help students with vengeful impulses? Not by overlooking actions or delaying responses; that rarely helps the student and often leads to further harmful acts. Punishment is also rarely helpful; punishment typically further fuels impulses to do harm. Prompt, assertive, nonpunitive reactions to incidents are more appropriate, as by using respectful disapprovals, **honest I statements, visitor chair** and **temporary removal**.

In the long run, I recommend aiming to reduce inner emotional pain and increase self-acceptance and acceptance by others, as by using **whole self lessons**, cooperative learning, activities that increase group togetherness and strong demonstrations that the teacher remains accepting of all persons, even when not accepting certain behaviors.

Also consider encouraging humor as a safe vent for hostile emotions and vigorous exercises or high-energy sports as a safe vent for physical energies. In some cases a home situation can be modified, as when a student is being abused at home.

Strategy 20-12   Parent aides

> Inviting parents and other adults to visit often and, perhaps, act as teacher aides. **Purpose**: To strengthen the adult presence in a classroom and increase school-parent cooperation.

Many students who would readily misbehave if there were one adult in the room will rarely do so when two adults are present. Perhaps it is the extra pair of eyes. Or the lack of a single focus for their authority-figure resentments. Or the added mature energy in the room. Whatever the reason, having other adults in a room might reduce your behavior problems significantly.

But there are other reasons to welcome parents, grandparents or any adult visitor: It is good publicity for good education. Much public criticism of schooling might vanish if more adults saw how hard teachers work each day in classrooms.

Although it is often difficult to get parents to visit during the day, such visits generally bring parents closer to their children. Parents then share in their children's daily experiences and often, are in a better position to help their children with homework. Perhaps most importantly, parents can see a model of an adult interacting respectfully, productively with children, a model that might well inform some parents.

I expect to pass through life but once. If therefore there be any kindness I can show, or any good thing I can do to any fellow being, let me do it now and not defer or neglect it, as I shall not pass this way gain.
—William Penn

Besides, adults can be valuable aides. One teacher regularly sends a letter home to parents inviting them to visit anytime without making prior arrangements. She also sends an announcement to nearby service clubs soliciting volunteer aides. Whenever an adult shows up, a student monitor is instructed to give the visitor a sheet of Visitor Guidelines. It is simply a note of welcome and a suggested list of ways to help (just sit and enjoy watching the children, offer to help me assist individual students, join in at cleanup time, offer to run errands) and suggested things to avoid (giving special attention to your own child, assisting students who would do better to solve problems on their own).

Strategy 20-13   Discipline squad

> An arrangement whereby several other nearby adults respond in times of emergency. **Purpose**: To give teachers who feel vulnerable sufficient feelings of security.

A teacher in some schools can feel so threatened that calm, confident teaching is not possible. Canter (1976) suggests that such teachers consider asking three or four other teachers or administrators to be ready, when called, to come immediately to help handle extreme situations, as when one or more students are too violent. The wisdom of this strategy is that it can allay the anxieties of a teacher so that he or she feels secure enough to handle problems alone and, therefore, rarely if ever needs to summon the discipline squad.

The risk of the strategy is in weakening feelings of authority and student respect for the teacher who calls on the squad. When the problem situation is so extreme that students can see clearly why one adult alone could not handle it, that risk is minimal. It is further minimized by having the classroom teacher in control of the actions of the discipline squad. It might look like this:

1. A problem arises that is beyond the teacher's ability to safely manage.

2. The teacher calls loudly to the class, "Summon the discipline squad!" Students have been told in advance what to do. Following these directions, some might immediately, say, phone the office, notify all nearby teachers, or run to the counselor's office.

3. Sometimes that announcement alone settles the problem enough so the teacher can handle it. However, the discipline squad will soon arrive. As members arrive, they stand and wait for commands from the classroom teacher. They do not initiate any actions without directions. The classroom teacher is still to be clearly in charge. If the problem has by then eased enough so the teacher can handle it, the other adults can be thanked and dismissed. If not, the classroom teacher directs members of the squad, as by saying, "Separate those two young men. Remind all others to take their seats. Take the one with the red shirt to the hall. Help me check the room for weapons. I'll start here. Mr. Jenkins, please begin there."

I love to teach as a painter loves to paint, as a musician loves to play, as a strong man rejoices to run a race. Teaching is an art — an art so great and so difficult to master that a man or woman can spend a long live at it without realizing much more than his limitations and mistakes and his distance from the ideal.

—William Phelps

Strategy 20-14   Misbehavior reaction check

Checking to see if reactions to a misbehaving student remain in line with plans and intentions.   **Purpose**: To help gauge when and when not to change ones approach.

What is your experience when you see a student misbehave? Do you feel irritable, even upset, as if no student should ever misbehave?

Or, do you react as if handling misbehavior was simply another part of the job, feeling generally able to manage, not upset but rather in personal balance?

Irritable	Balanced
1. Tom should know better by now!	1. Tom doesn't yet know better.
2. Sue wants to make trouble.	2. Sue's lost self control.
3. I'm frustrated and angry.	3. I don't know how to handle this one.
4. He's a mean one.	4. His goodness is deeply buried.
5. Got to get her to change.	5. Is it time for her to change?

If students usually elicit a response from you that resembles the balanced variety, chances are you are on the right track. Your approach to discipline is probably working well. On the other hand, if your response is irritable, you might want to invest in an improvement plan.

Why do I say that? First, irritability is not good for our mental health or our professional effectiveness. Second, students usually sense our irritability, absorb some of that emotion, and that usually makes matters worse.

Most importantly, staying irritable is now unnecessary. Enough practical strategies exist that, once mastered, will allow any of us to manage students while staying well above the level of distress. We can handle misbehavior much like we handle traffic lights and turns in the road, as just parts of ordinary days, not at all as distressing personal affronts.

The inspiration approach in general is designed to lead to that result. Enough teachers report that it does that I am confident in recommending it to others. Yet some strategies serve personal balance in the face of misbehavior more directly that do other strategies. If you would like to look more closely at this possibility for yourself, I especially recommend experimenting with:

We can reveal our riches to others, but it's better to reveal their riches to themselves.

—Anonymous

- Truth signs
- Cushioning
- Leave them be
- Whole self lesson
- Be choices
- DESCA checkups
- Teacher balance step
- Self-accepting monologue
- Reality-accepting monologue

- Priority assertions
- Respecting your own stage
- Authority statement
- Calm reminder
- Silent response
- Honest I statements
- Apologizing
- Person to person dialogue
- Whole class problem solving

Strategy 20-15   Ask for ideas

Sharing persisting problems with other professionals and requesting suggestions. **Purpose**: To broaden the base of a teacher's options and supports.

A tradition has grown in schools that discourages teachers from asking for help with discipline problems. That is understandable. Many teachers, not knowing how to handle all the many problems they faced, sent so many students to others that it was easy to conclude they were not taking management responsibilities seriously. It became logical to press all teachers to handle all problems by themselves.

I believe such pressures are counterproductive. Teachers nowadays need no more pressure. They will do better with more support and more practical assistance and *less* pressure. And this is especially true in the case of serious discipline problems. Trained psychologists have difficulty knowing what to do with some of the students in schools today. It is unfair to ask teachers with all their other responsibilities to know better.

I recommend teachers ask for help early, not late, not to avoid management responsibilities, but to fulfill them most wisely, most humanely. I would include in my own discipline plan the names of two or three people, other teachers perhaps, but not necessarily teachers, whom I knew I could approach any time I needed new ideas or an additional viewpoint. The more consultation, and the sooner, the more likely a wise and effective approach will be fashioned, for the welfare of the students and the dignity of the teacher.

Bottom line: Share your concerns when we need and share your insights when asked. Or, as we said elsewhere, it's intelligent to ask for help. No one need do it all alone.

The good school sees the student, not as a vessel to be filled, nor a lamp to be lighted. Both metaphores suggest that the student is something to be done to, when in reality he or she is something that does, a body the moves, a mind that purposes, a spirit that soars, a life that lives. The good school sees the student as a life to be lived.

— Royce S. Pitkin

Selected References

OVERVIEW CHAPTER

Anderson, L.W., and J.C. Anderson, (April 1982). "Affective Assessment Is Necessary and Possible." *Educational Leadership* 39, 7: 524-525.

Anderson, R., E. Hiebert, J. Scott, and I. Wilkinson, (1985). *Becoming a Nation of Readers: A Report of the Commission on Reading*. Washington, DC: National Institute of Education.

Ashton, P.T., and R.B. Webb, (1986). *Making a Difference: Teachers' Sense of Efficacy and Student Achievement*. New York: Longman.

Carter, K. (1990). "Teacher's Knowledge and Learning to Teach." In *Handbook of Research on Teacher Education*, edited by R. Houston. New York: Macmillan.

Crump, C. (April 1970). "Teachers, Questions, and Cognition." *Educational Leadership* 27, 7: 657-660.

Dillon-Peterson, B. (1986). "Trusting Teachers to Know What is Good for Them." In *Improving Teaching*, edited by K. Zumwalt. Alexandria, VA: ASCD Yearbook.

Frick, W.R. (1981). *Humanistic Psychology: Conversations with Abraham Maslow, Gardner Murphy and Carl Rogers*. Bristol, IN: Wyndham Hall Press.

Good, T., and J. Brophy, (1990). *Educational Psychology: A Realistic Approach*. New York: Longman.

Goodlad, J. (1984). *A Place Called School*. New York: McGraw-Hill.

Hagerty, R. (1995). *The Crisis Of Confidence In American Education: A Blueprint for Fixing What is Wrong and Restoring America's Confidence in the Public Schools*. Springfield, IL: Thomas.

Henson, K. (1988). *Methods and Strategies for Teaching in Secondary and Middle Schools*. New York: Longman.

James, W. (1980). *Principles of Psychology*. Mineloa, NY: Dover.

Jourard, S. (1980). *Healthy Personality: An Approach from the Point of View of Humanistic Psychology*. Riverside, CA: Macmillian.

Joyce, B., and M. Weil, (1980). *Models of Teaching*, 2nd ed. Englewood Cliffs, NJ: Prentice-Hall.

McLeish, J. (1976). "Lecture Method." In *The Psychology of Teaching Methods, Part I* (75th Yearbook of the National Society for the Study of Education), edited by N.L. Gage. Chicago, IL: University of Chicago.

Maslow, A. (1968). *Toward a Psychology of Being*. New York: Reinhold.

Miller, J.P., B. Cassie, and S. Drake, (1991). *Holistic Learning: A Teacher's Guide to Integrated Studies*. Toronto, CAN: OISE Press.

Pedersen, E., T.A. Faucher, and W.W. Eaton, (February 1978). "A New Perspective on the Effects of First-Grade Teachers on Children's Subsequent Adult Status." *Harvard Educational Review* 48, 1: 1-31.

Piaget, J. (1983). "Piaget's Theory." In *Handbook of Child Psychology*, edited by J.A. Flavell and A.M. Markman. New York: Wiley.

Richards, J. (1982). "Homework," In *Encyclopedias of Educational Research*, 5th ed., edited by H. Metzel. New York: Free Press.

Rosenholtz, S. (1989). *Teacher's Workplace: The Social Organization of Schools*. New York: Longman.

Rosenshine, B. (December 1968). "To explain: A Review of Research." *Educational Leadership* 26, 3: 303-309.

Sylvester, R., and J.Y. Choo, (December 1992). "What Brain Research Says About Paying Attention." *Educational Leadership* 50, 4: 71-77.

Tyler, R. (1950). *Basic Principles of Curriculum and Instruction*. Chicago, IL: University of Chicago Press.

Zumwalt, K., editor, (1986). *Improving Teaching*. Alexandria, VA: ASCD Yearbook.

CHAPTER 1. HIGH-INVOLVEMENT LESSONS

Bellanca, J., and Fogarty, R. (1990). *Blueprints for Cooperative Learning in the Thinking Classroom.* Palatine, IL: Skylight.

Brandt, R. ed. (1989). *Readings from Educational Leadership: Teaching Thinking.* Alexandria, VA: ASCD.

Bruner, J., J.J. Goodnow, and G. Austin, (1956). *A Study of Thinking.* New York: Wiley.

Cornett, L., and G. Gaines, (1994). *Reflecting on Ten Years of Incentive Programs.* Atlanta, GA: Southern Regional Educational Board.

Costa, A., and L. Lowrey, (1989). *Techniques for Teaching Thinking.* Pacific Grove, CA: Midwest Publications.

Crump, C. (April 1970). "Teachers, Questions, and Cognition." *Educational Leadership* 27, 7: 657-660.

Dillon, J.T. (November 1984). "Research on Questioning and Discussion." *Educational Leadership* 42, 3: 50-56.

Dillon, J.T. (1988). *Questioning and Teaching.* New York: Teachers College Press.

Gabbert, B., D.W. Johnson, and R. Johnson, (1986). "Cooperative Learning, Group-to-Individual Transfer, Process Gain, and the Acquisition of Cognitive Reasoning Strategies." *Journal of Psychology* 120: 265-278.

Gall, M. (December 1970). "The Use of Questions in Teaching." *Review of Educational Research* 40, 5: 207-220.

Johnson, D.W., and R. Johnson, (1987). *Creative Conflict.* Edina, MN: Interaction Book Company.

Johnson, D.W., and R. Johnson, (1989). *Cooperation and Competition: Theory and Research.* Edina, MN: Interaction Book Company.

McTighe, J., and F.T. Lyman, Jr. (April 1988). "Cueing Thinking in the Classroom: The Promise of Theory-Embedded Tools." *Educational Leadership* 45, 7: 18-24.

Redfield, D., and E. Rousseau, (Summer 1981). "A Meta-Analysis on Teacher Questioning Behavior." *Review of Educational Research* 51: 234-245.

Riley, J. (1980). *The Effects of Teachers' Wait-time and Cognitive Questioning Level on Pupil Science Development.* Paper presented at the Annual Meeting of the National Association for Research in Science Teaching, Boston, MA.

Rosenshine, B. (1976). "Classroom Instruction." In *Psychology of Teaching: The 77th Yearbook of the National Study of Education,* edited by N. Gage. Chicago: University of Chicago Press.

Rosenshine, B. (1979). "Content, Time and Direct Instruction." *Research on Teaching,* edited by P.L. Peterson and H.J. Walberg. Berkeley, CA: McCutchan.

Rowe, M.B. (January-February 1986). "Wait Time: Slowing Down May Be a Way of Speeding Up!" *The Journal of Teacher Education* 31, 1: 43-50.

Slavin, R. (May 1981). "Synthesis of Research on Cooperative Learning. "*Educational Leadership* 38, 8: 655-660.

Taba, H. (May 1965). "Teaching of Thinking." *Elementary English* 42, 2: 534.

Taba, H., S. Levine, and F. Elzey, (1964). *Thinking in Elementary School Children.* San Francisco: San Francisco State College. Cooperative Research Project No. 1574.

CHAPTER 2. EVERYDAY INSTRUCTION STRATEGIES

Annis, L. (1983). "The Processes and Effects of Peer Tutoring." *Human Learning* 2: 39-47.

Baumann, J.F. (1992). "Effect of Think-Aloud Instruction on Elementary Students' Comprehension Monitoring Abilities." *Journal of Reading Behavior* 24, 2: 143-172.

Borko, H., K.H. Davinroy, M.D. Flory, and G.H. Hieberrt, (1994). "Teachers' Knowledge and Benefits about Summary as a Component of Reading." In *Beliefs about Texts and Instruction with Text,* edited by R. Garner and P.A. Alexander, pp. 155-182. Hillside, NJ: Lawrence Erlbaum Associates.

Crump, C. (April 1970). "Teachers, Questions, and Cognition." *Educational Leadership* 27, 7: 657-660.

Cummings, C. (1980). *Teaching Makes a Difference*. Edmonds, WA: Teaching Inc.

Hunter, M.C. (1976). *Rx: Improved Instruction*. El Segundo, CA: T.I.P. Publications.

Jones, B.F., M.R. Amiran, and M. Katims, (1985). "Teaching Cognitive Strategies and Text Structures." *Thinking and Learning Skills: Relating Instruction to Research. Vol. 1*, edited by J. Segal, S.F. Chipman, and R. Glaser. Hillsdale, NJ: Lawrence Erlbaum.

Jones, B.F., A.S. Palincsar, D.S. Ogle, and E.F. Carr, eds. (1987). *Strategic Teaching and Learning: Cognitive Instruction in the Content Areas*. Alexandria, VA: ASCD.

Joyce, B., and Weil, M. (1991). *Models of Teaching*. Englewood Cliffs, NJ: Prentice-Hall.

Palincsar, A.S. (October 1986). "Metacognitive Strategy Instruction." *Exceptional Children* 53, 2: 118-124.

Palincsar, A.S., and D.A. Brown, (February 1987). "Enhancing Instructional Time Through Attention to Metacognition." *Journal of Learning Disabilities* 20, 2: 66-75.

Rosenshine, B. (1979). "Content, Time and Direct Instruction." *Research on Teaching*, edited by P.L. Peterson and H.J. Walberg. Berkeley, CA: McCutchan.

Rowe, M.B. (Spring 1974). "Wait Time and Rewards as Instructional Variables: Their Influence on Language, Logic, and Fate Control." *Journal of Research in Science Teaching* 11, 2: 81-84.

Sanders, N. (1966). *Classroom Questions: What Kinds*. New York: Harper and Row.

Walberg, H.J. (September 1986). "What Works in a Nation Still at Risk." *Educational Leadership* 44, 1: 7-10.

Walberg, H.J. (March 1988). "Synthesis of Research on Time and Learning." *Educational Leadership* 45, 6: 76-85.

Wasserman, S. (1988). *The Asking of Wonderful Questions*. Bloomington, IN: Phi Delta Kappa.

Widaman, K.F., and S. Kagan, (Winter 1987). "Cooperativeness and Achievement: Interaction of Student Cooperativeness with Cooperative versus Competitive Classroom Organization." *Journal of School Psychology* 25, 4: 355-365.

CHAPTER 3. FOR SOLID STUDENT CONFIDENCE

Adams, A., and E.L. Bebensee, (1983). *Success in Reading and Writing*. Glenview, IL: Good Year.

Akin, T. (1992). *The Best Self-Esteem Activities for the Elementary Grades*. Spring Valley, CA: Innerchoice.

Caine, R., and G. Caine, (1991). *Making Connections: Teaching and the Human Brain*. Alexandria, VA: ASCD.

Canfield, J. (September 1990). "Improving Students' Self-Esteem." *Educational Leadership* 48, 1: 48-50.

Cummings, C. (1983). *Managing to Teach*. Edmonds, WA: Teaching Inc.

Emmer, E., and C. Everston, (December 1980/January 1981). "Synthesis of Research on Classroom Management." *Educational Leadership* 38, 4: 342-347.

Guetzloe, E. (1994). "Risk, Resilience, and Protection." *Journal of Emotional and Behavioral Problems* 3, 2: 2-5.

Harmin, M. (1990). *How to Plan a Program for Moral Education*. Alexandria, VA: ASCD.

Hart, L. (1975). *How the Brain Works*. New York: Basic Books.

Hart, L. (1983). *Human Brain, Human Learning*. New York: Longman.

Joyce, B. and M. Weil, (1992). *Models of Teaching*. Englewood Cliffs, NJ: Prentice-Hall.

Kindsvetter, R. and W. Wilen, (1989). *Dynamics of Effective Teaching*. New York: Longman.

Pilon, G. (1988). Workshop Way. New Orleans, LA: The Workshop Way.

Marzano, R.J. (1992). *A Different Kind of Classroom: Teaching with Dimensions of Learning*. Alexandria, VA: ASCD.

Nave, B. (December 1990). *Self-Esteem: The Key to Student Success. A Series of Solutions and Strategies. Number 3*. Clemson, SC: National Dropout Prevention Center.

CHAPTER 4. BEYOND PRAISE AND REWARDS

Brophy, J.E. (1981). "Teacher Praise: A Functional Analysis." Occasional Paper No. 28. East Lansing: Michigan State University Institute for Research on Teaching.

Deci, E.L. (1978). "Application of Research on the Effect of Rewards." In *The Hidden Costs of Rewards: New Perspectives on the Psychology of Human Motivation*, edited by M. Lepper and D. Greene. Hillsdale, NJ: Lawrence Erlbaum

Emmer, E.T. (1988). "Praise and the Instructional Process. "*Journal of Classroom Interaction* 23, 2: 32-39.

Gibbs, J. (1987). *Tribes: A Process for Social Development and Cooperative Learning*. Santa Rosa, CA: Center Source Publications.

Hunter, M.D., and P.V. Carlson, (1971). *Improving Your Child's Behavior*. Glendale, CA: Bowmar.

Lepper, M. and D. Greene, eds. (1978). *The Hidden Costs of Rewards: New Perspectives on the Psychology of Human Motivation*. Hillsdale, NJ: Lawrence Erlbaum.

Murray, F.B. (1989). "Explanations in Education." In *Knowledge Base for the Beginning Teacher*, edited by M.C. Reynolds. New York: Pergamon.

CHAPTER 5. RAISING STANDARDS OF EXCELLENCE

Anderson, L.M. (1989). "Classroom Instruction." In *Knowledge Base for Beginning Teacher,* edited by M.C. Reynolds. New York: Pergamon.

Brandt, R., ed. (1989). *Readings from Educational Leadership: Teaching Thinking*. Alexandria, VA: ASCD.

Crump, C. (April 1970). "Teachers, Questions, and Cognition." *Educational Leadership* 27, 7: 657-660.

Cummings, C. (1980). *Teaching Makes a Difference*. Edmonds, WA: Teaching Inc.

Cummings, C. (1983). *Managing to Teach*. Edmonds, WA: Teaching Inc.

Hunter, M.C. (1976). *Rx: Improved Instruction*. El Segundo, CA: T.I.P. Publications.

Johnson, D.W., R.T. Johnson, E.J. Holubec, and P. Roy, (1984). *Circles of Learning: Cooperation in the Classroom*. Alexandria, VA: ASCD.

Joyce, B., and M. Weil, (1992). *Models of Teaching*. Englewood Cliffs, NJ: Prentice-Hall.

CHAPTER 6. EVERYDAY GROUP STRATEGIES

Aronson, E., et al. (1978). *The Jigsaw Classroom*. Beverly Hills, CA: Sage.

Bellanca, J, and R. Fogarty, (1990). *Blueprints for Cooperative Learning in the Thinking Classroom*. Palatine, IL: Skylight Publishing.

Carr, E., and D. Ogle, (April 1987). "K-W-L Plus: A Strategy for Comprehension and Summarization." *Journal of Reading* 30, 7: 626-631.

Cummings, C. (1983). *Managing to Teach*. Edmonds, WA: Teaching Inc.

Gabbert, B., D.W. Johnson, and R. Johnson, (1986). "Cooperative Learning, Group-to-Individual Transfer, Process Gain, and the Acquisition of Cognitive Reasoning Strategies." *Journal of Psychology* 120: 265-278.

Johnson, D.W., R.T. Johnson, E.J. Holubec, and P. Roy, (1984). *Circles of Learning: Cooperation in the Classroom*. Alexandria, VA: ASCD.

Johnson, D.W., and R. Johnson, (1987). *Creative Conflict*. Edina, MN: Interaction Book Company.

Johnson, D.W., and R. Johnson, (May 1988). "Critical Thinking Through Structured Controversy." *Educational Leadership* 45, 8: 58-64.

Johnson, D.W., and R. Johnson, (1989). *Cooperation and Competition: Theory and Research*. Edina, Minn.: Interaction Book Company.

Schmuck, R. and P. Schmuck, (1988). *Group Processes in the Classroom*. Dubuque, IA: William C. Brown.

Sharan, Y., and S. Sharan, (December 1989/January, 1990). "Group Investigation Expands Cooperative Learning." *Educational Leadership* 47, 4: 17-21.

Slavin, R. (May 1981). "Synthesis of Research on Cooperative Learning." *Educational Leadership* 38, 8: 655-660.

CHAPTER 7. EFFICIENT GROUP PROCEDURES

Bellanca, J, and R. Fogarty, (1990). *Blueprints for Cooperative Learning in the Thinking Classroom.* Palatine, IL: Skylight Publishing.

Evertson, C. (1989). "Classroom Organization and Management." In *Knowledge Base for the Beginning Teacher*, edited by M.C. Reynolds. New York: Pergamon.

Johnson, D.W., and R. Johnson, (1989). *Cooperation and Competition: Theory and Research.* Edina, MN: Interaction Book Company.

Johnson, D.W., et al. (1984). *Circles of Learning: Cooperation in the Classroom.* Alexandria, VA: ASCD.

Kagan, S. (December 1989/January 1990). "The Structural Approach to Cooperative Learning." *Educational Leadership* 47, 4: 12-15.

Midkiff, R. Bostick, and R.D. Thomasson, (1994). *A Practical Approach To Using Learning Styles In Math Instruction.* Springfield, IL: Thomas.

Schmuck, R. and P. Schmuck, (1988). *Group Processes in the Classroom*, 5th ed., Dubuque, IA: William C. Brown.

Widaman, K.F., and S. Kagan, (Winter 1987). "Cooperativeness and Achievement: Interaction of Student Cooperativeness with Cooperative versus Competitive Classroom Organization." *Journal of School Psychology* 25, 4: 355-365.

Wittrock, M. (1986). "Students' Thought Processes." In *Handbook of Research on Teaching*, edited by M.C. Wittrock. New York: Macmillan.

CHAPTER 8. BASIC CLASS PROCEDURES

Brophy, J.E. (1982). "Supplemental Group Management Techniques." In *Helping Teachers Manage Classrooms*, edited by D. Duke. Alexandria, VA: ASCD.

Cooper, H.M., and D. Tom, (September 1984). "Teacher Expectation Research: A Review with Implications for Classroom Instruction." *Elementary School Journal* 85, 1: 77-89.

Corno, L. (1979). "Classroom Instruction and the Matter of Time." In *Classroom Management, The 78th Yearbook of the National Society for the Study of Education*, edited by D. Duke. Chicago: University of Chicago Press.

Cummings, C. (1980). *Teaching Makes a Difference.* Edmonds, WA: Teaching, Inc.

Cummings, C. (1983). *Managing to Teach.* Edmonds, WA: Teaching, Inc.

Fantuzzo, J.W. (Winter 1990). "An Evaluation of Reciprocal Peer Tutoring Across Elementary School Settings." *Journal of School Psychology* 28, 4: 309-23.

Good, T.L. (July-August 1987). "Two Decades of Research on Teacher Expectations: Findings and Future Directions." *Journal of Teacher Education* 38, 4: 32-47.

Johnson, D.W., and R. Johnson, (1987). *Creative Conflict.* Edina, MN: Interaction Book Company.

Rosenshine, B. (1970). "Enthusiastic Teaching, A Research Review." *School Review* 78: 279-301.

CHAPTER 9. FOR OPENING A CLASS

Bellanca, J., and R. Fogarty, (1990). *Blueprints for Cooperative Learning in the Thinking Classroom.* Palatine, IL: Skylight Publishing.

Emmer, E., and C. Everston, (December 1980/January 1981). "Synthesis of Research on Classroom Management." *Educational Leadership* 38, 4: 342-347.

Johnson, D.W., R.T. Johnson, E.J. Holubec, and P. Roy, (1984). *Circles of Learning: Cooperation in the Classroom.* Alexandria, VA: ASCD.

Rosenshine, B. (1979). "Content, Time and Direct Instruction." In *Research on Teaching*, edited by P.L. Peterson and H.J. Walberg. Berkeley, CA: McCutchan.

CHAPTER 10. FOR ENDING A CLASS

Emmer, E., and C. Everston, (December 1980/January 1981). "Synthesis of Research on Classroom Management." *Educational Leadership* 38, 4: 342-347.

Johnson, D.W., and R. Johnson, (1989). *Cooperation and Competition: Theory and Research*. Edina, MN: Interaction Book Company.

Rowe, M.B. (January-February 1986). "Wait Time: Slowing Down May Be a Way of Speeding Up!" *The Journal of Teacher Education* 31, 1: 43-50.

Walberg, H.J. (March, 1988). "Synthesis of Research on Time and Learning." *Educational Leadership* 45, 6: 76-85.

CHAPTER 11. HOMEWORK STRATEGIES

Annis, L. (1979). "The Processes and Effects of Peer Tutoring." *Human Learning* 2: 39-47.

Biddle, B. and D.S. Anderson, (1986). "Theory, Methods, Knowledge, and Research on Teaching." In *Handbook of Research on Teaching*, edited by M.C. Wittrock. New York: Macmillan.

Channon, G. (1970). *Homework*. New York: Outerbridge.

Cooper, H. (1989). *Homework*. New York: Longman.

Cooper, H.M. (1989). *Integrating Research: A Guide for Literature Reviews*. 2nd ed. Newbury Park, CA: Sage.

National Commission on Excellence in Education. (1983). *A Nation at Risk: The Imperative for Educational Reform*. Washington DC: U.S. Department of Education.

Richards, J. (1982). "Homework." In *Encyclopedia of Educational Research*, 5th ed., edited by H.E. Mitzel, J. Hardin Best, and W. Rabinowitz. New York: Macmillan.

Walberg, H.J. (April 1985). "Homework's Powerful Effects on Learning." *Educational Leadership* 42, 7: 76-79.

CHAPTER 12. HANDLING TESTING AND GRADING

Camp, R. (Spring 1990). "Thinking Together About Portfolios." *National Writing Project and the Center for the Study of Writing and Literacy* 12, 2: 8-14, 27.

Davinroy, K.H., C.L. Bliem, and V. Mayfield, (April 1994). "'How Does My Teacher Know What I Know?': Third-Graders Perceptions of Math, Reading, and Assessment." Paper presented at the annual meeting of the American Educational Research Association, New Orleans.

Farnan, N. and R. Kelly, (July-September 1991). "Keeping Track: Creating Assessment Portfolios in Reading and Writing." *Quarterly of the National Writing Project and the Center for the Study of Writing and Literacy* 14, 1: 14-17.

Flexer, R.J., K. Cumbo, H. Borko, V. Mayfield, and S.F. Marion, (April 1994). "How 'Messing About' with Performance Assessment in Mathematics Affects What Happens in Classrooms." Paper presented at the annual meeting of the American Educational Research Association, New Orleans.

Herman, J., P. Aschbacher, and L. Winters, (1992). *A Practical Guide to Alternative Assessment*. Alexandria, VA: ASCD.

Houston, P., and J. Schneider, (June 1994). "Drive-by Critics and Silver Bullets." *Phi Delta Kappan* 75: 779-782.

Knight, P. (May 1992). "How I Use Portfolios in Mathematics." *Educational Leadership* 49, 8: 71-72.

Olson, M.W. (January-March 1991). "Portfolios: Education Tools (Research into Practice)." *Reading Psychology* 12, 1: 73-80.

Roe, M.F. (December 1991). *Portfolios: From Mandate to Implementation*. Paper presented at the Annual Meeting of the National Reading Conference, Palm Springs, CA.

Roettger, D., and M. Szymczuk, eds. (1990). *Guide for Developing Student Portfolios*. Draft version. Johnston, IA: Heartland Area Education Agency 11.

Tierney, R.J. (1991). *Portfolio Assessment in the Reading-Writing Classroom*. Norwood, MA: Christopher-Gordon Publishers.

Wolf, D.P. (December 1987/January 1988). "Opening Up Assessment." *Educational Leadership* 45, 4: 24-29.

Wolf, D.P. (April 1989). "Portfolio Assessment: Sampling Student Work." *Educational Leadership* 46, 7: 35-39.

CHAPTER 13. FOR LEARNING MASTERY

Brandt, R. (December 1992/January 1993). "On Outcome-Based Education: A Conversation with Bill Spady." *Educational Leadership* 50, 4: 66-71.

Brophy, J. (1989). *Advances in Research on Teaching. Vol.I: Teaching for Meaningful Understanding and Self-regulated Learning*. Greenwich, CT: JAI.

Calkins, L. (1986). *The Art of Teaching Writing*. Exeter: Heinemann.

Costa, A.L. (November 1984). "Mediating the Metacognitive." *Educational Leadership* 42, 3: 57-62.

Cummings, C. (1983). *Managing to Teach*. Edmonds, WA: Teaching Inc.

Gabbert, B., D.W. Johnson, and R. Johnson, (1986). "Cooperative Learning, Group-to-Individual Transfer, Process Gain, and the Acquisition of Cognitive Reasoning Strategies." *Journal of Psychology* 120: 265-278.

Johnson, D.W., and R. Johnson, (1989). *Cooperation and Competition: Theory and Research*. Edina, MN: Interaction Book Company.

Kagan, S. (1980). "Cooperation-Competition, Culture, and Structural Bias in Classrooms." In *Cooperation in Education,* edited by S. Sharan, P. Hare, C. Webb, and R. Hertz-Lazarowitz. Provo, UT: Brigham Young University Press.

Marzano, R.J., et. al. (1988). *Dimensions of Thinking: A Framework for Curriculum and Instruction*. Alexandria, VA: ASCD.

Pinnell G. and D. Deford, (1988). *Reading Recovery: Early Intervention for At Risk First Graders*. Arlington, VA: Educational Research Service.

Rosaen, C. (1989). "Writing in the Content Areas: Reading its Potential in the Learning Process." *In Advances in Research on Teaching. Vol. I: Teaching for Meaningful Understanding and Self-regulated Learning*. Greenwich, CT: JAI.

Rosenshine, B. (1976). "Classroom Instruction." In *Psychology of Teaching, 77th Yearbook of the National Study of Education,* edited by N. Gage. Chicago: University of Chicago Press.

Slavin, R.E. (April 1989). "On Mastery Learning and Mastery Teaching." *Educational Leadership*, 46, 7: 77-79.

Slavin, R. (May 1981). "Synthesis of Research on Cooperative Learning. "*Educational Leadership* 38, 8: 655-660.

Whimbey, A., and J. Lochhead, (1986). *Problem Solving and Comprehension*. Hillsdale, NJ: Lawrence Erlbaum.

CHAPTER 14. STIMULATING THINKING

Bailis, P., and M. Hunter, (August 1985). "Do Your Words Get Them to Think?" *Learning* 14, 1: 43.

Bloom, B., and D.R. Krathwohl, (1977; reprint of 1956 edition). *Taxonomy of Educational Objectives, Handbook I: Cognitive Domain*. New York: David McKay Company.

Brandt, R. (September 1984). "Teaching of Thinking, For Thinking, About Thinking." *Educational Leadership* 42, 1: 3.

Brandt, R., ed. (1989). *Readings from Educational Leadership: Teaching Thinking*. Alexandria, VA: ASCD.

Bruner, J.S. and M.J. Kenny, (1966). *Studies in Cognitive Growth*. New York: John Wiley and Sons.

Bruner, J.S., J.J. Goodnow, and G.A. Austin, (1956). *A Study of Thinking*. New York: John Wiley and Sons.

Costa, A.L., ed. (1991). *Developing Minds: A Resource Book for Teaching Thinking and Programs for Teaching Thinking*, Revised ed., Vols. 1 and 2. Alexandria, VA: ASCD.

Costa, A., and L. Lowrey, (1989). *Techniques for Teaching Thinking*. Pacific Grove, CA: Midwest Publications.

Flavell, J.H. (1976). "Metacognitive Aspects of Problem Solving." In *The Nature of Intelligence*, edited by L. B. Resnick. Hillsdale, NJ: Lawrence Erlbaum.

Gall, M. (December 1970). "The Use of Questions in Teaching." *Review of Educational Research* 40, 5: 207-220.

Heiman, M., and J. Slomianko, eds. (1987). *Thinking Skills Instruction: Concepts and Techniques*. Building Students' Thinking Skills series. Washington, DC: National Education Association.

Hyde, A., and M. Bizar, (1989). *Thinking in Context: Teaching Cognitive Processes Across the Elementary School Curriculum*.

Marzano, R.J. (1992). *A Different Kind of Classroom: Teaching with Dimensions of Learning*. Alexandria, VA: ASCD.

Redfield, D., and E. Rousseau, (Summer 1981). "A Meta-Analysis on Teacher Questioning Behavior." *Review of Educational Research* 51: 234-245.

Resnick, L. (1987). *Education and Learning to Think*. Washington, DC: National Academy Press.

Taba, H. (May 1965). "Teaching of Thinking." *Elementary English* 42, 2: 534.

Taba, H., S. Levine, and F. Elzey, (1964). *Thinking in Elementary School Children*. San Francisco: San Francisco State College, Cooperative Research Project No. 1574.

Whimbey, A. (April 1980). "Students Can Learn to Be Better Problem Solvers." Educational Leadership 37, 7: 560-565.

CHAPTER 15. BEYOND FACTS AND DETAILS

Anderson L. (1989). "Implementing Instructional Programs to Promote Meaningful, Self-regulated Learning." In *Advances in Research on Teaching. Vol. 1: Teaching for Meaningful Understanding and Self-regulated Learning*, edited by J. Brophy. Greenwich, CT: JAI.

Applebee, A. (1986). "Problems in Process Approaches: Toward a Reconceptualization of Process Instruction," edited by A. Petrosky & D. Bartholomae. In *The Teaching of Writing* (85th yearbook of the National Society for the Study of Education), Chicago: University of Chicago Press.

Brophy J. (1989). *Advances in Research on Teaching. Vol. 1: Teaching for Meaningful Understanding and Self-regulated Learning*. Greenwich, CT: JAI.

Calkins, L. (1986). *The Art of Teaching Writing*. Exeter: Heinemann.

Cazden, C., and H. Mehan, (1989). "Principles from Sociology and Anthropology: Context, Code, Classroom and Culture." In *Knowledge Base for the Beginning Teacher*, edited by M.C. Reynolds. New York: Pergamon.

Grossman, P., S.M. Wilson, and L.S. Shulman, (1989). "Teachers of Substance: Subject Matter Knowledge for Teaching." In *Knowledge Base for the Beginning Teacher*, edited by M.C. Reynolds. New York: Pergamon.

Johnson D., and R. Johnson, (1975). *Learning Together and Alone*. Englewood Cliffs, NJ: Prentice-Hall.

Marzano, R.J. (1992). *A Different Kind of Classroom: Teaching with Dimensions of Learning*. Alexandria, VA: ASCD.

Newmann, F. (1988). *Higher Order Thinking in High School Social Studies: An Analysis of Classrooms, Teachers, Students, and Leadership*. Madison: University of Wisconsin, National Center for Effective Secondary Schools.

Nucci, L. (1989). "Knowledge of the Learner: The Development of Children's Concepts of Self, Morality and Societal Convention." In *Knowledge Base for the Beginning Teacher*, edited by M.C. Reynolds. New York: Pergamon.

Pinnell, G., and D. DeFord, (1988). *Reading Recovery: Early Intervention for At Risk First Graders.* Arlington, VA: Educational Research Service.

Redfield, D., and E. Rousseau, (Summer 1981). "A Meta-Analysis on Teacher Questioning Behavior." *Review of Educational Research* 51: 234-245.

Rosaen, C. (1989). "Writing in the Content Areas: Researching Its Potential in the Learning Process." J. Brophy (Ed.). In *Advances in Research in Teaching, Vol. 1: Teaching for Meaningful Understanding and Self-regulated Learning.* Greenwich, CT: JAI.

Wasserman, S. (1991). *Serious Players: Empowering Children in the Primary Grades.* New York: Teachers College Press.

Wasserman S., and G. Ivany, (1988). *Teaching Elementary Science: Who's Afraid of Spiders?* New York: Harper Row.

CHAPTER 16. FOR A COMMUNITY OF LEARNERS

Banks, J.A., and C.A. McGee Banks, (1995). *Handbook of Research on Multicultural Education.* New York: Macmillian.

Bugental, J. (1967). *Challenges of Humanistic Psychology.* New York: McGraw-Hill.

Gendlin, E. *Focusing.* New York: Bantam.

Hirsch, E.D. (1987). *Cultural Literacy: What Every American Needs to Know.* Boston, MA: Houghton Mifflin Company.

Hoyle, J.R., F.W. English, and B.E. Steffy, (1990). *Skills for Successful School Leaders.* 2nd ed. Arlington, VA: AASA

Marzano, R.J. (1992). *A Different Kind of Classroom: Teaching with Dimensions of Learning.* Alexandria, VA: ASCD.

Owens, R. (1991). *Organizational Behavior in Education,* 4th ed. Englewood Cliffs, NJ: Prentice-Hall.

Perls, F., R.F. Hefferline, and P. Goodman, (1977). *Gestalt Therapy: Excitement and Growth in the Human Personality.* New York: Bantam.

Redfield, D., and E. Rousseau, (Summer 1981). "A Meta-Analysis on Teacher Questioning Behavior." *Review of Educational Research* 51: 234-245.

Schults, D. (1977). *Growth Psychology: Models of Healthy Personality.* New York: Van Reinhold.

CHAPTER 17. INSPIRING PERSONAL GROWTH

Allport, G. (1955). *Becoming: Basic Considerations for a Psychology of Personality.* New Haven: Yale University Press.

Ames, C., and J. Archer, (1982). "Achievement Goals in the Classroom: Students' Learning Strategies and Motivation Processes." *Journal of Educational Psychology* 80, 260-267.

Annis, L. (1979). "The Processes and Effects of Peer Tutoring." *Human Learning* 2: 39-47.

Bandura, A. (1986). *Social Foundations of Thought and Action: A Social Cognitive Theory.* Englewood Cliffs, NJ: Prentice-Hall.

Berliner, D.C. and R.C. Calfee, (1995). *Handbook of Research on Educational Psychology.* New York: Macmillan.

Berliner, D.C. (1984). "The Half-Full Glass: A Review of Research in Teaching." *Using What We Know About Teaching,* edited by P.I. Hosford. Alexandria, VA: ASCD.

Berliner, D.C. (1979). "Tempus Educare." *Research on Teaching,* edited by P.L. Peterson and H.J. Walberg. Berkeley, CA: McCutchan.

Deci, E. and R. Ryan, (1985). *Intrinsic Motivation and Self Determination in Human Behavior.* New York: Plenum.

DiCaprio, N.S. (1983). *Personality Theories: A Guide to Human Nature.* New York: Holt.

Fox, L. and F.L. Weaver, (1990). *Unlocking Doors to Self-Esteem.* Torrance, CA: B.L. Winch.

Frazer, R. and J. Fadiman, (1984). *Personality Theories and Personal Growth*. New York: Harper.

McWaters, . (1977). *Humanistic Perspectives: Current Trends in Psychology*. Monterey, CA: Wadsworth.

Moustakas, C. (1967). *Creativity and Conformity*. Princeton, NJ: Van Nostrand.

Purkey, W. and J.M. Novak, (1984). *Inviting School Success: A Self-Concept Approach to Teaching and Learning*. Belmont, CA: Wadsworth.

Royce, J.R. (1981). *Humanistic Psychology: Concepts and Criticisms*. New York: Plenum.

Walberg, H.J. (September 1986). "What Works in a Nation Still at Risk." *Educational Leadership* 44, 1: 7-10.

Welch, D. and G.A. Tate, (1987). *Self Actualization: An Annotated Bibliography of the Theory and Research*. New York: Garland.

CHAPTER 18. MAINTAINING OUR OWN BALANCE

Bateson, G. (1972). *Steps to an Ecology of Mind*. New York: Ballantine.

Borko, H. and J. Niles, (1987). "Descriptions of Teacher Planning." In *Educators' Handbook: A Research Perspective*. White Plains, NY: Longman.

Bridges, W. (1980). *Transitions: Making Sense of Life's Changes*. Reading, PA: Addison.

Brophy, J. (1986). "Teacher Socialization as a Mechanism for Developing Student Motivation to Learn." *Social Psychology Applied to Education*. Cambridge, MA: Cambridge University Press.

Bugental, J. (1989). *The Search for Authenticity: An Existential-Analytic Approach to Psychotherapy*. New York: Irvington.

Bugental, J. (1990). *Intimate Journeys: Stories from Life Changing Therapy*. San Francisco, CA: Jossey-Bass.

Goldenburg, C. (1985). *The Paradox of Expectations: Two Case Studies*. Paper presented at the Annual Meeting of the American Educational Research Association, Chicago, IL.

Grof, S. (1988). *The Adventure for Self Discovery*. Albany, NY: SUNY.

Jourard, S. (1963). *Personal Adjustment: An Approach through the Study of Healthy Personality*. New York: Macmillian.

Maeroff, G. (1988). *The Empowerment of Teachers*. New York: Teachers College.

May, R. (1984). *The Courage to Create*. New York: Bantam.

Miller, J.P. (1981). *The Compassionate Teacher: How to Teach and Learn with Your Whole Self*. Englewood Cliff, NJ: Prentice-Hall.

Mohrman, S.A., and P. Wohlstetter, et. al. (1994). *School-Based Management: Organizing for High Performance*. San Francisco, CA: Jossey-Bass.

CHAPTER 19 AND 20. DISCIPLINE

Adkins, G. (1990). "Educating the Handicapped in the Regular Classroom." *The Educational Digest* 56, 24-27.

Ames, C., and R. Ames, eds. (1985). *Research on Motivation in Education: Vol. 1. Student Motivation*. Orlando, FL: Academic Press.

Augustine, D.K., K.D. Gruber, and L.R. Hanson, (1990). "Cooperation Works!" *Educational Leadership* 47, 4-7.

Bandura, A. (1969). *Behavior Modification Through Modeling Procedures*, In L. Krasner and L.P. Ullman.

Biehler, R.F., and J. Snowman, (1990). *Psychology Applied to Teaching*, 6th ed. Boston, MA: Houghton Mifflin.

Brandt, R. (1989). A Changed Professional Culture. *Educational Leadership* 46, 2.

Brendtro, L., and J. Banbury, (1994). "Tapping the Strengths of Oppositional Youth." *Journal of Emotional and Behavioral Problems* 3,2: 41-45.

Brody, N. (1983). *Human Motivation: Commentary on Goal-Directed Action*. New York: Academic Press.

Brophy, J.E. (April 1979). *Advances in Teacher Effectiveness Research*. The Institute for Research on Teaching, Michigan State University.

Brown, D. (1971). Changing Student Behavior: A New Approach to Discipline. Dubuque, IA: W.C. Brown.

Cangelosi, J.S. (1990). Designing Tests for Evaluating Student Achievement. New York: Longman.

Canter, L., and M. Canter, (1976). Assertive Discipline: A Take-Charge Approach for Today's Educator. Santa Monica, CA: Lee Canter & Assocs.

Canter, L., and M. Canter, (1989). Assertive Discipline for Secondary School Educators: Inservice video package.

Charles, C.M. (1992). Building Classroom Discipline: From Models to Practice, 4th ed. New York: Longman.

Cooper, H. (1989). *Homework*. New York: Longman.

Cooper, H. and T. Good, (1983). *Pygmalion Grows Up: Studies in Expectation Communication Process*. New York: Macmillan.

Curwin, R.L., and A.N. Mendler, (1988). Discipline with Dignity. Alexandria, VA: ASCD.

Dewey, J. (1933). *How We Think*. Boston, MA: D. C. Heath.

Doyle, W. (1986). "Classroom Organization and Management." In *Handbook of Research on Teaching* 3rd.ed.,pp. 392-431. New York: Macmillan.

Dreikurs, R. (1968). *Psychology in the classroom* , edited by M.C. Wittrock, 2nd. ed. New York: Harper & Row.

Dreikurs, R., B. Grunwald, and F. Pepper, (1982). *Maintaining Sanity in the Classroom,* 2nd ed. New York: Harper & Row.

Elkind, D. (1988). *The Hurried Child*. New York: Addison-Wesley.

Firth, G. (1985). *Behavior Management in the Schools: A Primer for Parents*. New York: Thomas.

Flanders, N. (1960). "Teacher Effectiveness." In *Encyclopedia of Educational Research,* 4th ed., edited by R. Elbell. New York: Macmillan.

Ginott, H.G. (1972). *Teacher and Child*. New York: Avon.

Glasser, W. (1985). *Control Theory in the Classroom*. New York: Perennial Press.

Glasser, W. (1990). *The Quality School: Managing Students Without Coercion*. New York: Harper & Row.

Gordon, T. (1989). *Teaching Children Self-Discipline-At Home and at School*. New York: Times Books.

Harmin, M. (1990). *The Workshop Way to Student Success*. Educational Leadership, 48: 1, 43-47.

Harris, T.A. (1969). *I'm OK-You're OK: A Practical Guide to Transactional Analysis*. New York: Harper & Row.

Hunkins, F.P. (1989). *Teaching Thinking Through Effective Questioning*. Boston: Christopher-Gordon.

Johnson, D.W., and R. Johnson, (1994). *Teaching Students to Be Peacemakers: Results of Five Years of Research*. Minneapolis: University of Minnesota, Cooperative Learning Center.

Jones, F. (1987a). *Positive Classroom Discipline*. New York: McGraw-Hill.

Jones, F. (1987b). *Positive Classroom Instruction*. New York: McGraw-Hill.

Jones, V.F., and L.S. Jones, (1990). *Comprehensive Classroom Management: Motivating and Managing Students* (3rd ed.) Boston, MA: Allyn & Bacon.

Joyce, B., and M. Weil, (1991). *Models of Teaching*. Englewood Cliffs, NJ: Prentice-Hall.

Karlin, M.S., and R. Berger, (1972). *Discipline and the Disruptive Child: A Practical Guide for Elementary Teachers*. West Nyack, NY: Parker.

Kerman, S., and M. Martin, (1980). *Teacher Expectations and Student Achievement*. Bloomington, IN: Phi Delta Kappa.

Kerr, M.M., and C.M. Nelson, (1983). *Strategies for Managing Behavior Problems in the Classroom*. Columbus, OH: Merrill.

Kobrin, D. (1992). *In There with Kids: Teaching in Today's Classrooms*. Boston, MA: Houghton Mifflin.

Kohut, S., and D.G. Range, (1979). *Classroom Discipline: Case Studies and Viewpoints*. Washington DC: National Education Association.

Kounin, J. (1970). *Discipline and Group Management in Classrooms*. New York: Holt, Rinehart, and Winston.

Kounin, J. (1971; 1977). *Discipline and Group Management in Classrooms*. New York: Holt, Rinehart and Winston.

Krumboltz, J.D., and H.B. Krumboltz, (1972). *Changing Children's Behavior*. Englewood Cliffs, NJ: Prentice-Hall.

Krisberg, B., and J. Austin, (1993). *Reinventing Juvenile Justice*. Newbury Park. CA: Sage.

Lasley, T.J. (1985). "Fostering Nonaggression in the Classroom: An Anthropological Perspective." *Theory into Practice* 24, 247-255.

Lasley, T.J., and W.W. Wayson, (December 1982). "Characteristics of Schools with Good Discipline." *Educational Leadership* 40, 28-31.

Lemlich, J. (1988). Classroom Management: Methods and Techniques for Elementary and Secondary Teachers, 2nd ed. White Plains, NY: Longman.

Males, M. (March/April 1994). "Bashing Youth: Media Myths About Teenagers." *Extra*: 8-11.

Martin, G., and J. Pear, (1983). *Behavior Modification: What It Is and How to Do It,* 2nd ed. Englewood Cliffs, NJ: Prentice-Hall.

Maslow, A. (1962). *Toward a Psychology of Being*. New York: Van Nostrand.

Maurer, R. (1988). *Special Educator's Discipline Handbook*. West Nyack, NY: The Center for Applied Research in Education.

McIntyre, T. (1989). *The Behavior Management Handbook: Setting Up Effective Behavior Management Systems*. Boston, MA: Allyn & Bacon.

Moorman, C. and N. Moorman, (1989). *Teacher Talk*. Bay City, MI: Personal Power Press.

Murphy, J. (August 1988). "Contingency Contracting in Schools: A Review." *Education and Treatment of Children* 11, 3: 257-269.

Newman, J. (1991). *Interwoven Conversations*. Portsmouth: Heimann.

Ornstein, A.C. (1990). *Strategies for Effective Teaching*. New York: Harper & Row.

Pilon, G. (1988). Workshop Way. New Orleans, LA: The Workshop Way.

Pulaski, M.A.S. (1980). Understanding Piaget: An Introduction to Children's Cognitive Development, 2nd ed. New York: Harper & Row.

Pysch, R. (1991). *Discipline Improves as Students Take Responsibility*. NASSP Bulletin, 75, 117-118.

Redl, F., and W. Wattenberg, (1951; 1959). *Mental Hygiene in Teaching*. New York: Harcourt, Brace and World.

Render, G., J. Padilla,, and H. Krank, (1989). *What Research Really Shows About Assertive Discipline*. Educational Leadership 46, 6: 72-75.

Rogoff, B. (1990). *Apprenticeship in Thinking*. New York: Oxford University Press.

Rosenshine, B. (1971). *Teaching Behaviors and Student Achievement*. London: National Foundation for Educational Research in England and Wales.

Rosenthal, R., and L. Jacobson, (1968). *Pygmalion in the Classroom: Teacher Expectations and Pupils',* New York: HOH.

Schuster, C. and W. Van Pelt, eds. (1993). *Speculations*. Englewood Cliffs, NJ: Prentice Hall.

Skinner, B.F. (1953). *Science and Human Behavior*. New York: Macmillan.

Skinner, B.F. (1971). *Beyond Freedom and Dignity*. New York: Knopf.

Slavin, R.E. (1991). "Synthesis of Research on Cooperative Learning." *Educational Leadership,* 48, 71-82.

Swartz, R.J., and D.N. Perkins, (1990). *Teaching Thinking: Issues and Approaches,* Pacific Grove, CA: Midwest Publications.

Swick, K.J. (1985). *Disruptive Student Behavior in the Classroom* , 2nd ed. Washington DC: National Education Association.

Tillman, M. (1982). *Trouble-Shooting Classroom Problems*. Glenview, IL: Scott, Foresman.

Tolan, P., and N. Guerra, (1995). *What Works in Reducing Adolescent Violence: An Empirical Review of the Field.* Denver: Center for the Study of Prevention of Violence, University of Colorado.

Van Dyke, H.T. (1984). "Corporal Punishment in Our Schools." *The Clearing House*, 57, 296-300.

Walker, H., and R. Sylwater, (1991). "Where is School Along the Path of Prison?" *Educational Leadership*, 49, 14-16.

Walker, J.E., and T.M. Shea, (1984). Behavior Management: A Practical Approach for Educators, 3rd ed. St. Louis, MO: Times Mirror/Mosby College Publishing.

Wilde, J., and P. Sommers, (1978). "Teaching Disruptive Adolescents: A Game Worth Winning." *Phi Delta Kappan* 59, 342-343.

Glossary Index

Conflict resolution lesson A lesson to teach students how to talk honestly about a conflict and, if talk alone does not ease the problem, how to brainstorm a list of possible solutions. 20-5 Page 240

Connecting subject matter to values A lesson or unit connecting an academic topic to an issue students personally care about. 15-2 Page 170

Consult time Time set aside for individual students to visit briefly with the teacher. 8-11 Page 125

Cool-quick-certain control Forcefully taking control and managing a problem situation. 20-7 Page 244

Cooperative planning Announcing a topic or problem and asking students to help you think about the best ways to deal with it. 16-2 Page 180

Create groupings An assignment in which students create their own categories for a set of items and sort the items by those categories. 14-2 Page 162

Creative reports Reports given by students that are designed to be creative, not routine. 13-4 Page 158

Cushioning Questions or statements of a teacher designed to reinforce the meanings on truth signs, such as: "Is it okay if someone gives us a wrong answer today? Why?" or "Do you have to understand everything we talk about today? Why not?" 3-2 Page 55

DESCA challenges Challenges that stretch students' capacity to live with full dignity, high energy, wise self-management, in respectful community, or with open awareness. 5-5 Page 85

DESCA checkups Checking yourself occasionally to see how you are doing at serving student dignity, energy, self-management, community and awareness. 18-1 Page 205

DESCA inspirations Teacher comments to stir appreciation of the inherent dignity of all; the appropriate use of personal energy; the exercise of intelligent self management; healthful community relationships; and searching, open awareness. 4-9 Page 70

Diagnosing student motivations Considering what might be motivating a misbehaving student and, when appropriate, making a plan to ease the problem. 20-11 Page 250

Discipline squad An arrangement whereby several other nearby adults respond in times of emergency. 20-13 Page 253

Dramatic distraction Dramatically turning student attention away from problem behavior, as by getting students to talk or by posing a surprising question. 20-6 Page 243

Easing student distress Modeling someone who reaches out to ease class members in distress. 16-4 Page 184

Experience before concepts Giving students a meaningful experience of a concept before talking about it abstractly. 2-16 Page 46

Focus on learning statement Explaining that the focus in the class is on learning, not on grading, inviting students to adjust accordingly. 12-3 Page 148

Good living target Inspiring students to consider what they can do to live and work well together and occasionally urging them to keep moving in that direction. 16-1 Page 179

Grading plan A plan for grading that considers both the teacher's current grading responsibilities and the students' long-term welfare. 12-2 Page 146

Guided practice Students practicing a skill with teacher guidance, so students gradually move toward excellence. 2-12 Page 40

Hand raise signal The teacher raising a hand to signal the end of small group discussions, students who see the hand then raise one of their own hands, with the process continuing until all discussion has ceased. 7-3 Page 111

High expectations Maintaining an expectation that students will do excellent work, even when there is not yet evidence that students will do so. 5-4 Page 84

Homework hearing The teacher meeting briefly with each student to hear about completed homework. 11-2 Page 138

Homework sharing groups Student groups, usually pairs, sitting together to review or correct homework. 11-1 Page 136

Personal challenges   Inspiring students to activate their best intentions. 17-2 Page 193

Physical movement   Opportunities for students, especially younger students, to move about in the classroom. 8-8 Page 123

Plain corrects   Simply informing a student an answer is correct. 4-4 Page 65

Plain incorrects   Simply informing a student an answer is not correct. 4-5 Page 65

Portfolio   A collection of student work designed to increase self-responsible student learning and provide evidence for teacher evaluation. 12-1 Page 144

Positive parent schedule   A schedule that makes it easy to send home positive messages to all parents. 20-10 Page 249

Power inspirations   Comments that inspire students to activate their personal power. 17-3 Page 195

Praise and rewards for all   Praise or rewards offered to the group as a whole. 4-7 Page 67

Priority assertion   Noticing when you feel overburdened and then back off to see the whole picture and make plans in line with priorities. 18-6 Page 211

Project work   Students working on a task for an extended time period, alone or in small groups, usually to produce a tangible product. 6-6 Page 100

Question, all write   Students each writing an answer to a question before the teacher calls on one student or announces the correct answer. 2-1 Page 23

Quick pace   A classroom pace that moves fast enough to keep all students actively involved. 1-2 Page 18

Reality-acceptance monologue   Taking a moment to remind yourself that not all bothersome behavior can be eliminated. 18-4 Page 209

Redirect student energy   Turning the attention of a misbehaving student to something that is not disturbing. 19-2 Page 222

Report card plan   Planning to handle report cards in a way responsive both to professional requirements and the best interests of students. 12-4 Page 152

Respecting your own stage   Reminding yourself that teachers go through stages of development, and it is unwise to expect more of yourself than is now appropriate. 18-7 Page 212

Review test   The teacher asking a question about prior material, all students writing an answer, the teacher then either writing or orally announcing the correct answer, with the process continuing so students reinforce learnings and correct misunderstandings with high attention and low anxiety. 2-13 Page 42

Risk reminders   Reminding students that learning often involves risks, with perhaps some encouragement to consider risking in class today. 9-5 Page 129

Rotating pairs   Pairs of students sharing ideas and then rotating, so each student hears ideas from two or three other students. 6-8 Page 105

Selecting group size   Criteria for selecting the best size for group work, which usually recommends the smallest size feasible, often pairs. 7-1 Page 107

Selecting members for groups   Criteria for selecting members for groups, which usually recommends some form of student self-selection. 7-2 Page 108

Self-accepting monologue   Reminding yourself that you cannot expect to behave perfectly at all times. 18-3 Page 208

Self-management contract   A discussion with a misbehaving student that starts with a person-to-person dialogue, is followed by brainstorming a written list of possible next steps, aiming to produce a written agreement on exactly what is to be done next. 20-3 Page 236

Sensible risk taking   Teacher reminding students of risk-taking possibilities, allowing students to advance their rise-taking abilities according to their own timeclocks. 17-7 Page 201

Set of speakers   Requesting volunteers to speak and then, from all volunteers, choosing those who will then have a turn. 8-2 Page 116

Sharing pairs   Students pairing up to share thoughts. 2-5 Page 30

Silent response   Making a mental note of a misbehavior and leaving until later the consideration of what, if anything, is to be done about it. 19-6 Page 224

Silent response to errors   Making a mental note of a student error and leaving until later the consideration of what, if anything, is to be done about it. 4-6 Page 66

Simple discovery lesson   Asking students to ponder a topic or question and later leading them toward understanding. 2-15 Page 45

Solve a problem   Asking students to solve a problem which lacks an obvious solution. 14-8 Page 165

Sort the items   Students placing a set of items into categories the teacher announces. 14-1 Page 161

Speak-write   A lecture procedure containing occasional pauses that students know are for writing personal reactions, a summary of what was heard, questions, or anything else students choose. 2-9 Page 35

Star of the day   Each student has a turn to be the star of that day, with whatever special responsibilities or privileges might be appropriate. 17-6 Page 201

Student procedure mastery   Spending enough time teaching classroom procedures to insure that all students will be able to follow procedures easily and efficiently. 8-7 Page 121

Support groups   Groups of students, usually four's, who regularly sit together and offer appropriate support to each other. 6-5 Page 99

Task and team skill group   Small groups working at a task while simultaneously practicing an interpersonal skill. 6-7 Page 103

Task group, share group   Students considering a problem in small task groups and then regrouping, so each student can share task group work with students who were in different task groups. 6-2 Page 95

Teacher balance step   Taking steps to keep a comfortable personal balance and, when balance is lost, to regain it. 18-2 Page 206

Teacher talk chart   Keeping handy a list of comments to make that are preferred and not preferred. 18-5 Page 210

Teaching in layers not lumps   Returning to topics from time to time rather than aiming for mastery at any one time, so learnings get reinforced over time and the risk of losing student involvement is minimized. 1-3 Page 20

Temporary removal   Instructing a student to leave the group temporarily. 20-9 Page 248

Think aloud   Talking aloud while working through a problem, so students have a model of how the teacher's thinking proceeded. 2-11 Page 39

Thought-feel cards   Notes students make of personal thoughts and/or feelings currently in awareness, usually anonymously. 10-2 Page 133

Three structure weave   Regularly blending into the class time whole class lessons, small group work and time for individual work. 8-9 Page 123

Truth signs   Posted signs that remind students of important truths about learning. 3-1 Page 49

Tutor training   Lessons teaching students skills for effectively giving and receiving help. 8-6 Page 118

Underexplain and learning pairs   Explaining only enough to get some students fully understanding the material and then asking pairs to work together to help each other learn it. 2-3 Page 26

Undone work response   Avoiding blaming students who fail to do required work and, instead, aiming to respond in a growth-producing way. 5-8 Page 89

Validations   Showing all students including those who upset you, that you see them as worthy human beings. 17-5 Page 199

Visitor chair   Without communicating any displeasure, the teacher asks a student to sit in a chair near the teacher as "time out." 19-8 Page 227

Voting   Asking question to which students can respond by raising hands or giving another nonverbal signal. 2-14 Page 44

Waiting place   A place where a student can conveniently wait until the teacher has time for a private conversation. 19-11 Page 231

What know and want to know   In preparation for study, asking students to note what they already know and might want to know about a topic. 15-4 Page 175

What might explain Asking students to think back and consider what might explain an event. 14-7 Page 165

What's the difference Asking students in what ways two items are different. 14-3 Page 163

What's the same Asking students in what ways two or more items are the same. 14-4 Page 163

Whip around, pass option Asking each student in turn to speak to an issue or to say, "I pass." 2-6 Page 31

Whole class problem solving Asking students to brainstorm a list of possible solutions to a class problem and then seeking agreement on what options are best for all concerned. 20-4 Page 240

Whole self lesson A lesson to teach students how to accept themselves and others and how to open up more of their good selves. 17-1 Page 187

Write a summary Asking students to write a summary of certain material. 14-5 Page 164